D1411679

John Dos Passos

Twayne's United States Authors Series

Joseph M. Flora, Editor

University of North Carolina, Chapel Hill

TUSAS 700

JOHN DOS PASSOS

Courtesy of Lucy Dos Passos Coggin and Elizabeth H. Dos Passos

John Dos Passos

Lisa Nanney

North Carolina School of Science and Mathematics

Twayne Publishers
An Imprint of Simon & Schuster Macmillan
New York

Prentice Hall International
London • Mexico City • New Delhi • Singapore • Sydney • Toronto

Twayne's United States Authors Series No. 700

John Dos Passos
Lisa Nanney

Twayne Publishers
An Imprint of Simon & Schuster Macmillan
1633 Broadway
New York, NY 10019

Library of Congress Cataloging-in-Publication Data
Nanney, Lisa.
   John Dos Passos / Lisa Nanney.
      p.   cm. — (Twayne's United States authors series ; TUSAS 700)
   Includes bibliographical references (p.   ) and index.
   ISBN 0-8057-3971-8 (acid-free paper)
   1. Dos Passos, John, 1896–1970—Criticism and interpretation.
   I. Title.   II. Series.
   PS3507.0743J64   1998
   813'.52—dc21   98-34787
                                 CIP

This paper meets the requirements of ANSI/NISO Z3948–1992 (Permanence of Paper).

10 9 8 7 6 5 4 3 2 1

Printed in the United States of America

Contents

Preface

When he contributed his study of John Dos Passos to the Twayne United States Authors Series in 1961, John H. Wrenn enjoyed the "friendly cooperation"[1] of his subject in the form of correspondence, conversations, and even Dos Passos's editorial advice on the study. The resulting edition provides a clear and succinct introduction to Dos Passos's career written with the benefit of its subject's own perspective. Wrenn's study ends with the publication of *Midcentury*, a novel in which Dos Passos returned to the techniques of *U.S.A.* but which, as his future volumes testified, signaled the end of his hopes that American culture would ever realize its promise of individual liberty and self-determination. Nevertheless, he continued writing his chronicles—*Century's Ebb* was published posthumously—and, before his death in 1970, he completed a memoir, *The Best Times* (1966), several histories on subjects ranging from Thomas Jefferson to Easter Island, and a volume of essays. Even though Wrenn's study stops nearly 10 years before Dos Passos died, it establishes the dichotomy critics have perceived between the political and artistic radicalism of his earlier works and the increasing traditionalism of those after *U.S.A.*

With an artist's career still in process, however, a critic lacks the historical and critical perspective that enables him to place the artist's work in a larger context. In the years since Dos Passos died, a critical reappraisal of his work has been made possible by the appearance of some previously unpublished letters and works, three differently focused biographies, and new critical approaches to his work. Such additions to the context within which his place in American literature can be evaluated have underscored the value of his attempts to portray the dynamics of American life in the twentieth century. This expanded context also has reaffirmed the view that dominated much of the criticism at the time of the publication of *Manhattan Transfer* and *U.S.A.*, his best-known works: that what secured Dos Passos's place in the canon of American literature, what in 1938 led Jean-Paul Sartre to proclaim him "the greatest writer of our time,"[2] was his innovative modernist style.

This introduction to his career, the second Twayne series book devoted to Dos Passos, explores his development as one of the most important modernist writers of the twentieth century. This volume places him in a historical and critical context by drawing on materials by and about the writer that have become available since Wrenn's volume in 1961. Invaluable among these new resources are visual works Dos Passos produced as a practicing painter throughout his life; they constitute primary sources that provide important insights into the process by which his revolutionary narrative structures evolved. With the benefit of such fresh materials and recent critical methods, this new look at Dos Passos chronologically explores his development as an artist whose narrative innovations and acute portrayals of American culture were central to the definition of a distinctively American modernism.

Acknowledgments

I would like particularly to express my gratitude to the late Elizabeth H. Dos Passos and to Lucy Dos Passos Coggin for their remarkable and gracious generosity in providing me access to the paintings and other visual works of John Dos Passos, for permission to quote from his writings and to publish his photograph, and for their assistance throughout my research. For sound editorial advice, I thank the academic editor for this series, Professor Joseph Flora of the University of North Carolina at Chapel Hill. Likewise, many thanks to Professor Townsend Ludington of the University of North Carolina at Chapel Hill for valuable advice on the manuscript at several stages and for the use of materials in his collection by and about Dos Passos.

Chronology

1896   Born John Roderigo Madison on January 14 in a Chicago hotel, illegitimate son of John Randolph Dos Passos and Lucy Addison Sprigg Madison.

1897–1900   Childhood spent with mother traveling in Europe, where visits from his father can be discreet.

1901   Returns to America with his mother and settles in Washington, D.C., where he is enrolled at the private Sidwell Friends School.

1904–1906   Attends Peterborough Lodge, a boarding school in Hampstead, England.

1907–1911   Attends Choate School in Wallingford, Connecticut, where he publishes his first work in the school newspaper, which he edits.

1911   Assumes the name John Roderigo Dos Passos Jr. after his father's first wife dies in 1910 and his parents marry. Passes entrance exams for Harvard but postpones college to travel in Europe and the Near East with a tutor.

1912   Enters Harvard College and establishes friendships with fellow students including E. E. Cummings, Gilbert Seldes, and Dudley Poore, who are also interested in modern literature.

1913   Visits the Armory Show in Boston, where his first encounter with European modernist painting has a major impact on his aesthetics. Publishes first story in *Harvard Monthly*.

1914–1915   Continues editing and contributing to *Harvard Monthly* and joins its editorial board. Joins Poetry Society with Cummings, Robert Hillyer, and Stewart Mitchell. His mother dies in 1915.

1916   Works on autobiographical novel, which later becomes *Streets of Night*. Graduates with honors from Harvard in June. Publishes "Against American Literature," his first national publication, in the *New Republic*. Attempts to join ambulance corps but father blocks efforts and sends him instead to Spain to study architecture.

1917 Death of his father and return to United States in January. Enlists in Norton-Harjes Ambulance Unit and departs for duty in France. Seven of his poems included in *Eight Harvard Poets*. While on duty in France and Italy, collaborates with Hillyer on "Seven Times round the Walls of Jericho"; Dos Passos's contributions will later become *One Man's Initiation—1917*.

1918 On duty in Italy, experiences bombardments but also manages to absorb Italian art. Meets Ernest Hemingway. Joins Red Cross ambulance corps but is ordered to return to United States after his letter criticizing the war is intercepted by censors. Enlists in U.S. Army Medical Corps and returns with his unit to France.

1919 Discharged from army in France and remains in Europe to attend classes at the Sorbonne, to arrange for English publication of *One Man's Initiation—1917* by Allen and Unwin, and to travel and write in Spain, where he works on *Three Soldiers*.

1920 Completes *Three Soldiers*. *One Man's Initiation—1917* published in October after he agrees to expurgate offensive passages. Settles in New York City, where he takes art lessons, sees literary friends, and contributes to journals such as *The Dial* and *The Nation*.

1921 Travels in Near East while working for the Red Cross Near East relief organization. *Three Soldiers* published in New York by George H. Doran.

1922 Returns to New York where he remains until 1925; works seriously on painting and writing and becomes involved in the city's literary life, associating with such writers as F. Scott and Zelda Fitzgerald, Edmund Wilson, and Sherwood Anderson. Publishes American edition of *One Man's Initiation—1917, Rosinante to the Road Again,* and *A Pushcart at the Curb,* all with Doran.

1923 First exhibition of paintings at Whitney Studio Club. Publishes *Streets of Night* with Doran. Completes first play, *The Moon Is a Gong*. Spends spring and summer traveling in France and Spain. In Paris, becomes friends with cultured expatriates Gerald and Sara Murphy; through them meets painter Fernand Léger, poet Blaise Cendrars, and other modernist artists. Begins *Manhattan Transfer* late in the year after returning to New York.

1924   Travels again in Spain, where he becomes engaged to Crystal Ross and attends the Fiesta of San Fermin with Hemingway and his circle of friends.

1925   Becomes member of the executive board of *New Masses,* a journal of the radical left. *The Moon Is a Gong* produced by Harvard Dramatic Club. *Manhattan Transfer* published in November by Harper and Brothers.

1926   Becomes one of the directors of the New Playwrights Theater, which produces *The Garbage Man,* a revision of *The Moon Is a Gong.* Becomes involved with defense of Sacco and Vanzetti; covers their case for *New Masses.* Crystal Ross breaks their engagement.

1927   Continues work with New Playwrights as writer, director, producer, and designer. Publishes *Facing the Chair: Story of the Americanization of Two Foreignborn Workmen* with the Sacco-Vanzetti Defense Committee, but despite his and other writers' efforts, Sacco and Vanzetti are executed August 23. Begins work on *The 42nd Parallel.* Publishes *Orient Express,* based on travels in Near East.

1928   Meets Katharine "Katy" Smith during visit with Hemingway in Key West. Travels in Europe before extensive stay in USSR, where he meets filmmakers Eisenstein and Pudovkin, talks with them about film techniques, and comes into contact with work of other Soviet filmmakers.

1929   Second play, *Airways, Inc.,* produced by New Playwrights. Resigns from New Playwrights to devote more time to writing second work of *U.S.A.* Marries Katy in August and they settle in Provincetown, Massachusetts.

1930   Publishes *The 42nd Parallel* with Harper and Brothers to positive reviews. Travels in Europe and Mexico.

Buys small farm in Truro, near Provincetown. Letters and journalism, such as publications in *New Republic*, reveal growing disillusionment with leftist political movements.

1931   Translates, illustrates, and writes introduction to long poem by Blaise Cendrars, *Panama, or The Adventures of My Seven Uncles*. Joins National Committee for the Defense of Political Prisoners and travels to Harlan County, Kentucky, to investigate the plight of striking miners.

1932   Publishes *1919* with Harcourt, Brace after Harper refuses to publish the satirical portrait of J. P. Morgan that comprises one of the book's biographical segments. Contributes reportage of the Bonus Army, Republican and Democratic National Conventions to journals such as *Common Sense* and the *New Republic*. Votes for Communist candidate William Z. Foster in presidential election.

1933   Visits the Murphys in France. Travels in Spain and works on *In All Countries,* reportage of travel.

1934   Publishes *In All Countries* and *Three Plays: The Garbage Man, Airways, Inc.,* and *Fortune Heights*. Signs open letter protesting Communist disruption of Socialist Party meeting in Madison Square Garden; *New Masses* replies with critical letter addressed "Dear Comrade Dos Passos." Spends summer in Hollywood working on screenplay for Josef von Sternberg's film *The Devil Is a Woman,* a vehicle for Marlene Dietrich.

1936   Despite health problems that delay completion of *The Big Money,* publishes it in 1936 with Harcourt, Brace. Dos Passos featured on cover of *Time* magazine for August 10; new novel highly praised although reviewers on the Left criticize its pessimism. Backs Roosevelt for presidency.

1937   Works with Hemingway, Lillian Hellman, Archibald MacLeish, and others to organize Contemporary Historians, a group formed to produce a documentary about the Spanish Civil War. Travels to Spain to meet Hemingway and the film's director, Joris Ivens. Becomes disillusioned with the Republican cause when he learns that his friend José Robles, a Republican official, has been executed by Communists allied with Republicans. When Hemingway warns him not to write about the incident because of potential harm to the Republican cause and to Dos Passos's reputation, their friendship ends. The film, *The Spanish Earth,* does elicit support for the cause. Dos Passos returns to United States and publishes "Farewell to Europe!" in *Common Sense,* praising "Anglo-Saxon democracy" as "the best political method of . . . any." One-man show of 30 of his sketches in New York.

1938   The *U.S.A.* trilogy—*The 42nd Parallel, 1919,* and *The Big Money*—published in January by Harcourt, Brace. Publishes *Journeys between Wars,* a book of travel essays. Travels in Europe.

1939   Publishes *Adventures of a Young Man* with Harcourt, Brace to weak reviews by leftist critics, who attack its anti-Communist stance. Wins Guggenheim Fellowship to write history that will become *The Ground We Stand On.*

1940   Edits and introduces the anthology *The Living Thoughts of Tom Paine—Presented by John Dos Passos.* Wins second Guggenheim. Represents New World Resettlement Fund in effort to help Spanish Republican refugees to Ecuador. Votes again for Roosevelt but later regrets it.

1941   Publishes *The Ground We Stand On.* Delivers address at P.E.N. Club conference in England. Publishes articles in *Harper's* on British war effort and necessity for American industrial strength.

1942–1943 Travels in United States reporting for *Harper's* on home war front. Publishes *Number One* with Houghton Mifflin, his new publisher. Sells house in Truro.

1944   Publishes *State of the Nation,* based on *Harper's* articles. Begins work on biography of Thomas Jefferson. Wins lawsuit over his father's property at Spence's Point in Westmoreland County, Virginia, and gains land and income from the estate. Travels to Pacific to report on war for *Life*. Votes for John Dewey in presidential election.

1945 Continues as war correspondent for *Life* and reports also on the Nuremburg war-crime trials after the war.

1946 Publishes "Americans Are Losing the Victory in Europe" in *Life*, expressing pessimism about U.S. containment of fascism abroad. Begins restoring house at Spence's Point.

1947 In September, Katy is killed in an automobile accident in which Dos Passos loses an eye. Reports for *Life*. Election to American Academy of Arts and Letters.

1948 Publishes "The Failure of Marxism" in *Life*. Travels to Caribbean and South America to write about political situations.

1949 Publishes *The Grand Design*. In August marries Elizabeth "Betty" Hamlin Holdridge, whom he met through friends in New York, and settles with her and her child at Spence's Point.

1950 Daughter Lucy Hamlin Dos Passos born in May. Publishes *The Prospect before Us*, a book of political essays.

1951 Publishes *Chosen Country*, an autobiographical novel.

1952 Publishes the trilogy *District of Columbia—Adventures of a Young Man, Number One*, and *The Grand Design*.

1954 Publishes *The Head and Heart of Thomas Jefferson* with Doubleday. Publishes *Most Likely To Succeed* with Prentice-Hall.

1956 Publishes *The Theme Is Freedom*, a volume of political essays.

1957 Publishes *The Men Who Made the Nation*, early American history. Accepts Gold Medal for Fiction from National Institute for Arts and Letters.

1958 Publishes *The Great Days*, an autobiographical novel, with Sagamore Press. Researches labor unions for *Reader's Digest*.

1959 Publishes *Prospects of a Golden Age*, another early American history. Adapts *U.S.A.* for stage with Paul Shyre.

1961   Publishes *Midcentury* with Houghton Mifflin to excellent reviews and sales.

1962   Publishes *Mr. Wilson's War,* American history covering 1901–1921. Receives award from conservative Young Americans for Freedom.

1963   Becomes writer-in-residence at University of Virginia. Publishes *Brazil on the Move.*

1964   Attends Republican National Convention in San Francisco and documents support for Barry Goldwater's nomination in *National Review.* Publishes *Occasions and Protests,* another book of political essays, and *Thomas Jefferson: The Making of a President,* a biography for children.

1966   Publishes *Shackles of Power: Three Jeffersonian Decades* and *The Best Times,* a memoir.

1967–1968   Travels in Portugal, Italy, the United States.

1969   Travels to Easter Island and South America. Publishes *The Portugal Story.* Works on *Easter Island: Island of Enigmas,* published posthumously in 1971. Works on *Century's Ebb,* a final novel, published posthumously in 1975.

1970   Hospitalized for continuing heart problems. Dies of congestive heart failure in Baltimore, September 28. Buried at Yeocomico Church near Spence's Point on October 7.

Chapter One
Dos Passos and the Modernist Impulse

As early as 1916, the year he graduated from Harvard, John Dos Passos had already clarified for himself and articulated for his readers the issues he would wrestle with during his entire career—a career occupying and fundamentally defining more than 50 years in the middle of the twentieth century. Yet, politically and literarily, he never rested in the middle: during his literary life, his stances on the same central issues he outlined in "A Humble Protest" and "Against American Literature," two defining essays he wrote and published as a senior at Harvard, propelled him from fervent activism for the far Left during the mid-1920s to public support for Joseph McCarthy and the work of the House Un-American Activities Committee 25 years later, in the early 1950s. The darling of the Left as a young writer, he was decried by leftists as a traitor to their causes from midcentury until his death in 1970. But Dos Passos himself regarded the beliefs that charged his early and later work as entirely consistent; they were as carefully considered in defense of Sacco and Vanzetti as they were in attacking communism, and they were founded on the same principles.

These principles, these concerns, were first defined for public readership in the two most fully developed and important of the early essays he wrote at college. The, first, "A Humble Protest," he published in the *Harvard Monthly* of June 1916, the month he graduated. Although it bears the marks of diffuse undergraduate writing—it asks, for example, "What is the end of human life?"—it raises concrete questions that would inform his great modernist works *Manhattan Transfer* and the *U.S.A.* trilogy: "What is the goal of this mechanical, splendidly inventive civilization of ours?" "How do [thought and art] fare under the rule of . . . Industrialism, and Mechanical Civilization?" How can twentieth-century culture reconcile its sense of accomplishment through science and industrialization with the method of its achievement, a "human pyramid where the few at the top are in the sunlight while the rest sweat in the filthy darkness of meaningless labor"?[1] "Has not the world

1

of today got itself enslaved by this immense machine, the Industrial system?" And, observing the relative benefits and costs of this modern system, can we call "this ponderous suicidal machine civilization"? He answers his own questions by citing the example of Germany, the "one modern nation which, as well as having developed the industrial system to its highest degree, has a really great living art"; yet that "same civilization has produced [both] . . . the Eroica Symphony and the ruins of Rheims" ("Humble," 120).

The purpose and nature of life in the modern industrial age, the human toll of mechanization and its threat to individualism, the pernicious, inevitable application of technology to systems that destroy civilization—these are the themes that echo through Dos Passos's mature modernist work. The second precursor to his fully realized work more specifically applies these concerns to his own nation and its literature. "Against American Literature," his first national publication, appeared in the *New Republic* in October 1916. This essay refracts the problem of the modern to illuminate what Dos Passos sees as an emptiness at the core of American writing. In a less confrontational but no less critical tone than that of "A Humble Protest," he takes his country's culture and writers to task for lacking a distinctive identity and for not challenging American readers to seek what is substantial, unique, and deeply spiritual in their own intellectual heritage. As "sincere, careful, and . . . shrewd" as the better American novels are, he asserts that it would be impossible for "anyone to confine himself for long to purely American books without feeling starved."[2] The vitality and the revolutionary conception of democracy ("our jumble of races") that were the foundations of this civilization, he believed, could yield something more meaningful than "steel and oil and grain" ("Against," 271), something more significant than the pallid, interchangeable books American writers were currently producing.

Essays such as these, other writing Dos Passos was crafting at Harvard and after, and his first novels were all expressions of his belief that the core of American democracy was the principle of individual liberty. Literature that was truly American, then, would stress the primacy of the individual. As he searched for this definitively American idiom whose lack he decried in these apprentice essays, his own writing would confront the powerful systems in his culture that threatened liberty and self-determination. Early in his career, as a young radical who came of age during the Great War and reached artistic maturity in the 1920s, he found the most imminent danger in the economic, governmental, and political structures of his own country. As fascism spread throughout post–World War I Europe, however, he began to detect disquieting evidence that the leftist organizations he had once regarded as defending individual liberties were instead more insidious threats to them than the forces he had earlier opposed. After experiencing Stalinism firsthand in Russia; seeing the American Communist Party's manipulation of the Harlan County, Kentucky, miners' strike; witnessing the Communists' disruption of a Socialist Party meeting in Madison Square Garden; and, finally, supporting the Republican cause in the Spanish Civil War only to lose a friend to Communist treachery, Dos Passos concluded that "America has got to be in a better position to work out the problem: individual liberty vs. bureaucratic industrial organization than any other part of the world."[3] He saw no incongruity between this stance and his earlier beliefs: his career had been an investigation of the effect of "superpower" of whatever kind on the individual and an attempt to use the forces at his disposal to affect the issue. Now that he focused on democracy as the only form of government that could protect the common person from manipulation, he came under fire from leftists who had formerly regarded him as one of their own. They bitterly denounced both his politics and his writing, but characteristically remaining committed to his beliefs, he put them into writing as he always had, creating for the remainder of his life political nonfiction, histories, and historically based fiction—the "chronicles" of his "chosen country," as he titled one of his later books.

From the beginning of his vocation, his art and politics had been inseparable. From his earliest exposure to the arts that constituted the beginnings of modernism, at Harvard and at the 1913 Armory Show of modern European and American painting, he had understood the revolutionary nature of modernist aesthetics, experiencing in the upheavals of the early twentieth century the culture that created modernism. Not only did modernism recreate that culture, but modernist arts had the potential to make powerful statements about the culture, even to change it, as Dos Passos realized in the artistic ferment of post–World War I Paris and New York. American and Russian filmmakers were exploiting innovative visual narrative forms in the service of politics; in Russia, Dos Passos exchanged ideas about the uses of montage with Sergei Eisenstein. Radical playwrights were staging experimental dramas about the plight of the proletariat; Dos Passos wrote plays and designed and created stage sets for the New Playwrights Theater with which many of his politically dedicated artist friends were associated. Mexican artists were unionizing and painting public art to explain the agrarian revolution to the common people, most of whom were illiterate; Dos Passos traveled to Mexico City to learn from the huge murals of Diego Rivera and write about them for *New Masses*, the reincarnation of the radical journal popular during the writer's Harvard days. While his political stances shaped his style throughout his career, the years during which he created his most fully realized modernist works were also the years of his most outspoken and active radicalism on the left. And just as modernism itself developed out of a dynamic interchange among the arts, his expressions of his leftist politics and groundbreaking modernist aesthetics crossed boundaries between disciplines. Such intertextuality in his work, however, is not surprising, since he not only maintained working relationships with many painters, wrote about the visual arts, and adapted their techniques into his literary style, but throughout his life he was also a practicing painter whose work was shown publicly both during his life and posthumously.

In the catalog accompanying a 1971 exhibition of visual art by writers, the listing of Dos Passos's paintings begins with this statement from the author: "The aim of every art is transmission of feeling, fashioned to the point of beauty, whether it be in the form of sound or shape or color or words on a page."[4] The title of this showing at the Arts Club of Chicago was "A Second Talent," implying that Dos Passos's first talent was writing, what he was best known for, even after some periods of critical dismissal over the course of a long, varied career until his death in 1970. In actuality, these two talents developed concurrently during the years of apprenticeship that enabled Dos Passos to produce *Manhattan Transfer* (1925) and the *U.S.A.* trilogy (1930, 1932, 1936), the modernist works for which he is best known. As a writer and a painter, he absorbed, reflected, and often anticipated the literary and visual movements that marked the evolution of modernism in the first third of the twentieth century. The parallel transformations of his narrative and visual techniques during these years illustrate how his involvement in World War I and his exposure to the burgeoning modernist movements just after the war generated the themes and verbal and visual structures that characterize his modernist innovations.

During the 1920s and 1930s, when he had fully achieved the innovations in narrative technique to which all his later work was inevitably compared, his paintings and drawings had merited several public exhibitions: at the Whitney Studio Club in 1923 (along with works by Adelaide Lawson and Ruben Nakian); in the New Playwrights Theater and at a nearby studio in 1927 and 1928; in the Provincetown Art Association Gallery in 1929; and at the Pierre Matisse Gallery in New York City in 1937. Later, in 1960, his paintings were included in the United Nations Art Club's Tenth Anniversary Exhibition, and after his death a few appeared in a 1975 University of Virginia Library display of his manuscripts and artifacts and in a 1979 Gallery Odin exhibition entitled "Innovators and Organizers of Modern Art—The 1913 Armory Show Thru the Thirties."

As the title of this exhibition implies, the paintings for which Dos Passos most often received critical praise were those he executed during what he termed "the creative tidal wave that spread over the world" during the years between World War I and the mid-1930s, the years during which modernism transformed all the arts.[5] Since 1979, the only two public recognitions of his painting have focused almost exclusively on his works from that period. A 1980 retrospective exhibition of 54 of his paintings and drawings at the Virginia Museum of Fine Arts in Richmond included few paintings from after the mid-1930s. *Doubly Gifted: The Author as Visual Artist,* a 1986 collection by Kathleen G. Hjerter of paintings by well-known writers, features two sketches by Dos Passos from 1918 and one of the paintings he produced in 1926 as part of his set design and publicity work for the expressionist New Playwrights Theater in New York.[6]

This featured painting, probably a poster for John Howard Lawson's satire about a labor dispute, is among Dos Passos's most completely modernist visual expressions. In bold reds, blues, and yellows, Dos Passos layers the play's name, *Processional,* an almost abstract marching parade, and a man's figure distorted by its tension against dark bars that suggest a jail cell or ladder. The painting's dynamic colors, content, and design evoke some of the most important artistic movements associated with American and European modernism—expressionism, cubism, precisionism, synchromism. As is usually the case when Dos Passos's "second talent" is publicly recognized today, Hjerter features a painting whose techniques parallel the techniques he evolved in his novels of the 1920s and 1930s to express his modernist themes. Because his writing constituted such a definitive contribution to the development of literary modernism in America, and because *Manhattan Transfer* and the *U.S.A.* trilogy pioneered the American "cubist novel," it is not surprising that the occasional appraisal of his other talents should discover in them the characteristic strengths of his literary style.

Today, his reputation rests largely on the "technical brilliance and mastery of language" of his "massive achievement" *U.S.A.,* as the

Reader's Encyclopedia summarizes his accomplishment.[7] As late as 1922, however, Dos Passos himself was unsure "whether [he] wanted most to paint or write," as he noted in his memoir, *The Best Times*.[8] By then, although he was still deliberating about his direction, he had already published four books and had spent several months in Spain studying art and architecture. In an interview in 1968, two years before his death, he expressed regret at not having developed his architectural ability more extensively. Instead, he noted, he had channeled that ability into the "objective painting" that interested him.[9]

The choice of a vocation seems to have been made for him, however, before 1922, by his experiences in World War I. As a driver for the Norton-Harjes ambulance corps, he was stationed first, in 1917, in Paris, where the architecture "moved [him] like music" (*Best*, 49), then at the French front, then on to the Italian front with a Red Cross unit. There, he was excited by the architecture, by the "sight of Venice across a lagoon sheathed with a thin scrim of ice," and by the thirteenth- and fourteenth-century paintings he saw.[10] But he had also seen "the grey crooked fingers of the dead, the dark look of dirty mangled bodies," had heard "their groans & joltings in the ambulances, the vast tomtom of the guns," as he wrote in one of the journal entries collected in *The Fourteenth Chronicle*.[11]

The incongruity of such horror amid the ancient culture and beauty in these European theaters of war convinced him that he must "be able to express . . . all the tragedy and hideous excitement of it . . . , must experience more of it, & more." He knew even then what he needed to express was not just the ugliness and brutality of war on a foreign continent; it was the inhumanity of a civilization or a government that would, through "lies & hypocritical patriotic gibber" such as he had heard in America, perpetuate a conflict that could in an instant destroy the intellectual and cultural achievements of "long generations toiling" (*Fourteenth*, 90–95). He needed, in short, "to try to describe in colors that would not fade . . . our America that we loved and hated" ("What," 30).

Yet the very wording of his declaration of purpose reveals that while he may have chosen to express what he saw and felt in writing instead of in painting, Dos Passos still thought like a visual artist, conceiving his writing in visual terms and informing his work with what he had learned of form, dynamic, color, and space through the painting he had done and seen. Throughout his career he used the vocabulary of the visual arts to express himself. At first, in his Harvard writing and in his early writing about the war, he drew on the classical and romantic traditions with which he was familiar from his extensive travels and from his Harvard education. Even the "feverish notes" he scribbled between battles and campaigns read like paintings: "[A] pearly glow lights up the pedimented facades of the houses on the hills and the square pointed church that rises above them, etching them curiously against the dark hills behind the town, where the lights, . . . match those in the brilliant night sky" (*Best,* 59). His impressions of the war were all the more intense for his feeling "that perhaps we were the last men who would ever look on [the] masterpieces" of Europe, and "that perhaps [those masterpieces] might be the last thing we would experience on this earth" ("What," 30).

Modernism

As Dos Passos's vision of the world and America became more complex, so did the visual sensibility underlying his writing. In his early writing, he had used overtly representational descriptions to communicate the subjective impressions of an individual protagonist; but once he confronted a fragmented "civilization . . . torn and battered by every nightmare scourge" imaginable, he felt that only "objectivity" could express the nature of such a life. Later, in *U.S.A.,* after the apex of his modernist style and sensibility in *Manhattan Transfer,* he would try to reclaim something of the old values, something of the romantic mind-set of his prewar writing. Even as he developed into a fully modernist writer, his guiding principle was still romantic: "Keats was right when he exclaimed that beauty was truth and truth beauty" ("What," 30).

Just after the war, however, that truth demanded methods reflecting its multiplicity, complexity, dynamism, and speed. He instinctively turned to the same kinds of techniques the visual artists of the day were experimenting with, because his goals were the same. To relate "the lives of the men [he] had known so intimately in the army, of their women friends and mine . . . to the bloody panorama of history" required the kind of "simultaneity" he found in the cubism "of the painters of the school of Paris." To make the life "stand up off the page" required the direct emotion he found in the poetry of Rimbaud and the symbolists. To "record the fleeting world the way the motion picture film recorded it" required the "rapportage[,] . . . juxtaposition, montage" of Griffith's and Eisenstein's innovations ("What," 31). The war, the resultant despair and loss of traditional religious faith, and the urban industrial revolution that followed in America had rendered nineteenth-century beliefs, values, and mimetic artistic modes obsolete. Dos Passos searched for narrative techniques that would free literary expression from outmoded linearity into the space, time, and motion previously thought possible only in the visual arts.

But it was not simply his association with visual artists, or the artistic ferment of the time, or even his painter's eye that led Dos Passos to infuse his writing with a visual vocabulary. It was his realization that words were inadequate to express the world as he had seen it become. Words used in old ways were not equal to his purposes and vision in the war's aftermath. Like Jimmy Herf, the writer who is the closest approximation to a protagonist in the welter of characters in *Manhattan Transfer,* Dos Passos no longer "had faith in words."[12]

Dos Passos was not alone in his realization that a new language was necessary to convey modern experience. That realization, the "determination to invent a new style . . . to express the . . . change in the modern world," was "the primary gesture of modernism," as Stephen Spender noted.[13] Modernist artists perceived "a frightening discontinuity between the traditional past," with its reassuring verities and faiths, "and the shaken present," with its disquieting scientific and technological revelations. They believed that, in the aftermath of the war's brutality, "[h]uman nature," too, had irrevocably "changed" (Howe, 15). The gulf they felt between past and present seemed to undermine the comfortable notion of linear historical development and to throw into discomfiting relief the dislocated, fragmented rhythms of contemporary life.

Dos Passos observed much later in his career that the near chaos of modern existence in postwar America had completely invalidated what he called "the great formulations of the generation of 1776," the expressions of belief out of which the American Republic was constructed.[14] These "old words," such as "Life, liberty, and the pursuit of happiness," had become "dusty and hung with the faded bunting of a thousand political orations," he believed (*Occasions,* 13–14). For individuals trying to maintain identity and integrity while the impersonal forces of government, capitalism, technology, and urban life threatened to overwhelm them, the "old words" had become meaningless and fragmented. Like Jimmy Herf, each individual struggles just to remember and hear, let alone trust or live by, expressions of what the Republic promised in its beginning. By the time of *Manhattan Transfer,* via Herf's fragmented point of view, Dos Passos showed these words and promises as syntactically and actually broken: "Pursuit of happiness, unalienable pursuit . . . right to life liberty and . . ." (365). A new world, disjunctive and insecure as it might be, required a new language, one that transcended the limitations of verbal expression.

The Interartistic Analogy

Dos Passos, like other modernists, sought that revolutionary language in the formal techniques of the visual arts. These forms, they hoped, would prove more capable of capturing modern existence precisely because they purported to be only one person's vision of "reality." In response to the destruction of the notion of absolute external "reality," modernist writers sought in their own consciousnesses a way to reconstruct the world "out of [their] own creativity" (Gottfried Benn quoted in Howe, 15). What had been thematic issues in the romantic art that nurtured these modernists became structural issues to them. Whereas romantic writers such as Wordsworth explored the power of the individual consciousness to transform experience, Dos Passos and other modernist writers recreated for the reader in their narrative forms the actual working of the transforming consciousness. The subjective perception became the epistemology of modernist art. Similarly, the romantic "discovery that the field of human experience is time" impelled the modernists to seek narrative techniques that did not simply tell about time's effect, but actually created it.[15] As Georges Braque had declared, they believed that "one must not imitate what one wants to create."[16]

Thus, the modernists, by abandoning mimesis, tried to depict the simultaneity of time in space—of a modern world full of isolated individuals acting in individual realities. Alone, a temporal medium—words—seemed inadequate in this attempt to dissolve "the traditional duality between the world and its representation . . . [and] the commonly accepted distance between subject and act of representation." The result of this concentration on form as message, the modernists hoped, would be a creation of one individual world, a self-sufficient work, one of the "central direction[s] in modernist literature" (Howe, 27–28). The self-contained artwork, concomitantly, was a reflection of the "self-contained individual" one had to be to survive modernity, the modernists ruefully asserted.[17]

The modernist preoccupation with form—form as message rather than representation—elicited a dizzying variety of responses from early modernist writers. James Joyce's single day in Dublin immerses the reader into the associative mind of Leopold Bloom and the physical intelligence of Molly Bloom. T. S. Eliot's mythical landscape bristles with such personal and universal significances that the reader needs a map of notes to navigate among them. And Gertrude Stein's essential portraits of figures and locales slowly emerge for the reader from the accumulation of a complex of visual and verbal detail. These are only some of the best known of the multiplicity of modernist attempts to produce icons that are simultaneously free of mimesis yet partake of the spirit of the world that produced their creators—artists who would, above all, "make it new," as Ezra Pound decreed. Critics have found that the modernist idea of painting-as-object, resembling literary work at least in its intent, provides a useful metaphor for the work of some of these writers, particularly those, like Gertrude Stein, whose training and milieu included several artistic modes.

While critics have found the interartistic analogy helpful in exploring modernist writers such as Stein and Joyce, more often they have used historicist approaches to writers such as Dos Passos, Hemingway, or Fitzgerald, whose work comments explicitly on social and political issues of their day. A glance at the most comprehensive and recent of the three Dos Passos bibliographies, for instance, reveals the historicist or Marxist slant of most of the writing about him.[18] Of more than 40 doctoral dissertations written in the United States since 1930 dealing solely with Dos Passos, half deal with historical or political aspects of his work. The titles of his own works, both early and late—from *Manhattan Transfer* to *Century's Ebb,* his final chronicle, posthumously published—suggest his consciousness of his times and his historical and political context. Neither the critics' nor Dos Passos's historicist orientation is surprising, however, for the modernists were always acutely aware that their era marked the irrevocable loss of past verities and the resultant possibility for—the urgent need for—an "aesthetic revolution."[19] When Dos Passos wrote explicitly about modernism, he defined it in social and political as well as artistic terms. Its influences and movements, he said, were "borne in the air" of that time ("What," 30). He called it "an explosion . . . that had an influence in its sphere comparable with that of the October revolution in social organization and politics" ("Foreword," 30).

But Dos Passos's definition of modernism stresses also its manifestations in all the arts of the period. The "artistic ferment" ("What," 30) that characterized the movement produced "most of the best work in the arts of our time," he wrote in 1931:

> [Blaise] Cendrars and Apollinaire, poets, were on the first cubist barri-
> cades with the group that included Picasso, Modigliani, Marinetti, Cha-

gall; that profoundly influenced Maiakovsky, Meyerhold, Eisenstein; whose ideas carom through Joyce, Gertrude Stein, T. S. Eliot. . . . The music of Stravinsky and Prokofieff and Diageleff's Ballet hail from this same Paris already in the disintegration of victory, as do the windows of Saks Fifth Avenue, skyscraper furniture, the Lenin Memorial in Moscow, the paintings of Diego Rivera in Mexico City and the newritz styles of advertising in American magazines. ("Foreword," vii–viii)

This eclectic catalog of modernist practitioners appeared in Dos Passos's explanatory foreword to *Le Panama et mes sept oncles,* a book by the French avant-garde poet Blaise Cendrars. Dos Passos not only translated the poems into English but also illustrated them with a series of watercolors, bearing out his observation of the pervasiveness of modernism in the various arts and of the interrelatedness of all manifestations of modernism.

Such interartistic analogies have traditionally been based, as is Dos Passos's, on "historical criteria," on "the presence of a zeitgeist illuminating all the arts," the same criteria that provide the basis for most criticism of Dos Passos's work.[20] When critics have tried to extend the interartistic analogy beyond the grounds of periodization, they have been met with serious objections from prominent quarters. Rene Wellek points out that "the various arts . . . have each their individual evolution, with . . . a different internal structure of elements."[21] More recently, Jean Laude declares, "Absolutely everything distinguishes a literary text from a painting or a drawing: its conception, its method of production, its modes of appreciation, its identity as an object irreducible to any other object, and its autonomous functioning."[22]

Equally prominent voices, however, assert that analogical thinking is among the most natural human methods of inquiry. M. H. Abrams, in his important study *The Mirror and the Lamp,* explains that "critical thinking" is often "thinking in parallels, and critical argument" is often "argument from analogy."[23] "[M]etaphors, analogies, models, diagrams, [and] pictures," Wendy Steiner argues in *The Colors of Rhetoric: Problems in the Relation between Modern Literature and Painting,* "allow[ ] a system to be explored in depth or a notion to be followed in all its relations and implications"—"a dynamic process." This kind of dynamic interchange among artists, their ideas, and their works obviously underlay the modernists' efforts. William Carlos Williams, for instance, defined modernism as "a fusion of the goals of poetry and painting." Modernist writers, Williams explained, strove to go "beyond the mere thought

expressed" to discover "the tactile qualities [of words], the words themselves. . . . [That] is the reason why painting and the poem became so
closely allied" (Steiner, 1, 72, 380).

Not only did modernist artists in different media seek the same goal,
as Williams explained, but their essential conception of the relation of
the work of art to the world was the same despite their varying media. A
"preoccupation with the art-life relation" was characteristic of the modernists, as Steiner observes, as it was with the romantics before them.
But in modernist art, mimesis was not necessarily a primary goal. For
the modernists, the work of art became "an independent object with the
same degree of 'thingness' as objects in the world." Modernists
attempted to go beyond representing reality "to create a portion of reality itself" in the work of art (Steiner, 17). As F. T. Marinetti passionately
expressed in his 1909 manifesto, the goals of the Italian futurists were
not to reproduce a "fixed moment" but to make of the work "the
dynamic sensation itself."[24] In keeping with this concept of the work,
modernists emphasized the tangible properties of whatever medium
they used (Steiner, 17). In literature, this emphasis resulted in words
that could "stand up off the page," as Dos Passos characterized his modernist technique ("What," 30).

Chapter Two
A "Double Foreigner":
The Shaping of a Writer

John Dos Passos is one of the first generation of writers whose themes and techniques announced the coming of modernism to American literature and art. Born out of wedlock to Lucy Sprigg Madison and John Randolph Dos Passos on January 14, 1896, he experienced a childhood that gave him a unique perspective on America and directed him into the changing cultural currents of his time and nation. As a "double foreigner," a phrase he later used to characterize the generally autobiographical protagonist of *Chosen Country,* Dos Passos could see clearly the promise and cost of the life twentieth-century America was breeding; emotionally, he could sense how compelling it was to claim American identity and all that it implied, since as a boy he had no sure national identity.

The illegitimate son of a Virginia gentlewoman and a prominent corporation lawyer, Dos Passos grew up in Europe, where his parents could travel together discreetly for weeks at a time. Discretion was necessary since his father, John R., was a Catholic married to a New York socialite, and his mother, Lucy, was married as well, although long estranged from her husband. Soon after his birth, Lucy took her child, whom she called Jack, to Brussels, where they remained until 1901, when they returned to Washington, D.C., where John R. frequently had business and where he maintained a household for Lucy and Jack. The boy began his schooling at the Sidwell Friends School in 1901, but when he and his mother moved to London, he entered Peterborough Lodge, a boarding school.

John R., largely self-educated, had ambitious plans for the development of his son's intellect. Because he believed the English educational system superior to the American, he chose Peterborough Lodge with an eye toward enrolling Jack later at Oxford or Cambridge. In fact, the father was the definition of many of the forces that would become the focus of the son's literary career. The son of a Portuguese shoemaker whose immigrant father had settled in Philadelphia, John R. embodied the opportunity for self-determination that emerges as the essence of

13

American ambition in many of Dos Passos's characters—the opportunistic French immigrant Congo in *Manhattan Transfer,* for instance,
who arrives in the United States as a mess boy on a ship and becomes a
millionaire entrepreneur with a Park Avenue address. John R. himself
rose from the position of office boy in a Philadelphia law firm to become
one of the most successful corporate lawyers and writers on economic
practice in the Gilded Age. Among other works, he published *A Treatise
on the Law of Stockbrokers and Stock Exchanges* in 1882, a book that became
a standard text for brokers. Most of his work at the apex of his career,
however, was directed toward building and defending trusts. He acted
on behalf of H. O. Havemeyer in developing the Sugar Trust, which
controlled 98 percent of the sugar refined in the United States. This
effort, for which he reportedly earned the largest legal fee on record up
to that time, resulted in an 1895 Supreme Court decision allowing such
exclusive control of an industry. Like the social Darwinists of the same
period, John R. advocated—and practiced—the belief that the fittest
had a right to amass wealth: he wrote, "[T]he road to fortune is open to
us all, and if we have not individually been successful enough to acquire
a great amount of property, we should not belittle the men who have
been more fortunate. . . . [They are] men who . . . by hard work, skill
and luck have acquired fortunes . . . , types of American citizenship, and
. . . incentives to young people."[1]

If in his self-creation John R. anticipated those characters in his son's
work who respond to the ideal of unlimited possibilities in America, his
unswerving capitalism provided his son with a model of the economic
forces that in novels such as the *U.S.A.* trilogy undermine integrity and
overwhelm individualism. Given his father's career and beliefs, Dos Passos's literary themes and his political leanings until late in the 1930s
may be interpreted partly as rebellions against what this paternal figure
represented.

Moreover, since John R.'s sporadic intrusions into young Jack's life
with his beloved mother diverted the lavish attention she otherwise paid
him, it is little wonder that even as a boy he felt ambivalent about this
powerful authority figure whose very role was purposely ill defined in
his life. This aggressive, self-confident man whose own biases controlled
Jack's schooling was known to him as his "guardian"; John R. did not
marry Lucy until his wife's death in 1910, whereupon Jack was finally
able to change his name from his mother's Madison to Dos Passos.

Although John R.'s ambitions for his son had dictated Peterborough
Lodge for Jack, the boy concurred with his mother's wish to return to

the country of his birth, of which Lucy spoke so wistfully. While his marks at Peterborough were respectable, Lucy nevertheless opposed her lover's wish that their son continue there. Instead, the rootless pair asserted their desire to live permanently in America, the land Dos Passos called his "chosen country" later in his life. This term, given his early expatriation and his adult peregrinations all over the world, assumes great significance for a writer whose central concern was what his chosen country was becoming during his lifetime.

In 1906, he and his mother returned to America and settled in Washington, largely because of the proximity to his father, but also because of the boy's yearning to feel less of an outsider: he had been one of only two American boys at Peterborough Lodge and, in any case, had spent most of his childhood with his mother and her older female relatives and friends, and was unused to the rough-and-tumble play among young boys. Summers brought Lucy and Jack to John R.'s large estate, a working farm in Sandy Point, Virginia, near the mouth of the Potomac in the Tidewater region. But before long, John R.'s ambitions for the boy's education dictated another relocation: Jack was sent in 1907 to the Choate School in Wallingford, Connecticut. The sound classical curriculum there, John R. hoped, could fit the boy for a career in law.

"I hated boardingschool," Dos Passos wrote years later in *The Best Times* (15). It was not merely his opposition to his father's choice of his school that evoked such a reaction, however. Amid Choate's confident, competitive, and prominent students, all of whom were older than he, the shy, bookish boy whose paternity was unclear felt even more alienated than he had at Peterborough Lodge. In one of the autobiographical "Camera Eye" sections of *U.S.A.,* he characterized the boys at Choate as "clean young . . . Rover Boys."[2] There, he felt keenly his position as a "double outsider": too long in Europe to sound or act entirely American, he felt himself "an Englishman in America and an American in England."[3] Although he disliked competitive sports, he relished hiking or canoeing trips by himself or with his one close friend, Franklin Nordhoff. And young Jack became active in the school's publications and dramatics.

But his primary interest was books: by the end of tenth grade, he had won the Class Day prize for "Excellence in English" and an honorable mention for excellence in classics; and in the eleventh grade, he was editor in chief of the *Choate News* as well as literary editor. The Class Day of the year of his graduation, 1911, he again took the top award in English and was commended as well for his continuing editorship of the school paper. As literary editor of the paper that year, he had organized and edited a special literary supplement to it. Besides the works of Choate's most notable student writers, the publication contained one of Jack's own stories, "The City of Burnished Copper"—his first work in print. The story appeared without his name, however, perhaps because of his characteristic modesty or because he was suddenly unsure of how to represent his legal name. Less than a year earlier, in June 1910, his mother had very quietly married Jack's "guardian": Lucy's former husband had been deceased since 1903, and Mary Hays Dos Passos had died in March 1910. When John R. and Lucy chose to make the marriage public in October 1910, after what they felt was a decent interval following the death of his first wife, John R. rapidly instructed Jack never again to address letters to his mother under the name of Madison. "We will attend to yours later," John R. wrote, adding the advice that Jack inform his headmaster of the event "quietly," but leaving the choice to Jack.[4]

The young Jack Madison must have felt some ambivalence about both his mother's marriage and his guardian's advice: he finished out his term at Choate through June 1911 still calling himself Madison, even though his name had legally become Dos Passos when his parents married—and, by that time, he apparently knew that John R. was his father. But the potential embarrassment of assuming that name must have been painful for the deeply self-conscious boy, despite his longing to resolve the ambiguous status of his parentage. Were he to assume the name Dos Passos, he would draw attention to the irregularity of his parents' previous relationship by potentially affirming publicly what many both within and outside of the families already suspected: that John R. was Jack's real father, that Lucy was his natural mother, and that Jack was not, as Lucy had given the world and her family to understand, an adopted foundling. Jack's ambivalence about his public status was surely reinforced by John R.'s own extreme sensitivity about the matter. At the top of the letter giving Jack instructions about his mother's name change and about Jack's name, John R. wrote *Détruissez* (Destroy).

A sense of distance from the society he inhabited, a feeling of not belonging, a consciousness of the weight of large cultural forces on people's lives, such as the burdens propriety imposed on his and his parents' lives—these products of his childhood became central issues in his adult work. The rebellion against paternal authority that had shaped his adolescence would emerge in his maturity as an impulse toward artistic and political experimentation and a rejection of traditional aesthetics.

Certainly, his father's ambitions for him continued to direct his life powerfully once he graduated from Choate. Although Jack had taken and passed the entrance exams for Harvard immediately after graduation, his father believed that, at barely 15, Jack would benefit from a year of travel and experience before undertaking college. For once, Jack agreed with his father, especially since he was to go abroad not with either parent, as he had so often before, but with a companion, a Mr. Jones, who was to serve as tutor.

The summer before they were to sail in November 1911 Jack spent preparing for the journey at his father's farm in Sandy Point. As much as he came to love the peace and long-standing traditions of the Northern Neck area, during that summer the rural South seems to have exacerbated in the adolescent the restlessness and craving for adventure that had already been burning in him, as his recollections of the time betray. His autobiographical voice in a "Camera Eye" segment remembers how he "wanted to go away and to foreign cities Carcasonne Marakesh Isfahan" (*42nd,* 209). And he experienced longings not just for adventure but, like any 15-year-old, for more adult kinds of knowledge. Both in this "Camera Eye" and later in the experiences of his autobiographical hero, Jay Pignatelli, in *Chosen Country,* Dos Passos relates how the proximity of the girls with whom he came into contact—one, a young servant, another, the daughter of the household cook—made him long for intimacies: "If I only had the nerve breathless nights when the moon was full" (*42nd,* 209). He wrote movingly about these unrealized desires even before *U.S.A.,* however, in a short story published in 1924 in *transatlantic review.* In this story, "July," he depicts the urge of his autobiographical protagonist, Jimmy Herf, to seek some intimate connection after his passions have been stirred by chance encounters—brushing against a girl's breast when he teaches her to swim, noticing the bulge of a pregnant woman's stomach. Tellingly, in this story, the refinements of class and education become restrictions as potent as his own acute shyness on Herf's behavior. As Dos Passos, early the romantic artist, must have also done, Herf transforms his longings into fantasy: he creates an alter ego who rescues a beautiful maiden from danger and escapes with her "naked in each other's arms in the brocaded love barge among the lotus flowers."[5]

Even though the adolescent Jack shied away from sexual experience out of reticence and a rigid sense of propriety, he was receptive to a broadened perspective on the world. In fact, the six-month tour he took under the guidance of his tutor, Mr. Jones, encouraged the growth of some directions and practices that would become central to his mature work. The habit of keeping a journal, from which the summer in Virginia had distracted him, he renewed the day he and Mr. Jones sailed from New York for England. In the entries about his travels from November 1911 until their return in May 1912, he begins to demonstrate a perspective on history that, enlarged by his political thinking as an adult, underlies his "chronicles" (*Fourteenth,* 631) of the United States and other nations, as he began calling his novels and commentaries in the 1960s.

The journal of this grand tour also records the beginnings of Dos Passos's lifelong involvement in the visual arts, whose techniques would become so dynamic and integral a part of his brand of modernism. Already in this journal small sketches illustrate architectural or painterly details he describes; and as his journals more and more served as the basis for his fiction during the Great War and into the 1920s, likewise his sketches and pastels began to capture and interpret what he was seeing and experiencing. Dos Passos, who was to become an accomplished painter as an adult, an acute critic of contemporary art, and a friend and supporter of some of the most important painters of the twentieth century, reveals in these adolescent journals the beginnings of an aptitude that became a vital avocation for him.

A few years after this trip, in an unpublished manuscript, he proclaimed that art consists of "a revolt against the excessive finiteness of life"—a revolt against traditions and forms that inhibit or proscribe individual expression.[6] Certainly, his growth as a modernist represents his own rejection of received aesthetic notions and their concomitant cultural assumptions. But before he or any other American artist in any medium could revolt against tradition, there had to *be* a tradition. And, for Dos Passos, what constituted traditional art, from classical to romantic, provided both the basic elements against which he would revolt and the impetus for his need to innovate. Ironically, romanticism—the very complex of ideals, icons, and techniques from which the artists of the early twentieth century would depart into modernism—was itself a revolution in the beginning.

It was a revolution against classicism and against its eighteenth-century manifestation, neoclassicism. In general, the term *classicism* encompasses the stable, authoritative, unified, essentially mimetic formalism that informed the arts during the rationalist late seventeenth century, especially in France. Seventeenth-century classicism, drawing its values from an idealized Greco-Roman civilization, sought "greatness through the adoption of common forms which it tried to make exclusive."[7] Thus, the classical aesthetic regularized expression and established orthodoxy. For the classicist, the imposition of order on chaos, the valuation of reason over emotion, produced an aesthetic tradition of restraint and balance.

Ancient architecture, art, and literature, the models for this classical aesthetic, underlay the earliest formalized attempts at design and literature in America, formed the basis of a "proper" education for a young American man, and dictated the course of his broadening education outside the walls of the university as well. The grand tour of Europe and the repositories of ancient, classical civilization were de rigueur for the sons of nineteenth- and early-twentieth-century upper-class families. This ritual of travel exposed young Americans to the artifacts and manifestations of the classical philosophical and literary aesthetic still perpetuated in universities of the era.

Likewise, Dos Passos's education exposed him to the breadth of the world's cultures. He received during his years at Harvard solid grounding in Greek and Latin literature, Greek philosophy, and Italian medieval and Renaissance art, as the records of the Office of the Registrar report. Such course work only reinforced the classical education Dos Passos had begun at Choate and continued in his own grand tour in 1911 and 1912, primarily visiting Italy, Greece, and France. Already unwilling to genuflect before a work of art simply because of its reputation for greatness, Dos Passos at the age of 15 nevertheless recorded all the works he saw with exacting detail that suggests his sensitivity to the techniques of visual art. From the young journalist's fascination with the marble mosaics of the Medici Chapel in Florence's Church of San Lorenzo, for instance, emerges a concern for composition and color that informs much of his commentary, distinguishing it by its nascent critical faculties and painter's sensibility.

Similarly, Dos Passos's enthusiasm over a Greco-Etruscan artifact he saw in Florence at the Archaeological Museum illustrates both his solid background in and understanding of classical aesthetics. The journal entry demonstrates his leaning, even at 15, toward a realistic, expressive visual style similar to the literary styles he would favor and assimilate later. The "very fine Graeco-Etruscan painted sarcophagos [*sic*]" he viewed there was "the only real specimen of Greek painting" he had ever seen.[8] He knew, obviously, that the once-vivid colors of Greek paintings, bas-reliefs, and statuary had been effaced by time, as the 1748 discovery of Pompeii, for instance, revealed. The focus of nineteenth-century

artists on Pompeii as subject and model, however, ignored the often garish painting on the architecture found in the preserved city, and they
chose to emulate only the solemn, regular, and unpainted rectilinear
forms that had become the nineteenth century's idea of antiquity.[9] Confronted by an example of the art as it actually appeared, Dos Passos
appraised it on its own terms despite his evident knowledge of it as
"classical art": "The features of the men and women—it represented a
battle between Greeks and Amazons—were bold and very true to life.
The horses and clothing were as good as anything I have seen anywhere
and the coloring was excellent and very soft. In short it was one of the
finest paintings I have ever seen anywhere, of any kind, and interested
me more than all the old masters and their pupils put together"
("Diary," 97–98).

The young traveler did, in fact, have grounds for such a declaration.
Besides all the art he had been exposed to in his earlier travels with his
mother in Europe and the ancient world, on this tour he saw the architecture and cathedrals of Rome, the ancient buildings and works of art
of Athens, Mycenae, Corinth, and Delphi, and the churches and palaces
of Venice and Florence. In each of these and the smaller cities in
between, he looked at the masterpieces of Andrea del Sarto, Fra Angelico,
Michelangelo, Raphael, Titian, Tintoretto, Bellini, and Reni, among
others. As indefatigable a chronicler as he was a tourist, Dos Passos
painstakingly recorded each site's historical and artistic significance,
writing with self-confidence, if usually without inspiration, born of his
extensive aesthetic training. The journal does acknowledge warmly the
superiority of some of those works that comprise the classical canon: St.
Paul's in Rome is "most beautiful and . . . most inspiring"; the theater of
Dionysius at Athens is "very handsome"; the Doges Palace in Venice is
"very interesting" ("Diary," 27, 65, 80).

But what jolts the young writer out of his respectful yet often unen-
thusiastic compendium of names and facts is, as in the case of the
painted sarcophagus, the occasional obscure work in which he sees
reflected the individual and the culture that formed it. Of the original
state of Greco-Etruscan paintings, he remarks "how wonderful the
art must have been when at its height" and observes how "wonderfully
lifelike" are the enamel inlaid eyes of a bronze charioteer in Delphi
("Diary," 98, 77). Already, in these small recognitions of the human consciousness expressing itself in the work and of that consciousness's individual relationship to and perception of his time, Dos Passos was in
revolt against the objective aesthetic limits of a classicism that valued

unity, universality, and reason as correctives to the transitory relativism of spontaneous expression.

Dos Passos's isolated, expatriate childhood and his unusually immediate education in European and classical art sharpened his awareness of the gap between classical values and individual experience. Certainly, the breadth of his early experiences gave him a sensitive imagination, while the irregular circumstances of his upbringing may have created in him an emotional sensitivity to the precarious instability of his life with his mother. As a result of these exposures to foreign cultures and his enforced awareness of himself as a foreigner, the direction of his earliest work constitutes a paradigm of the process by which American writers and painters began their evolution out of European influences toward a national art.

When he recalled his childhood as a "double foreigner" (*Chosen*, 26), for instance, in writing of the autobiographical protagonist of a 1951 novel, it was in images of color and light that suggest an early sensitivity to those elements of his environment that eventually became the most characteristic aspects of his style up to *Manhattan Transfer*. In his recollections in later novels such as *Chosen Country*, in memoirs such as *The Best Times*, and in college essays such as the 1916 "Les Lauriers Sont Coupés," France, Belgium, Portugal, and England, where he began school, emerge in landscapes suffused with a luminist radiance suggesting that earlier American school's emphasis on a nostalgic but objective representation of "time stilled."[10] Impressionist effects also convey the young observer's keen sense of the moment and suggest the writer's awareness of the applicability of that European technique to his subject matter: "I never can get down into the roaring cave of the Gare du Nord without feeling the thrill of early memories of trains and stations. The hissing of the white clouds of steam and the corpse-like glare or arc-lamps shrouded in smoke, bring back inevitably my first exultant awe and wonder at the swiftness of trains and the hugeness of crowds."[11]

In this description written in 1916, Dos Passos, nonetheless, conveys something of the aesthetic and the perception of a transient time evidenced in J. M. W. Turner's painting of a train nearly a quarter of a century earlier. Certainly, Dos Passos's mise-en-scène and effects recall the Gare St. Lazare of Monet, whose techniques engaged the young writer's interest.[12] When Dos Passos recalled in 1916 the scenes of his childhood, he invested them with "a dim halo, a pale, intense light . . . suffusing them with strange beauty."[13] Like his prose and poetry of that era, his adult memoirs acquire an impressionist mistiness suggesting the writer's consciousness of technique during that apprentice period. But his earliest aesthetic impressions, set down in the journal he kept during his grand tour, by comparison constitute a kind of plein air, concrete style that hints at the immediacy and realism that would characterize his early modernist works. As Townsend Ludington notes in his 1980 biography, "Dos Passos's comments in his diary [and his] letters to his parents [suggest] the writer he would become."[14] Besides their interest as examples of his earliest style and experiences, these entries constitute a valuable record of the young Dos Passos's exposure to European art and culture and of his nascent critical faculties.

Italian Art

An inveterate chronicler even at 15, Dos Passos kept the journal almost daily on his grand tour from November 1911 to April 1912, perhaps to be able to relate his experiences to his mother, by this time an invalid. The works, techniques, and artists that impress the young writer convey his acute responses even then to color and design and his sure intuition for the human and the real. For instance, although he catalogs hundreds of works he viewed, he comments favorably and in detail about relatively few. Usually, he devotes his longest descriptions to works, such as Titian's *Assumption of the Virgin* and Tintoretto's *Last Supper*, or groups of works that he perceives as organically integrated into their settings. Two repositories in particular caught his attention because of their synthesis of color, design, and technique—the Medici Chapel in the Church of San Lorenzo, and the Convent of Saint Mark, both in Florence. These impressions remained with him. When he returned to Florence—"drab olive grey with bright green shutters" (*Fourteenth*, 164)—during his wartime service, those sites evoked from him the assertion that they were among "the great places in Italy": "How they could paint[,] those . . . Florentine masters!"[15]

It was not just the paintings that interested Dos Passos at 15. In the case of the Medici Chapel as well as several other sites he singled out for comment, it was the vibrancy of the mosaics. Originally a pagan art, mosaic inlay had over the centuries been adapted to the purposes of the Christian church, but its practitioners still employed many of the pagan designs.[16] Precious or semiprecious stones often constituted the working materials, as in the unusually colorful Filippo Lippi mosaic *Jacob and Abraham* (c. 1497), inlaid with lapis, malachite, and cinnabar to form dynamic figures that Dos Passos admired.

The Medici Chapel mosaics, however, employed precious marbles to form panels interspersed with the tombs of the Medicis embedded in the walls. Dos Passos perceived the semiological implications of the juxtaposition of the art commissioned by the powerful family and their tombs, commenting on the "pride of a proud family" that produced this "rich jewel" of a chapel but likening it to an "Egyptian tomb"—a monument to death—in a connection recalling Shelley's "Ozymandias" ("Diary of Italy," 94). Dos Passos's fascination with the ornate work prefigures his leanings during his Harvard days toward the work of the aesthetes and the symbolists.

By the time Dos Passos revisited Florence in 1918, his experiences in the war had shown him the artificiality of that aesthete sensibility. Yet something drew him back to the Medici tombs and to the Convent of St. Mark as well. What had attracted him in 1912 to the convent-turned-museum, "where Fra Angelico and Savanarola lived," were "Fra Angelico's beautiful frescoes which illustrate the different public rooms and many of the cells" ("Diary," 88). Typically packed with activity and variety, often portraying an accurate cross section of society, and usually created to enhance the aesthetics of worship or simply to decorate a household, frescoes constitute visual narratives whose panels function both as autonomous works and as integrated segments of a larger design, the structure that houses them. Given these functions, they naturally interested Dos Passos, who later attempted, in his own way, to create a representative panorama of his own culture in discrete parts that nevertheless depended on their interrelationship for their meaning. Similarly, he naturally gravitated toward the works of Fra Angelico, who achieved what Dos Passos recognized as "wonderfully ethereal" effects with suffusing light that helped convey the narrative significance of, for instance, the *Annunciation.* This painting the young traveler found one of the painter's "most beautiful" ("Diary," 88).

Returning to St. Mark's during the war, however, Dos Passos was less impressed by the ethereality of the master's works than by the "frenzy of life" that leaped from them ("Diary of Italy," 46), was drawn not to the sublime, light-filled *Annunciation,* but to the apocalyptic *Last Judgment* that Fra Angelico painted to decorate the chair priests used during the celebration of High Mass.[17] With his drive into Italy with his ambulance corps, the "tragedy and hideous excitement" of the French front, the "dark look of dirty mangled bodies . . . [and] the vast tomtom of the guns" fresh in his mind (*Fourteenth,* 95), Dos Passos's changed perspective forecasts his evolving modernist sensibility. His revision provides an example of his growing ability to find the life in art as a way of learning to express life *with* art, however dark the vision. Whereas at 15 he saw the work merely as an artifact, he now saw the connection between its color and dynamics and the mind and culture that produced it.

Fra Angelico's *Last Judgment* (c. 1430) is one of the finest examples of a common Renaissance theme. And most churches displayed a depiction of its scene, the consignment of souls to heaven or hell depending on their virtue or vice during life. This admonitory image, to which preachers routinely referred during Mass, was "a powerful agent of social control, which tempered the lives of all who lived in Renaissance society." Fra Angelico's scene, like many of the other paintings Dos Passos notes, portrays a microcosm of the various ranks of the society that produced it, because this apocalyptic judgment was envisioned as completely "egalitarian" (Cole, 272–73). Likewise significant and egalitarian are the cultural forces that control the inhabitants of Dos Passos's *U.S.A.*, itself intended as a representative microcosm. Of Fra Angelico's work, Dos Passos wrote in 1918 of the "hard colors . . . [,] scornful vividness, . . . [and] scorching fury" of the judgment scene ("Diary of Italy," 46), terms that easily apply to Dos Passos's satiric, scathing, painterly view of his own society 500 years after the Florentine master's. In Fra Angelico's scene, Dos Passos writes in his journal, "Only the paradise is flat" ("Diary of Italy," 46). Speaking as a painter himself on the spatial perspective of the scene, he suggests nonetheless an underlying irony born of his recent battle experiences, an irony that grew stronger as his modernist vision developed.

Another Italian painter whose work attracted the young journalist was Raphael; as in the case of Fra Angelico, a comparison of Dos Passos's early affinity for the painter to his 1918 reassessment sketches a pattern in the modernist' writer's development. The grand tour diary mentions Raphael more often than almost any other artist. It declares the *Coronation of the Virgin,* the *Transfiguration,* and the Sistine Chapel frescoes "perfectly magnificent" ("Diary," 49). The work of Raphael, the Renaissance's foremost *madonniere,* unites with rare sensitivity the human and the ideal in the image of the holy mother.[18] The young traveler, keenly aware of his own mother's failing health and, by this time, of the difficulties she had endured during the nearly 20 clandestine years before she and John R. were able to marry in 1910, wrote dutifully to her from his travels, addressing her at times as the "dear Princess" (*Fourteenth,* 20). Dos Passos's wartime reappraisal of Raphael's work and of "Italian fresco painting" (*Fourteenth,* 169) in general provides a revealing contrast to his youthful, romantic attraction to the maternal images in Raphael's work and his romantic tendency to connect art and life.

Although in 1918 he enthuses in a letter to Rumsey Marvin, a younger friend, that he has "never seen such gorgeous, unimaginably interesting" painting as that of the Italian Renaissance masters, he calls it "decoration," clearly distinguishing that art from the life he now saw around him. He then extends his adolescent fervor for the Italian painters with a critical comment that suggests the turn toward greater realism and consciousness of technique that his work took on its way to modernism around 1920: "[W]ith Raphael all Italian painting seems to go smash in vapid banality and a coloratura sort of ease" (*Fourteenth,* 169). After experiencing the horror of the front lines and no longer willing to accord as art what he now perceived as the sentimental and facile, he has begun clearly to distinguish between mere decoration and art that conveys some greater truth by means of the vitality of its techniques.

Chapter Three
An Education in the Arts: Harvard

As his journals and letters from the grand tour of 1911 to 1912 reveal, by the time the young Dos Passos returned from his travels in the spring of 1912, he had begun to acquire a sound background in ancient, classical, and Renaissance art and some critical sense of the kind of art that engaged him and the reason for its appeal. He was now ready for a more systematic education in the liberal arts and for an opportunity to begin crafting his own aesthetics. Besides the tour's influence on his visual and cultural perceptions, his reading, his viewing of art, and the intellectual atmosphere at Harvard during his four years there helped direct his writing and his sense of the visual as his style metamorphosed.

Well prepared intellectually by Choate and by his independent reading and travels for the academic rigors of Harvard, the initial challenge of adjusting to college life was social for the 16-year-old Dos Passos—"Dos," as his college friends came to call him. Although the university, headed at that time by A. Lawrence Lowell, was busy augmenting its academic prestige with innovative curricula and a distinguished faculty, it was still an institution whose social systems were the legacy of its generations of socially elite alumni. Being a good athlete, belonging to the right social club, and cultivating the friendships that would carry one into the social and professional circles that would secure one's position—these were markers of a certain kind of success whose significance would have been impossible for a boy of Dos Passos's educational and cultural background to ignore completely. Yet he was not interested in organized sports, he failed to be elected to any social club, and his social isolation was exacerbated by his unwitting choice, as a freshman, of a dormitory intended for seniors and graduate students only. Malcolm Cowley, a few years behind Dos Passos at Harvard, remembered him as "a lonely figure, standing outside the terribly snobbish social system of those days."[1]

But if social success eluded Dos Passos—or, more accurately, if he did not care enough to pursue it—academic success came fairly easily, given his abilities and the encouragement Harvard offered him to explore his astonishingly broad range of literary interests. He began a detailed reading journal in his first month at Harvard in September 1912, and the three volumes it comprises before its conclusion in 1916 show an omnivorous reader honing his critical skills, seriously gauging what makes writing work, and searching for writing that accomplished what would later become his own literary goals. The sheer scope of the reading reveals much about the young man's intellectual breadth and democratic mind: Anton Chekov, Henry James, George Sand, the British romantic poets, Oscar Wilde, Mary Antin, Lady Gregory, John Reed, Guy de Maupassant, D. H. Lawrence, French writers, and the Dutch writer Louis Couperus were among the vast number of writers whom he read and, in brief or detailed entries, critiqued in these journals. About John Reed's *Insurgent Mexico,* he noted its "lack of prejudice and humanity"; in Henry James's *The Europeans,* he admired the "wonderful" characterization; in Thackeray's *Vanity Fair,* which he read more than once, he found "the inimitable characters, the satire, the wit, . . . universality of the book is overwhelming!" (*Fourteenth,* 21–22) These affinities show the beginnings of Dos Passos's own stylistic goals.

His course work, too, extended his breadth of knowledge and showed him the directions in which his skills might take him. During his college career he studied languages—advanced French literature, since he was already fluent in the language; German; Latin; Greek; and Spanish—as well as history, for which he had a decided aptitude. Except for a very few science courses, he focused on literature, philosophy, and the arts in his later course work. Studying composition and literature with some of Harvard's most distinguished professors, Dos Passos quickly demonstrated his nascent talent as a writer and was encouraged by his teachers. Working with one of Harvard's best-known members of its English department, Bliss Perry, Dos Passos delved into the forms of eighteenth- and nineteenth-century fiction; with another professor, the unorthodox but immensely popular Charles Townsend Copeland, the student began writing essays and stories that became the basis of some of his earliest published prose in the *Harvard Monthly.* Copeland praised his gift for sensory detail, while another composition teacher, Le Baron Russell Briggs, commented on one of the student's papers, "You show the feeling that, with hard work, makes an artist."[2] Although his training in composition was providing Dos Passos with some guidelines toward achieving his vocation, his education in literature did little to construct a framework to help him evaluate the direction of his own country's literary products. As was the case generally in American academics at the time, Harvard communicated the view that American writing was insufficiently developed to warrant much critical study. Barrett Wendell, one of Harvard's noted professors whose lectures Dos Passos sometimes attended, asserted that "there is no American literature."[3] This perception of the rootlessness of American literature would generate the critical explorations into that problem and its possible solutions that constitute one of Dos Passos's first post-Harvard publications, "Against American Literature," which appeared in the *New Republic* in October 1916, just after the writer graduated.

Perhaps as much as the teaching at Harvard, the intellectual atmosphere outside the classroom stimulated Dos Passos initially. There were abundant opportunities to publish and edit as a student—among them the *Advocate,* the *Illustrated Magazine,* and especially the *Harvard Monthly.* His first publications were in this serious literary journal; he published 28 pieces in it during his years at Harvard—13 stories, 5 poems, 5 book reviews, and 5 essays or editorials. As a senior, he was one of its most frequent contributors, and he served on its editorial board as well, following in the tradition of such writers as George Santayana, who had founded the journal in 1885. Some of Dos Passos's early pieces for the *Monthly* show the influence of some of the literary movements that affected Harvard as well as American writing of the day. Dos Passos had read and admired the French symbolist poets of the previous century, such as Verlaine and Rimbaud, and was particularly impressed with the poetry of the Belgian Emile Verhaeren. Growing out of the symbolist movement, imagism used common language, created new rhythms, chose its subject matter freely and did not confine itself to the conventionally "poetic," and created clear, concentrated, concrete images. These artistic goals, delineated in *Some Imagist Poets* (1915) by Amy Lowell, self-appointed spokesperson for the imagists, are echoed by Dos Passos both in his own impressionistic techniques in the *Harvard Monthly* fiction and in his articulation of his own beliefs about what made poetry powerful. He wrote to Rumsey Marvin, like Dos Passos a beginning writer: "[A]n idea or an emotion has usually to be tied up in a picture, a figure of speech or something like that, before it is readily available for poetry. . . . Admitted that excessive & artificial use of 'sweat and swear' to make poems seem manly and modern is abominable and heinous . . . still, I insist that every subject under the sun which has any thing to do with human beings—man, woman, or child—is susceptible of poetic treatment" (*Fourteenth,* 26).

Typical of many of the authors who would reach artistic maturity during the war, in his college writing Dos Passos showed the effect of literary movements, imagism and symbolism particularly, that enlivened the collegiate intellectual atmosphere. But even when he assimilates images or stylistic elements of literary or visual movements into his writing, Dos Passos frequently shows their influence by reacting *against* them, often trying both uses of an element in the same piece. As a consequence, much of his college work illustrates the pattern by which Dos Passos worked through influences and stylistic trends to evolve his own style, a process strikingly similar to the one by which American artists evolved a "national" school in the visual arts in the late nineteenth and early twentieth centuries.

Dos Passos's earliest extant poetry and stories, both published and unpublished, illustrate his attempt to infuse into his patently romantic style a more original use of the materials, themes, techniques, and pictorial elements characteristic of romanticism. In working toward an individual style, he assimilates and finds new uses for the European artistic traditions he knew well, in the same way that American landscape painters transformed European romantic landscape-painting conventions into a style that would express the American perspective.

For all its influences from early modernist styles and movements, Dos Passos's collegiate work shows the marks of his exposure to the classical and romantic in writing and art. In the records of his voluminous reading at Harvard, Dos Passos returns often to British romantics; for example, he notes Byron's "Childe Harold" (*Fourteenth*, 24) and Keats's "Hyperion" and "Endymion" (Ludington 1980, 62). These works deal with a theme that often preoccupies Dos Passos's apprentice fiction, the conflict between the life of the imagination and life in the concrete world. His fascination with Henry James's work prefigures another recurrent theme in his early Harvard writing. The uneasy coexistence of the New World's spirit with the Old World's values and aesthetics that concerns James in such works as *The Europeans* and *Daisy Miller* elicits from Dos Passos a comparison between James's portraits and "the delicacy of Fra Angelico, or . . . of some of the more refined Dutch portrait painters" (quoted in Ludington 1980, 63). Dos Passos's interartistic analogy suggests his earliest method of trying to deal with this theme: by incorporating allusions to European classical art into stories and poems in which he tries to develop his own experience of Harvard and of America into an individual style.

The results are sometimes incongruous. Thematically exploring from different angles the dichotomy between feeling and intellect, between the experience of life and the aesthetic expression of it, the apprentice writing of the early Harvard days often uses romantic iconography to suggest a lost arcadian age in which art and life were integrated and the artist, or simply the sensitive individual, was less divided from the world and from himself. Typical of the stories' pattern, for instance, is a January 1916 *Harvard Monthly* contribution, "The Shepherd."[4] In it, the 15-year-old protagonist contrasts the blandness of security with the romance of adventure. The boy's feelings about security emerge in his images of the "tedium of [his] long years at school" and the safety of his family, of his mother as a "fragrant shrine of `... sweetness and gentleness," an image recalling Dos Passos's early fascination with Raphael's Madonnas. But the boy longs for the "exultation at . . . adventure" represented by a gruffly cordial, intensely masculine shepherd he meets when "lost in the mountains," a phrase that sounds "marvelous to his ears" (116–17). In fact, as the shepherd entertains the boy during the night they spend by the campfire, the boy recasts all the shepherd's "harsh, brutal tales" into "scrolls of gold and purple," seeing embodied in them "the old stories of mythology" and "all the passion of the ancient world." The gruff rustic's story of swimming a river at night "to go an' see a girl" becomes "Hero and Leander!" to the boy, and the already picturesque shepherd himself, ultimately, is transformed by the boy's imagination into Pan. When the boy is reunited with his mother in the morning, however, the "dazzling vision of freedom" fades in the face of her solicitous tears, and the boy feels, romantically, "the dim pleasure of renunciation." "[T]he memory of the . . . firelight in the black eyes of the shepherd" (120–21), however, persists.

The story's slight plot prefigures the central situation in *Streets of Night*, the first novel Dos Passos worked on, which he began at Harvard. In it, a sensitive, bookish young man, devoted to his mother, romantically idealizes a tougher, more adventuresome "man of the world." The change in the overlay of aesthetic borrowings and mise-en-scène, however, even in the few years between story and novel, reveals Dos Passos's growing awareness of his own aesthetic direction and aptitudes. While in those few years both the aesthetic and the psychological threads would become more complex and varied, in "The Shepherd" the romantic strain emerges not only in the boy's imaginative transformation of ordinary events and appearances into high adventure and misty perspectives but also in the role time plays in this recreation. The "old stories of mythology," the classical elements the boy adds, and the allusions to a past golden age constitute an idealized status quo ante that lives on in the boy's memory, as the story's last line insists.

Other stories of the 1915 to 1916 period that ultimately appeared in the *Harvard Monthly* create other romantic arcadian pasts. Dos Passos still uses these idyllic referents, however, as a kind of aesthetic or emotional standard against which the present and its artistic expressions fall grossly short or look cheaply ridiculous. The wide range of the arcadia Dos Passos creates bespeaks the catholicity of his youthful imagination and artistic tastes. In "An Aesthete's Nightmare," a fifth-century "temple of Aphrodite" houses the still-complete Venus de Milo, an icon of classical culture, "whole as the day she came from the sculptor's chisel."[5] In "First Love," a schoolboy whose mind wanders from the *Aeneid* "tell[s] himself a story" in a creative transformation similar to the boy's in "The Shepherd."[6] "[C]lothed in cloth of gold, with a sword like Excalibur by his side," the schoolboy imagines himself pursuing "a woman clothed in white samite . . . embroidered with seed pearls" (23), a Pre-Raphaelite vision of Camelot rudely dispelled by a headmaster's reprimand.

The "art-life relation" that later preoccupied the modernists, as Steiner notes (17), obviously concerned Dos Passos in his premodernist work as well, although it emerges at this stage in his career as a romantic struggle with the division between art and life. Romantic iconography, a focus on time and memory, and the characteristic romantic validation of the individual's point of view mark his early Harvard poetry as well.

In "The Past," a Harvard poem never published, Dos Passos creates an archetypally romantic hymn to the power of nature to inspire in the speaker a recognition of how mutable but, simultaneously, how rich were the past lives with which he feels momentarily connected. Besides its quintessentially romantic mise-en-scène, themes, and focus on both the "I" and the "eye," the poem suggests explicit borrowings from the fountainhead of British romanticism, William Wordsworth. In 151 alternately rhyming lines interspersed with couplets, Dos Passos places his speaker first in a pastoral landscape reminiscent of the picturesque mode in European romantic painting, a mode defined in England partly by the reciprocal influence of landscapists and poets. The speaker's point of view from a "high hill" yields the same perspective the viewer of a landscape painting might have of a painted scene—distant and panoramic.[7] Herds of sheep, shepherds' fires, and mountains' "dull white spires" stretch before the speaker (l. 26). Like the viewer of a painting, the speaker feels drawn into the scene, a desire that shifts his thoughts to other times when "In the woods of terror" he stood (l. 41). Like Wordsworth's young persona in *The Prelude*, Dos Passos's speaker senses and fears an ambient spirit in nature: "Eyes in the mottled dance of light and shade, / Eyes in the smooth-trunked trees around, / Eyes in the brown leaf-strewn ground; / [And I] . . . stood in icy terror bound" (ll. 46–50). The speaker allows himself to participate in several other imagined "old lives" in the course of the poem. The lives that Dos Passos chooses, such as that of the sacrificial devotee to some unnamed but—for Dos Passos at this point—quite sensual goddess of beauty, continue the Wordsworthian sense of a presence in nature. Another scene from the past, in which the speaker is a reaper among "stooks new-built" (l. 111), visually evokes the antique rural homages of the Barbizon painters. Corot creates just such a landscape in *Farm at Recouvrieres* (1831) and Millet in *The Buckwheat Harvest* (1868–1874), even down to the shocks' "purple shade" that, in Millet's scene, is characteristic of ripe buckwheat. The poem searches romantically for the "grey / [c]onglomerate past" (ll. 44–45) and mourns romantically the "changing substance of this flesh" (l. 49). Its language, too, is still very hyperbolic and self-conscious. Dawn is a "fulgent flame / [that] fire[s]" the "welkin" (ll. 15–18); noon is a "twang[ing] . . . / . . . drowsy lyre" (ll. 27–28); in a "leaping aureate glow," days "swoon[ ] with delight" (ll. 141–42).

A similarly idyllic, romantically anthropomorphized pastoral scene provides the setting for another unpublished poem of this period, "Bubbles and the Sea Wind," subtitled, apparently at a date later than composition, "To a certain small boy." The mise-en-scène elicits a memory from the speaker in a process similar to the speaker's imaginative recreations in "The Past." In "Bubbles," the clouds "gallop" over reeds that "plunge and rear" like the "necks of galloping horses."[8] The windy scene sends the speaker's "spirit . . . / . . . whirl[ing] like thistledown away" (ll. 16–17) to a seascape from some past day impressionistically misted over by sea spray. Again, Dos Passos combines a concern about the effects of time on memory with romantic scenery to comment somewhat self-consciously on the fragility of dreams. His convoluted metaphor for them is bubbles from a child's toy pipe, bubbles he *then* compares to ships that sail an "opal sea" (l. 39), an image that recurs to quite different—and far less romantic—effect in a 1918 poem written aboard ship bound for France and the war.

The art-life conflict emerges also in some published poems, in even more typically romantic iconography and in equally as unadventuresome diction. A conventional poem alternating regular iambic tetrameter and trimeter lines, "From Simonides" invokes such classical symbols as the "garland of bay" on the speaker's brow.[9] The speaker enjoins the "friend" addressed in the recurring refrain to "embrace with me" the "madness of youth" (ll. 15–16) but to "be wise with me" when "leaden with wisdom and thought" (ll. 17–18).

Slightly more metrically imaginative but no less conventionally classical is "Saturnalia," included in the 1917 collection *Eight Harvard Poets* by Dos Passos, E. Estlin Cummings, S. Foster Damon, Robert Hillyer, R. S. Mitchell, William A. Norris, Dudley Poore, and Cuthbert Wright.[10] This poem does try to create the energy of an ancient pagan celebration of "the life gods" (l. 7) who sing "Saturn's orisons" (l. 18), but in sestets whose first two and last two lines rhyme exactly and with diction that depicts "woodland spirits" (l. 24) carrying "tapers . . . / [a]-dance, like strayed fireflies" (ll. 16–17). The limitations of these slight works suggest not only the writer's youthfulness but also the stylistic confinements imposed by the classical and romantic European aesthetics still propagated by a "good" American education in Dos Passos's time.

American Art against the Background of Europe

Perhaps Dos Passos, like the nineteenth-century American landscape painters before him, borrowed symbols and techniques from the tradition of European art because, simply, America lacked the stable and established aesthetic background, the *native* diversity, from which artists might proceed to innovate and yet still produce an art recognizably distinct from Europe's. As Dos Passos defined the problem in 1916, in journal notes working toward his first novel and first publicly published essay, "Against American Literature," America had "no ghosts . . . to give overtones to life."[11] The result of this "constant need to draw on foreign sources" in American literature, he ultimately concluded in the published essay, was a "hybrid" literature, "which, like the mule, is barren and must be produced afresh each time by the crossing of other strains." This "hybrid" quality he bemoaned in his notes as a "thinness," a "lack of richness and texture" ("Book," 47) that left the reader of American literature "starved, . . . pining for the color and passion and profound thought of other literatures" ("Against," 269).

And his own writing up to this point had certainly borne out his conclusions, for even as he reached this realization about what American art and life lacked, he was producing stories and poems that, for all their technical care, still relied for their aesthetic basis on European traditions and allusions. Yet sometimes, even when writing in the romantic mode about the conflict between experience and aesthetics and about the transformational power of the imagination, he began to cast those prob-

lems in the context of the issues he finally articulated in his senior year
in the *New Republic* essay—of the "rootless" quality of American life and
art, "its lack of depth" ("Against," 270).

Two 1915 *Harvard Monthly* stories in particular, both set in Europe,
express that emerging concern. In "Malbrouck: A Sketch," Dos Passos
depicts once more the power of art to elicit strong feelings often predicated on memories. This time, although the setting is Paris, he ventures
into new territory that hints of a growing awareness of an issue that
would transform his work and the work of all the modernists: World
War I. But while he acknowledges for perhaps the first time in his writing the tragedies of war, he nevertheless expresses that acknowledgment
in a resolutely romantic plot. A young mother living in a shabby garret
overlooking Paris sings to sleep her fretful young son with a folk song
about a lady in a high tower awaiting the return of her husband, Malbrouck. The first stanzas of the song promise that he will return by
Easter, but the last stanza admits that "Le sieur Malbrouck est mort."[12]
As the woman sings her lullaby, its parallels to her own situation overcome over her and, clutching a rosary, she finally "let[s] herself go [in] a
flood of sobbing" (194). Dos Passos makes her keenly aware of the whis-
tles of trains in the distance "carrying . . . more eager, hopeful young
men . . . toward the cold mud flats of Flanders" (192), thus delicately
cueing the reader to the reason for her anxiety.

The progress of her rising fear is fairly subtly keyed to the song's
progress, but for all the signs of a developing awareness of how to mod-
ulate narrative and vary narrative techniques, Dos Passos's basic stance
here is still romantic. No authorial irony seems to underlie the woman's
perception of the war or the narrator's final comment as the story steps
back from the woman, leaving her "weeping silently" beside the "sweet
regular breathing of her son asleep": "And outside the trains rumbled on
towards the north . . . where the army was fighting in the midst of
blood and cold and wet, for the glory of France" (194). The setting, the
characters, the work of art that acts as catalyst, and, for the most part at
this point, the concern about the war are all European, and the story is
certainly an example of the "foreign-inspired writing" that Dos Passos
labeled most of American literature ("Against," 269).

The other *Harvard Monthly* story, "An Interrupted Romance," defines
more overtly the relative cultural and spiritual impoverishment of
American life compared to Europe's environment. In fact, in this story
Dos Passos begins to confront fictionally the need for America and its
literature to break free of their European antecedents in order to define

themselves. The acknowledgment is perhaps unconscious and certainly metaphorical, but shows a hint of the satiric detachment that would help define his war novels written within the next five years. Ironically, while he writes here with amused detachment about the crude pragmatism of the American spirit that disallows the kind of romance that encourages imaginative creation, he nevertheless depicts the whole situation in romantic visual and literary conventions. The story's protagonist, Francis Thomas, goes to Paris where "he [is] supposed by his relatives in America to be studying."[13] Actually, however, he is soaking up the ambiance of springtime Paris, loitering all day on a bench "under the trees of the Champs Elysees" (119). The Paris that passes before him is the Paris of the impressionists. Dos Passos's nursemaids and "*bébés* . . . wreathed in stiff laces" and the "*grandes dames* . . . in carriages along the crowded driveway" (119) recall Renoir's 1872 *The Pont Neuf, Paris,* or Monet's 1867 *Le Jardin de la Princesse,* two Right Bank scenes in which the viewer has a somewhat removed perspective on the frothy figures of ladies and the sensual, sun-drenched stream of passers-by set against the gentle, orderly charm of Parisian architecture. In that pattern common to so many of Dos Passos's works of this period, the protagonist imaginatively transforms what he sees around him, "dreamily construct[ing] little stories" about "the other habitues" of the promenade, especially about a young woman who catches his interest. Thomas first sees her when "a few stiff spikes of white bloom were beginning to appear" (119–20) on the chestnut trees. This iconographic detail is common to other impressionistically romantic depictions of Paris, such as American painter Childe Hassam's *Tuileries Gardens* (1893). The chestnut trees frequently serve also as a compositional element, their foliage often framing the scenes in Monet's 1876 paintings of the Parc Monceau, also along a fashionable promenade.

Dos Passos describes the young woman who excites Thomas's attention in painterly, impressionistic terms of shapes and lines. At first, Thomas can only see the back of her "delightfully-shaped fair head," her "charmingly mignon profile," and the "charming curve" of her coiffure "half hidden by her veil" (120). Always accompanied by an elderly gentleman, whom she seems to cater to, she so stirs Thomas's romantic fancy that he begins to frequent his observation place more assiduously, not even bringing a book, so absorbed is he in creating stories about the pair. Together they compose a visual unit—seated on iron chairs under trees surrounded by other fashionable Parisians—distinctly reminiscent of the haute bourgeois couples who people Manet's 1862 *Music in the*

Tuileries Gardens. Manet's perspective in this seemingly casual, contemporary scene, like Thomas's in Dos Passos's depiction of Paris, is that of the "idle stroller who absorbs impressions and captures the tone and atmosphere of the moment."[14]

Two twists distinguish this story from the other romantic, "foreign-inspired" works in which Dos Passos dwells on the art-life relation, however. First, in this story, the protagonist ceases briefly to be merely the imaginative voyeur that other point-of-view characters have usually been in these early works. When Thomas rescues a lace handkerchief the lady has left behind her, he feels tremendous anxiety about the move, as any dreamer might about finally acting. Kissing the handkerchief and inhaling its "faint perfume of lilacs," he feels guilt about his ardor, as any American product of a Puritan ancestry and a Yankee upbringing might about allowing himself what seems to him such voluptuous participation in Parisian life. Nevertheless, he plans to use the handkerchief's return as an excuse to meet the lady, confident that she'll "like [his being] very American" (121).

That very Americanness provides the other twist, however. In this story, Dos Passos suggests that the practical, raw American spirit is somehow definitively antiromantic and can never blend comfortably with European customs or sentience. The implications of this contrast for American literature Dos Passos articulates the following year, in the *New Republic* article calling for American authors to break free of European aesthetic antecedents. Thomas, Dos Passos's callow protagonist, has no choice but to resign himself to his Americanness. At the crucial moment when he has finally gathered his nerve to introduce himself to the couple, his stout Aunt Jane from Chicago and her two "giggly" daughters, Baedeker guides in hand, appear, lost in the city, and press him into service as a tour guide. The chance to realize his romantic dream is shattered by reminders of his Americanness in the person of his aunt and cousins, whom Dos Passos describes with the stolidly pragmatic image of "a liner being towed . . . by officious tugs" (122), hardly the lilting impressionism of the story's early visual images.

American Impressionism and Luminism

That pretty, sheerly visual impressionism often served as the raison d'être for some of Dos Passos's slighter earlier works. Although a movement toward modernist art in that it eschewed mimetic representationalism and initiated a new concern with technique for its own sake,

impressionism is still romantic in its focus on the individual consciousness as the most legitimate agent for perceiving and communicating
reality, as in some uses of the first-person point of view in literature, for
instance. Likewise romantic is impressionism's preoccupation with time.
Impressionist artists tried to present the immediacy of a visual impression. They often worked outdoors, like the Barbizon artists whose concern with the effects of natural light immediately preceded the impressionists and to whose "atmospheric effects" Dos Passos attributed the
beginning of his interest in this visual technique (Knox, 23). Additionally, impressionist paintings often depend on the viewer's eye to fuse the
colors in an interpretive process analogous to the role of the reader's
transformational imagination that the romantics insisted upon. Impressionist painters do not paint the world as we presumably "see" it; rather,
they record their own sensations of color and light, validating them the
way romantic writers validate what might be termed their subjective
perceptions of the world.

Dos Passos, even through the war years that brought a new modernism to his style, continued to use some impressionist techniques, a
lingering sensibility that emerges in his paintings and sketches of the
same period. Those post-Harvard writings develop a tension between
technique and theme or between juxtaposed styles, a tension suggesting
a growing narrative expertise. But the Harvard works most impressionistic and descriptively visual in technique are simply that—descriptively
visual, and for effect. Those characteristics align poems that are visual in
conception—such as "Whan That Aprille ..." (39), included in the
1917 *Eight Harvard Poets,* and "Prairies," published in the November
1915 *Harvard Monthly*—with those late-nineteenth- and early-twentieth-
century American painters whose "atmospheric romanticism" constituted a brief transitional movement between the influence of the French
impressionists on American painting and the complete flowering of the
essentially American luminists.[15]

Romantic intention, native materials, and "diaphanous" (Novak
1969, 245) visual effects clearly define these transitional American
works such as John Twachtman's 1902 *Hemlock Pool,* depicting dense
New England woods, or George Inness's 1893 *Home of the Heron,* blur-
ring the demarcation between marsh and sky yet using marsh water and
foliage to direct the eye to the rising heron. The compositional focus of
these works suggests a conceptualism that distinguishes them from the
works of the impressionists, even though they use many impressionist
techniques (Novak 1969, 245). In effect and intent, Dos Passos's visual

poems resemble such paintings. Both "Aprille" and "Prairies" use form—fairly regular iambic blank verse—but abandon rhyme and precise thematic focus in favor of romantic evocation.

The opening lines of "Aprille" recall Inness's scene: "Is it the song of a meadow lark / [o]f the brown, sere, salt marshes . . . ?" (ll. 1–2) Later images, such as "the bare branches of elm trees / [t]wined in the delicate sky," hinting of Oriental design, link Dos Passos's visual sense to the work of James A. McNeill Whistler, who at times incorporated Japanese artistic influences into swirling, amorphous "nocturnes" that ultimately came to define "an indigenous romantic conceptualism" in America (Novak 1969, 247), despite Whistler's expatriatism. These nocturnes French symbolist writers such as Mallarmé later labeled visual analogues of their poems. Given Dos Passos's brief leaning in his college days toward *art pour l'art* and the influence of the symbolists, an affinity with Whistler is not surprising.

"Prairies," an even more persistently visual poem than "Aprille" (and an earlier one), evokes the sumptuous natural palette and suffusing light of some French impressionists. Such effects characterize Pisarro's paintings, such as *A Cowherd on the Route du Chou, Pointoise* (1874) and *Poplars, Eragny* (1895), and some of Seurat's prepointillist plein-air studies. Dos Passos's poem, too, depicts a sun-filled natural world; his first line—" 'Tis green and gold the world is"—establishes with its color images and inverted syntax his impressionistically romantic intent.[16] The green "of waving, feathery grasses" "verges to greyness / [w]here shadows of faint mists roam" (ll. 3, 7–8), diction that gives a sense of impressionistic indistinctness. The air's "[p]ale, laughing and luminous gold" (l. 14) saturates the prairie's rolling grasses, light and line conveying a romantic visual sensibility. Such painterly insistence on the transformative power of light recalls as well the American luminist painters, one step closer to the twentieth century than the impressionists and as consciously American as any painters had yet been.

The philosophical orientation and techniques of this "especially . . . American" movement (Wilmerding, 17) parallel important characteristics of Dos Passos's work in his last two years at Harvard. Particularly in the poems he contributed to *Eight Harvard Poets,* Dos Passos's gradual change from the cheerfully sunny, romantic landscapes of such poems as "Whan That Aprille . . ." to the dark ennui and nostalgia of such poems as "The Bridge" and "Night Piece" follows the pattern of the luminists' progression from "Jacksonian optimism" (Wilmerding, 11) and serenity to a brooding post–Civil War sense of loss.

"The Bridge" uses characteristically "cool . . . , planar" luminist light that "gleams" (Wilmerding, 25) rather than diffuses atmospherically, as in impressionist paintings. The speaker observes a "lonely bridge [that] cuts dark across the marsh / [w]hose long pools glow with . . . / . . . a flaring summer sunset" (ll. 1–3), a horizontal composition in which red tones from a sunken sun create depth by their graduated reflection.[17] The elements of this composition recur repeatedly in prominent late luminist scenes: Martin J. Heade's 1860s *Twilight on the Marshes* and 1887 *Great Florida Sunset;* Sanford Robinson Gifford's 1863 *Sunset;* and Albert Bierstadt's 1881 *Buffaloes on the Prairie.* Similarly luminist is the poem's sense of time stilled, of "repose."[18] As in many of Dos Passos's earlier romantic works, the speaker in "The Bridge" observes, "sitting quiet," and although "tired" (l. 15) of his stasis and speaking from a kind of dramatic ennui, he seems unmoved to act (unlike the impulse toward motion in "An Interrupted Romance"). Instead, he remains still as the "red sky-glory fades" (l. 23), the poem's final line an explicitly luminist image.

That sense of nostalgic, meditative repose characterizes also the speaker's stance in "Night Piece." A poem whose use of luminist light occurs in an *urban* setting and whose retrospective meditations veer into the self-consciously morbid pessimism affected by the Harvard aesthetes, this contribution to *Eight Harvard Poets* gives a glimpse ahead into the effects of the aesthetes and the symbolists on Dos Passos's writing in his senior year and just after.

The poem's central image suggests the melancholy theme. The moon has spun a "silver web / . . . [w]here the frail stars quiver . . . / [l]ike tangled gnats that . . . die" (ll. 2–4).[19] Also like entangled dying gnats are the speaker's soul, also caught in the moon's web, and his "[i]mportunate memories" (l. 11), an image introducing the characteristic romantic concern with time. The "huge . . . moon [that] broods on the night" (l. 8) is the central link among all the memories the speaker then enumerates, of nights when the moon was on the river or on the sea. Likewise, in luminist paintings such as Robert Salmon's 1836 *Moonlight Coastal Scene,* the centrally placed moon provides the composition's focus and touches specifically with its light every other object in the scene. The moon in Dos Passos's poem induces a "strange peace" on "town streets" in the "silent night" (ll. 14–15), a luminist hush of time arrested. This romantic ennui, the speaker's dramatic anguish over "broken loves" and "dead farewells" (ll. 32–33), and the controlling imagery of the moonlight "lovely as death" (l. 13) hint at the emergence in Dos Passos's college work of characteristics of another artistic movement, aestheticism, which succeeds these visual reminders of luminism, the "closing phase of romanticism."[20] Out of Dos Passos's reaction to the aesthetes came stories and poems whose styles and themes led eventually to the young writer's first attempt at a novel, published in 1923 as *Streets of Night.*

From Aestheticism and Symbolism to the Beginnings of Realism

If luminism was the "closing phase of romanticism" in America's late-nineteenth-century visual arts, aestheticism was America's brief revival of the desiccated European romanticism of the 1890s. The dramatically melancholy and disillusioned spirit in which its adherents carried out that final flirtation suggests the degree of self-consciousness with which they undertook the retrospective movement. Malcolm Cowley, who notes in Dos Passos's work up through the *U.S.A.* trilogy the effects of the Harvard aesthetes on the writer's development, defines the movement's qualities colorfully and, since Cowley himself attended Harvard during those years, perhaps authoritatively. To characterize this "after-image of Oxford in the 1890s" at Harvard, Cowley describes the mise-en-scène that the aesthetes carefully constructed for themselves: the *Yellow Book;* the teatime gatherings at the *Harvard Monthly* offices for "seidels of straight gin topped with a maraschino cherry"; the patchouli, incense, and religious icons in rooms whose inhabitants frequented picturesque dives and brothels.[21]

Dos Passos himself creates an even more detailed picture of the aesthetes' contrived ambiance in his wry 1915 story "An Aesthete's Nightmare," published in the *Harvard Monthly.* In it, a pallid "Aesthete"—Dos Passos gives him no other name—discovers within himself a "Berserker rage" to destroy the "artistic room" (79) he has painstakingly created as an aesthetic shrine. Despite Dos Passos's ironic portrayal of the Aesthete's discovery of his more primal, anti-intellectual nature, the story concentrates on setting the aesthetic mood. The Aesthete's "luxurious artistic atmosphere" features "carefully shaded lights"; a "divan—as he euphemistically called his cot bed" covered by "an eastern rug"; a "smiling Buddha" mantelpiece beside a "lotus-shaped burner" for incense; and a reproduction of Maxfield Parrish's "Pirate Ship." The protagonist, dressed in "Turkish slippers" and "pale crepe dressing gown," indulges in "a precious liqueur, of exotic name . . . only obtainable at one monastery, and that a small one, in Dalmatia" (77–78).

In this story, Dos Passos's obvious amusement at superficial aesthetic pretensions would seem to undermine the idea that the aesthetes were a clearly defined aesthetic movement with consistent philosophical beliefs. But their philosophy, although they would never have deigned to articulate it methodically, derived from Casanova, Pater, and Beardsley, among others. The poet, inevitably misunderstood by a world full of philistines, lives only by the charge to "[cultivate and express] . . . his own sensibility" in an art that, conceived in an "ecstasy . . . provoked by . . . alcohol, drugs . . . debauchery, madness, [or] suicide . . . exists apart from the world."[22]

Cowley defines, too, the kind of fiction the aesthetes produced from this milieu—the "art novel," as Cowley terms it. The art novel typically opposes two antagonists, an artist, whom Cowley calls "the Poet," and "the World" (Cowley 1936, 171). The World, or society, usually crushes the artist figure's dreams and tender individuality with its materialistic and insensitive stupidity, leaving only the artist's work to testify to his bitter struggle. The aesthetes' focus on the individual's expression in the art novel and their nostalgia place them firmly in the context of romanticism, albeit at the end of the spectrum, with their nostalgia having become cynical and backward-looking, and their individuality having sunk into solipsistic obscurity. As Cowley observes, only a few of the aesthetes grew out of their affectations into solid writers (Cowley 1934, 35). Dos Passos's own Harvard work, especially in his senior year, weaves both aesthetic mise-en-scène and art novel themes into stories that show him developing beyond his earlier callow classical romanticism and past his impressionist and luminist visual sensibilities, beginning to question the aesthetic assumptions those alignments imply.

Obviously, aesthetic strains emerge in Dos Passos's work of this period. But the way he used aesthetic elements, making something original of an established visual and literary trend, marked the first instance in his long career when he transformed a movement's techniques and materials into an unmistakably original product. Acknowledging Dos Passos's aesthetic tendencies, Cowley points out that the young writer counterposed against them a "hardminded" realism, that Dos Passos is "two novelists at war with each other" in his first books (Cowley 1936, 168). But the interaction of these two strains as early as the Harvard apprentice works is even more complex than Cowley discovers, more complex than a "quarrel" or "collaboration," as Cowley terms the interaction between Dos Passos's two facets (Cowley 1936, 168). Dos Passos certainly shows the opposition of romanticism and realism in his 1915 to 1916 stories, using the trappings of aestheticism to debunk the per-fervid romanticism they suggest.

Yet while these stories depict romanticism as a sham, they also question the power of realism, as an attitude or an aesthetic, to produce meaningful art or life. While Dos Passos ridicules the pretenses of the artist figures in these stories who prefigure the art novel's protagonist, the author also clearly pities them as they confront the bleakness of realism. Always unwilling to subscribe unquestioningly to any political cause, Dos Passos was equally unwilling to allow artistic doctrine to subsume his individuality. The tension between the aesthetic of the times and the expression of Dos Passos's individual sensibility creates an art that, because its perspective is detached from its own milieu, reflects more accurately the culture from which it emerges than any collective movement could.

As early as his freshman year, Dos Passos's writing for the *Harvard Monthly* was using aesthetic mise-en-scène to deflate the tone it created. He was, even at this point, an antiromantic romantic, as contradictory as that label seems. For instance, "The Almeh," a 1913 *Harvard Monthly* contribution, set in exotic Cairo, features backdrops, props, and characters that would have appealed to an aesthete: bazaars, the Pyramids, colorful Egyptian garb, Turkish coffee, and an "exquisitely fair" veiled woman.[23] A pair of young tourists, one English and one American, catch a glimpse of this young woman. The Englishman, Dick Mansford, this story's artist figure, is drawn to the Egyptians' "fatalistic ideas" (173) and also to this elusive beauty. Dos Passos makes the man who believes dramatically that the woman is his "fate" (177) a native of England. In terms of Dos Passos's development as an American artist, this designation recalls the fact that England was the source of the romantic visual and literary aesthetic that twentieth-century America was beginning to outgrow and the source also of the decadent affectations the Harvard aesthetes adopted. Mansford's brief sight of the woman precipitates an ecstasy of artistic activity during which he produces a portrait of "the lovely Almeh dancing in the light of a flaring torch." Continuing to search for her against the pragmatic protestations of his American companion, Hazen, Mansford eventually discovers her in a scene whose realism jars unevenly against the story's previous picturesquely idealized settings and jolts Mansford as unexpectedly as it does the reader: "Before them, a little group of grimy, naked brats were playing about a young woman, who sat in the doorway of a mud-hut, preparing the mid-day meal. Every now and then she would scream at the children in a harsh voice. Flies swarmed about her, and about the food. . . . It was the Almeh, the lovely *houri* of the bazaar" (179). The story ends with Mansford's realization that she is merely the purchased wife of the Egyptian "donkey-boy" (179) who has been the tourists' guide.

To label the story as antiromantic or anti-aesthetic is to oversimplify it, slight though it is. Certainly, in contrast to Hazen's refusal to romanticize Egypt and the Egyptians, Mansford's idealization and subsequent artistic recreation of the girl seem affected and ridiculous, just as Dos Passos said he found the aesthetes too "deadly serious" (*Best,* 23) about themselves to countenance for long. Although Dos Passos in his 1966 memoir, *The Best Times,* recalled that new influences in his Harvard years—Russian novelists, D. H. Lawrence, Diaghilev, the Armory Show—had "set [him] to panting for 'real life' " (23), the "real life" in "The Almeh" does not seem particularly preferable to aesthetic fakery. Dos Passos's depiction of Hazen, for instance, seems to exceed the degree of pragmatism necessary to make him the normative voice of reason. Where Mansford sees only picturesque charm in Egypt, Hazen perceives only the heat, the dirt, and the "smells," seeming almost xenophobic in his charge that Mansford must be a "regular heathen" to be attracted to one of those "disgusting-looking women" (173). Likewise, the realistic truth about the girl seems hardly preferable to Mansford's idealized fantasy. Even as a young writer, Dos Passos seems incapable of settling for easy answers or comfortable affiliations: while the aesthetic artist is phony, the reality that disillusions him is too harsh. And after all, at least when he is possessed of his romantic illusion, Mansford *acts.* He paints; he does not simply criticize condescendingly, as Hazen the realist seems to.

Ambivalence about the relative virtues of aestheticism and realism pervades Dos Passos's 1915 to 1916 work as thoroughly as do visual reminders of artists the aesthetes adopted and Dos Passos absorbed. The contrast of the gilt decadence and remote asceticism of the High Church with the homespun simplicity of peasant devoutness creates the tension in "The Cardinal's Grapes," another *Harvard Monthly* story. Here, Dos Passos dresses the coldly antisensual Cardinal in aesthetic costume— "red plush slippers . . . silk stockings . . . [and] flowered dressing gown"— and surrounds him with aesthetic objects—"a gilt tabouret . . . a Sevres bowl," for instance.[24] The Cardinal's cathedral, "with its huge melancholy frescoes telling their tales" (155), recalls the enthralled journalist Dos Passos was a mere four years earlier.

The great frescoes he then found so full of narrative life he now associates with an asexual priest who punishes a boy for bringing him

crushed grapes whose juiciness elicits unwanted memories of the physicality of his boyhood. A reader might suppose Dos Passos entirely critical of the priest's ascetic remoteness. Yet he connects the cleric with the
great frescoes, for Dos Passos surely not an entirely pejorative conjunction, and with imagery of bright tones: "air . . . rich and . . . full of . . .
sunlight and gleams of gold and brown from the frescoes." The peasant
boy, in this story the proponent of realism, one might suppose is
intended entirely as a positive character, except that, in his earthy simplicity, he is entirely submissive to the Cardinal's reprimand and ends
the story praying "earnestly to the blessed Virgin" (155). To Dos Passos,
surely such an unquestioning nature cannot be unqualifiedly endorsed.

Some stories express Dos Passos's ambivalence more lightly than "The
Cardinal's Grapes," however, making good-natured fun of both the aesthetic and the more realistic attitudes. A story whose primary interest
is in the humorous, perhaps slightly self-mocking tone with which it
depicts its theme is "A Pot of Tulips." This story places the shy aesthete
Stanhope Whitcombe in pursuit of the "modern" woman Mabel Fisher.
Although Whitcombe surrounds himself with the "oriental rugs and the
Japanese bronzes" requisite to aesthetic decor, and although he writes
aesthetic verse "of a very inflamed, purple order" in which "*{s}hame* and
flame always rhyme[ ] together," he pragmatically tailors his work to
popular tastes and is, as a result, successful.[25] For all of Mabel's emanci-
pated values and self-proclaimed lack of sentimentality, she pretentiously
calls the flower shop she runs "Chez Louise." Despite her avowal that she
has "no prejudices," she summarily dumps Whitcombe when she discovers that the reason for his regular visits to Chez Louise—to buy flowers
for a "sick friend" (80)—has been merely a ruse to visit her.

The phoniness of aesthetic values is turned to satire in another 1915
story, "Orientale." In this story, the recently widowed Angela Leviker
discovers that instead of being overcome with grief, as she feels she
should be at her husband's death, she no longer wants to be a "whited
sepulchre."[26] Falling under the influence of the Persian poet Hafiz, she
decides to redecorate her home in what turns out to be high-aesthetic
faux Oriental: " 'The hallways 'll be Japanese, the drawing room Sara-
cenic, the library Turkish, my bedroom Persian.' " In the process she dis-
cards what she evidently considers accoutrements of her staid, haute
bourgeois, respectable life—Dresden china, gilt chairs, and "Whistler's
'Portrait of My Mother' " (45–46).

Aside from Dos Passos's uncharacteristic misnaming of *Arrangement
in Grey and Black No. 1: The Artist's Mother* (1872), a painting he would

surely have seen in the Louvre during his extensive European travels, he also unexpectedly associates genteel cultural conventionality with this painting whose Oriental-influenced design and what Novak calls its "abstract" composition (Novak 1969, 252) would have placed it firmly within the aesthetic canon. The painting's early and continued popularity with the public, however, and its inclusion in the Louvre's collection, thus linking it with accepted academic artistic standards, perhaps suggested it to Dos Passos as a detail of setting that would evoke middle-class conventionality.

Eventually, the dealer from whom Angela buys her new furnishings, Kekronian's Art Gallery and Exhibition of Oriental Fabrics, turns out to be as bogus as her new decor and her penchant for "rice . . . and bamboo tips . . . candied rose leaves . . . and sake in a lacquer bowl." Kekronian's gallery is an aesthete's dream, furnished with "carved Turkish stools . . . , a brass coffee pot and some cups of silver filigree" tinted by "Persian stained glass" (45–46) over rich Oriental carpets. Enchanted by the ambiance, Angela invests a great deal financially and emotionally as well when Kekronian courts her. But the dealer in romance disappears abruptly, his firm bankrupt, and aesthetic values are once again revealed as foundationless. Angela responds by selling all her goods to recoup her losses, a turn to capitalism as a remedy for romance that Dos Passos used also in "A Pot of Tulips," suggesting this early perception of the inevitable opposition between economics and idealism.

Sometimes, however, Dos Passos shows the reality beneath the romance to be much more pernicious and sinister. In "Romantic Education," for the first time the sentimentally idealized woman, who here represents romantic values, descends precipitously from the heights to which Dos Passos usually elevated her. An exotic but distinctly mature Spanish woman, Madame d'Alvarina, whom John Ricker, a callow American, meets on a crossing to Europe, comes to embody for him the richness and romance of European life. She feeds his imagination with stories that open "the narrow walls of his life" into "a huge vista filled with glitter and merriment, even with poetry."[27] " 'Ah, you do not live, you Americans!' " (1), she warns him, so when Ricker lands in Europe he is determined to "see the world." What he sees, however, is the "nasty leering smile" beneath the powder and rouge that prettify coarse, "naughty" (4) women, just as Madame d'Alvarina's stories had likely glossed over considerably the reality of her experiences.

The visual qualities of this story are not as striking as those in most of Dos Passos's other romantic antiromances drawing on aesthetic details.

"Romantic Education" returns, however, to the familiar dichotomy between European and American values and the dissonance that results when Americans—adventurers or artists—try to adopt, but not adapt, European sensibilities. These themes reiterate the young writer's ambivalence about both romantic and realistic attitudes. The story ends inconclusively and with evidence of Dos Passos's growing narrative sense in two brief paragraphs that jump abruptly from Ricker aboard ship dreaming, to Ricker in a "hot garish" European cafe, regarding his companion's "dead white face and . . . vermilion lips" and comparing the reality of the moment to d'Alvarina's "glowing narrative." Ambivalently, Ricker doubts whether the tawdriness around him must be "the culmination of romance" (4). Dos Passos shows that Ricker, like the other romantic aesthetes who confront reality in these *Harvard Monthly* stories, still *needs* some hope of an aesthetic value neither as inflated as the Harvard aesthetes' nor as grim as the flat pragmatism of the American commercial middle class.

Dos Passos's romantic aesthetic background had begun to conflict tellingly with his attempts to make more original use of materials at hand, of realistic images and themes. The resulting dissonance creates in his work a wary tension that gradually becomes more controlled, foreshadowing the innovative skill with which he would later deliberately combine disparate elements in a collage or cubist composition to jolt the reader. In particular, Dos Passos's poetry in his final year at Harvard illustrates the process by which he was developing beyond romantic tendencies into modernism. Even when a poem's tone is predominantly aesthetic, as in "Incarnation," eventually published in *Eight Harvard Poets,* Dos Passos carefully chooses and exploits the resonances of his central visual image.[28] Often, he opposes the image against his own developing brand of realism to produce a work that clearly sets him apart from most of his *Harvard Monthly* counterparts. These aspiring young writers were still, in 1916, publishing poems of the nature of Ernest Benshimol's "To a Mad Poetess": "Daughter of Luna, sister unto death / Tell me of regions where I see thee fly," Benshimol's ode enjoins, ending "Frail winged wanderer of the awesome night, / Poor Nukteris, how lonely is thy flight!" [29]

Dos Passos's sentiment in "Incarnation" is romantic, dwelling on the lasting after-image in the speaker's mind of the face of an Italian woman. The poem's structure, built around that central image, is somewhat regular, occasionally interspersing alternately rhyming lines among exactly rhyming couplets. But Dos Passos, familiar as he was with the Italian

Renaissance art that forms the poem's visual basis, is able to suggest much more with the image of the Madonna he uses than one would expect from what might otherwise be a conventionally aesthetic invocation of a Pre-Raphaelite icon.

The Pre-Raphaelite painters, who self-consciously borrowed from earlier artistic movements, developed a highly personal system of symbols and conceived of themselves as addressing only a very restricted but sensitively select audience. In these ways they helped lay the foundations for the aesthetic movement in England in the 1880s, from which the Harvard aesthetes in turn derived, and for the symbolist artists of the late nineteenth and early twentieth century, whose work impressed Dos Passos in his senior year. The Pre-Raphaelite Brotherhood's idealization of women, especially in early works of the movement, produced paintings of iconic figures—Ophelia, Beatrice, and the Virgin Mary, among others. Dante Gabriel Rossetti's early depiction of the Annunciation, for instance, in the 1850 *Ecce Ancilla Domini,* introduces iconography that recurs in Dos Passos's "Incarnation": the "gleam" of the "white-robed angel" with the "garden's silver lilies" (ll. 12–13), suggesting luminous fire beneath a hazy white light. Looking backward for the spirit infusing the image, Dos Passos's poem finds an analogy typical of a young poet well versed in the visual arts: "An old Italian painter [who] . . . has played / . . . away . . . all his desire / For fragrant things afar from earth" (ll. 18–20). Such retrospection is as characteristic of the Pre-Raphaelites as it is of their successors, the aesthetes. Finding in this poem visual reminders of Pre-Raphaelite painting certainly validates Malcolm Cowley's analogy between "Incarnation" and "the virgin in Botticelli's *Annunciation"* (Cowley 1936, 170), with Botticelli's late-fifteenth-century "power to materialize . . . beautiful visions" having influenced the late-nineteenth-century revival.[30]

But Dos Passos's poem makes more complex use of the image than as mere visual allusion or nostalgic retrospection. Fascinated during his 1911 to 1912 grand tour among the Madonnas of Raphael himself, Dos Passos invests the quickly glimpsed face in his poem with a mixture of ethereality and sensuality more akin to the Renaissance master's ability to fuse "Christian devotion and pagan beauty" (de la Croix and Tansey, 489) than to the earlier Botticelli's delicate spirituality.

The poet achieves this complexity by juxtaposing images from the two conflicting strains that characterize this and other poems of this period—the romantic-aesthetic and the urban-realistic. The melancholy image of "long rain . . . / Slanting on black walls" (ll. 1–2) and the sug-

gestion of the "voluptuousness of the Church" (Cowley 1934, 35) create
the tone one might expect from a somewhat self-consciously decayed
romantic. But Dos Passos places his vision of the unforgettable face
amid a cityscape, crowding realistic details against the vision. The light
suffusing the "long rain," light that Dos Passos later translates into the
light from the Madonna's face that "[f]lames into [the speaker's] soul
. . . / . . . in the turbulent darkness" (ll. 7–8), comes from "gas-lamps
[that] shine / Greenish gold" on the "dark interminable streets" (ll.
28–30). Passing by a shopwindow "spangled in long lines" by raindrops
(l. 4), the speaker sees "An oval olive face" whose expression embodies
for him the "sweetly sullen grace" (l. 10) of the Virgin surprised by
God's messenger. This is an image of a reluctant, almost petulant young
woman, innocent but human—certainly not a Botticelli divine. Dos
Passos manages to imbue his description of Mary's response to the
angel's visit with delicacy that nevertheless hints of eroticism. To the
speaker, the Italian woman's face conveys what Mary experienced when
she felt "all her soul subdued unto the fire / And radiance of her ecstasy"
(ll. 14–15), an image recalling Bernini's *The Ecstasy of St. Theresa*
(1645–1652), which mingles religious and physical passion. As in the
baroque sculpture, Dos Passos depicts the sacred visitation as "a sultry
dream" (ll. 14–16), reinforcing the poem's play on heat from light and
from sexuality mingled with religious fervor.

Gradually, however, even as Dos Passos jostles romantic aesthetic elements and art novel preciousness against modern and modernist strains
in these 1915 to 1916 poems, the fresher, more original, and modernist
strains begin to emerge as the poems' undeniable strengths. Three
poems in particular from this period illustrate the beginning of Dos Passos's transition toward modernism. Each opposes a romantic concept
against a modernist setting, structure, or set of images that looks ahead
to the author's fully modernist work and constitutes the most memo-
rable aspect of the poem.

Perhaps the most essentially romantic poem of the three is "Memory," the only one of them ultimately to be published, appearing in *Eight
Harvard Poets*. The poem abandons the unimaginative use of regular
meter in favor of varying line lengths and occasional rhyme more suited
to the imagist-influenced visual vignettes whose pictorial effects employ
impressionist lighting. For all its studied irregularity and its impressionistic efforts to embody a moment's passage, the poem's very title, its
theme, its point of view, and even its visual effects still betray a romantic
imagination. The speaker recalls a girl with whom he spoke briefly dur-

ing a summertime steamer ride, focusing on shimmering, diffuse light effects—the river "green in the deeps" like the girl's eyes, the canal "full of dazzle and sheen," the "sunlight [lost] . . . among [her] hair, / . . . warm light caught and tangled . . . / Red gold amid [her] hair."[31]

This soft-focus idealization of femininity, typical of Dos Passos's work of this period, is common also to some of the turn-of-the-century American impressionists. For example, Thomas Dewing's evanescent "atmospheric romanticism" (Novak 1969, 246) in *The Recitation* (1891) presents misty female figures in a dreamlike nostalgia that Novak traces as a long tradition in American painting, as early as Washington Allston's reveries. In a typically romantic, nostalgic recreation, the transforming imagination of the speaker of "Memory" emphasizes the transitoriness of the encounter. He focuses on the effects of time, noting wistfully in a single line that comprises a separate stanza, "I never even knew your name" (l. 55). Following that romantic note, however, Dos Passos shifts scenes to a "dingy hotel room" (l. 56) the night following the encounter, where the speaker sees the moon "like a golden gong" looming "[r]edly" (ll. 57–58) across a lake. The ensuing color images of "lake waves . . . of red gold, / Burnished to copper," of the moon's "gong" as belonging to the temple of "some silent twinkling city" (ll. 62–64), recall Dos Passos's luminist twilights and voluptuously religious aesthetic images.

But the final images of "Memory" also look forward to the innovative work Dos Passos produced in the creative years just before and after World War I, work whose style, tone, and themes built toward his modernist novel *Manhattan Transfer* and his most modernist painting. A moon hanging like a gong over the "purple and lavender buildings of New York" was the backdrop Dos Passos envisioned in 1918 for the first act of a play—a "Fantasy" (Ludington 1980, 168), he called it in his journal—that the Harvard Dramatic Club eventually produced in 1925 under the title *The Moon Is a Gong*. In its original version, the play contrasted a couple's prosperous country life with their impoverished existence after their move to the city, a dichotomy Dos Passos used again, although more ambiguously, in *Manhattan Transfer*. In this later portrait of New York City, he suggests the potential for a meaningful life for only one central character, Jimmy Herf, a "survivor," by associating him with natural images as opposed to mechanical, urban ones. The play's second production, by the Greenwich Village Cherry Lane Theater, led to Dos Passos's invitation to join the New Playwrights, who also produced the play, although after revisions and under a new name, *The Garbage Man*. Its style still showed the "ambivalence between sentimen-

tal and hard-boiled modes" that begins to emerge in Dos Passos's writing during his final year at Harvard.[32]

But the revised play's differences from its earliest form reflect the
ways in which Dos Passos was developing artistically in these years.
Between 1916, the first time he used the image of the moon as a gong,
and 1925, when *The Moon Is a Gong* was produced, he began working
with expressionist and precisionist themes and literary and visual forms,
as closer study of the work of that period will reveal. The early-to-mid-
1920s saw Dos Passos's painting as well as his writing evolve into styles
that at times anticipated, at times assimilated, the most exciting aspects
of modernist art. A 1923 exhibition of his paintings at New York's
Whitney Studio Club showed elements of futurism and cubism, for
instance, emerging in Dos Passos's visual imagination, while such forms
emerged from his writing as well.

The Ashcan School

The modernist elements emerging from the poems of his senior year,
however, were still cautious, although, for their time and place, fairly
innovative. For instance, these poems persistently turn on romantic concepts placed in modernist settings. The two unpublished poems apparently written at about the same time as "Memory" use images echoing
those of the American realist painters who called themselves The Eight,
but whose popular label, the Ashcan school, more bluntly conveys the
tone of their work. Because they depicted scenes of urban lower-class
life, the Ashcan painters were allied in spirit and intent with French real-
ists such as Balzac and de Maupassant, to whom Dos Passos felt drawn
at this time. Ashcan painters Robert Henri and John Sloan bucked the
traditions of the Pennsylvania Academy, the closest American analogy to
the French Salon, in a challenge to establishment aesthetics.[33] Similarly,
Dos Passos attempted, in these senior year poems, to inject a fresh
breath of actuality into the hermetically sealed aestheticism of much of
what was published in the *Harvard Monthly* and other contemporary literary journals.

"The Ladies' Orchestra: Spring" is a vignette of urban culture that
reveals something of the life of the individual that often lies buried
beneath the city's impersonal, demanding movement, a theme to which
Dos Passos would return, far less romantically, in *Manhattan Transfer*. In
this poem, a chamber trio plays practically unnoticed amid a city restaurant's "[w]hite table cloths and yellow lights; / Clatter and glare; waiters

with trays; / laughter of women tinkling shrill" ("Book," ll. 1–3). The restaurant's "wanton gold" (l. 5) shimmers over "eating throngs" (ll. 26) who complacently dine "[a]mid the buzz of talk" (ll. 22) that overwhelms the halting waltzes and the "headlong swagger of ragtime songs" (l. 25) the trio plays. Such images appear in William Glackens's depictions of *Chez Mouquin,* busy compositions in which figures are surrounded by movement and light glinting off surfaces in the restaurant. In the center of the bustle of Dos Passos's composition are narratives that emanate from the memories of the musicians whose minds wander as they play.

The structure Dos Passos intended for the poem emerges even though it seems to be unfinished. The pianist's 24-line reminiscence, preceded by an 8-line stanza, begins, "Piano, harp and violin / Grind out old tunes, quavering, thin" (ll. 19–20) and establishes the surrounding din. The pianist's stanza is followed by a parallel stanza, only 5 lines this time, but beginning the same way: "Piano, harp and violin / Scrape out tunes that fruitlessly spin" (ll. 51–52). Following that variation on the theme, the violinist's story begins to unfold, but 13 lines into the narrative, it breaks off, and no harpist's story appears.

Both the existing narratives are set off from the refrains by a row of large dots in the manuscript, suggesting, as does the text's progress, that Dos Passos intended the structures to be parallel not only in content but in their structural function as well. Both narratives are essentially romantic, the complete one moving from the pianist's mechanical playing to her interior life as her mind wanders back to her son's birth, apparently the central event of her life. She pictures him, born on Easter, in terms suggesting a Byzantine icon or a Renaissance fresco. His golden hair is "[a]ureoled like the saints at church . . . like / The young St. John, who with fervid eyes adores / The Virgin at the altar, about whose throne / Gold glitters . . . and . . . / candles sway . . . [T]he woman feels her soul / Tremulous with sudden ecstasy" (ll. 38–43). The violinist's narrative is too incomplete to tell whether it would have used similarly aesthetic images to portray the romantic power of memory. But what exists of the composition seems to suggest Dos Passos's growing awareness, expressed both by this poem's theme and its structure, of how the depersonalizing and daily commerce of the city subsumes the individual, here essentially romantic in her need for memory to transform the grubby monotony of everyday life.

Creating a similar tension between theme and setting, expressing also a sense of the buried life adrift in the city, and looking forward also to more modernist, more pessimistic expressions of this theme, an unpublished poem headed "1916—Sonnet" sets a romantic point of view in an urban landscape. Amid "dinning city noises, dark throngs move / Monotonously" (ll. 2–3), their "faces in shadow . . . a jumbled stream" (ll. 5 – 6).[34] But the speaker sees the street lights illuminate individuals, "a boy's pale intense face" and "a girl's madonna profile, full of ruth" (ll. 8 –9). The lights illuminate for the speaker "one face / In every face" he sees: "dark mystic eyes / . . . longing . . . / For fragrant unknown things" (ll. 10 –13). With the poem's first-person point of view and its emphasis on "eyes" and individual vision, Dos Passos conveys a romantic recognition of the gap between human dreams and the mediocre, anonymous reality of city life.

That realistic image of city life, however, is a modernist perspective of the kind Dos Passos would create later in *Manhattan Transfer,* the kind the Ashcan painters created in their dark, spare portraits of city dwellers. Some of these portraits, such as Sloan's 1907 *Hairdresser's Window* and Glackens's 1908 *The Shoppers,* catch the vitality of individual lives in the city's rush. Some, such as Everett Shinn's 1890 *Sixth Avenue Elevated after Midnight,* with its artificial light barely tracing the individual features of tired, isolated train passengers, depict the dim enervation caused by the city's constant demands. Dos Passos's structurally perfect if formally unimaginative "1916—Sonnet" attests to the technical skill the writer had developed by the time he produced the poem to fulfill a senior English course requirement. Its glimpse into the face of the masses, however romantic, is precocious for a 20-year-old nurtured by Harvard's traditional academic curriculum and friendly with the college aesthetes whose elitist tastes shaped the *Harvard Monthly.*

Another response to a different English course assignment illustrates the growing intensity and predominance of Dos Passos's visual imagination at a time when he was consciously working to define his own style and consciously creating a tension between romantic and realistic elements in his work. "City Twilight" presents generally the same theme as "The Ladies' Orchestra" and "1916—Sonnet": the individual's identity and energy pitted against the anonymous city. But the extant drafts of "City Twilight" reveal a conscious if gradual movement toward greater realism in his depiction of the city and toward modernist poetic techniques. Dos Passos's revision of the title, from "The Park Benches" to "City Twilight" and later to "City Sunset," shows that he intended the poem to focus on the city, not the couple whom the speaker observes in "close embrace" (l. 18) on a park bench.[35] This interest in the small actors against the large setting, individuals placed in a perspective that threatens to overwhelm them, recalls Dos Passos's fascination, in his 1911 to 1912 European travels, with works of art whose composition depended on the dynamic between part and whole. He had seen how frescoes brought alive daily scenes in the larger context of their environment and times and how Italian mosaics created designs with their vibrant colors. Likewise, *Manhattan Transfer* would later cast the city as that novel's main character, depicting individual lives as scenes in a fresco and employing the juxtaposition of parts as an integral stylistic device.

That "City Twilight" later became "City Sunset" suggests another move away from idealization. The word *twilight* connotes a romantic evening mood, while *sunset* connotes ending, closure, the loss of natural light. The city once again is the closed, murky, grimy landscape of the Ashcan painters: "distant arclamps" flare "against the steely grey / of a harsh and wind-chilled sunset" touching "[a]brupt dusty house-piles . . . / Like obscene, angled cobwebs in the dusk" (ll. 1–7). Actually, Dos Passos's revisions of the city's image bring him even closer to the characteristic tone of the Ashcan painters' work. They more closely identified with realistic writers (Rose, 9), who depicted urban life without much commentary, than with naturalists, such as Stephen Crane, whose image of the city in *Maggie: A Girl of the Streets* is so sordid as to outrage the reader.

Dos Passos's third draft removes some naturalistic details, such as "smoky nauseous smells / Of burning litter" (ll. 12–13). It also removes one of the more overtly sexual references in his work to date. Perhaps, in omitting "lust" from the phrase "the fury of their lust and love" (l. 21), Dos Passos sought to avoid characterizing the couple too specifically; perhaps he simply retreated into characteristic excessive shyness about sexual matters; or perhaps he was trying to appease the reviewers—probably from the *Harvard Monthly*—whose initialed remarks on the back of the second draft suggest a similar prudishness. The commentators had rejected it, apparently for publication, on the grounds that it was "too hot"—a comment that was signed "e.e.c." Edward Estlin Cummings, who later signed his sometimes controversial poetry "e. e. cummings," served on the *Harvard Monthly* editorial board during this time.

The couple, so overcome by love (if not lust as well) that "there is for them no earth, no sky; / But only two hot bodies quivering" (ll. 19–20), for a romantic moment "annihilate[ ] the squalor and filth" with the "mad flame" (l. 22) of their love. They are nevertheless "frail" (l. 17) and, ultimately, merely "a grey brown shadow" (l. 26) against the lamp-lit glare of the city. The city surrounds them thematically, visually, and within the structure of the poem: the first 14 lines and the final 8, two separate stanzas painting the urban scene, predominate over the middle stanza of 8 lines about the couple. Metrically, the poem reaches for greater modernity and a more colloquial idiom. As Dos Passos's instructor, Dean Briggs, noted critically of the first version, it "goes off into no rhythm in particular" after "four five-accent verses like iambic pentameter docked for trochaic movement." But the revision shows Dos Passos's awareness of his use of rhythm—or lack of it—as he scans the first 20 lines, then quits.

Even less romantic is a poem that *did* see print in *Eight Harvard Poets.* "Salvation Army" mingles the "raucous monotone" (l. 29) of drums and cymbals in the shrill Salvation Army band with the city's noises—"endless rumble of carts, / The scrape of feet, the noise of marts" (ll. 5–6).[36] The only touch of sentiment is the inclusion of a "tired girl / [a] [s]lim wisp" (ll. 16–17), characteristic of Dos Passos's idealization of women. Still, she is less romantic an image than the girl in a poem such as "Memory," for instance, in that this Salvation Army waif constitutes only a two-line image before the "crowded streets" (l. 18) so typical of Ashcan paintings overwhelm her. She seems less a romantic symbol of the individual's struggle against the city's energy than merely another "Face[ ] . . . wan in the arc-light's livid glare" (l. 20). Briefly, here, the lighting effects suggest expressionist distortion and colors, predicting the direction Dos Passos's images would take past impressionist or luminist light into twentieth-century modernist technique and sensibility. Again, as in "City Twilight," an image that in an earlier poem might have been used to romantic effect becomes another image of the city's anonymous power. The poem's focus on the girl's face reinforces the importance of the individual. And again, as in "City Twilight," the rhyme scheme that begins regularly, as Dos Passos fairly unobtrusively forms couplets, becomes sporadic after 20 lines, as the band's noise dies away "[a]mong the silent, dark array / [o]f city houses where no soul stirs" (ll. 26–27).

The best of these senior-year poems, "Genre," is also the best paradigm for how Dos Passos used romantic elements, both in the process and the product of writing. Gaining confidence with realistic elements, he had learned by the time he left Harvard to control the tension between them to original effect. "Genre" is also the most potently visual of these college poems, abandoning "writerly," self-consciously aesthetic, or poetic diction and images in favor of bold colors in realistic images expressed simply and concretely. Although the poem draws a crowded cityscape such as Bellows or Glackens might depict, its colors are vibrant and primary fauvist splashes, no longer The Eight's dark palette. These are distinctly more postimpressionist images, evoking even the brilliant primary color interplays of the synchromist Robert Delaunay, whose city paintings of this same period directly influenced Dos Passos's own painting in the illustrations for his 1927 *Orient Express* (Knox, 27). The poem's dynamic settings predict the bright energy of Dos Passos's first fully realized modernist work, *Manhattan Transfer:* "Studded with orange, rippling with lemon-yellow light, / Spilled onto the blue-blackness of the city night, / The pavements laugh reflections under foot / Of crowds that bustle through the twinkling rain" (ll. 1–4).[37] Two small boys, "wet hair snaky on their foreheads" (l. 11), stand by a "fruit-store [that] glows" with "fragrant" (ll. 6–7) color. Transfixed by the greens, reds, and yellows, the boys' imaginations "gild with romance / The fruit piles" (l. 18), producing "[s]tories of pirates" and of "Crusoe's isle" (ll. 13–15) in a romantic transformation illustrating the best and most sustaining effects of imagination.

Although a romantic concept, the power of the memory here produces none of the pessimism, melancholy, or dissatisfaction of the imaginative forays in Dos Passos's early and aesthetic romantic writings. The poem's speaker is finally at sufficient distance to depict the images realistically enough to let *them* do the work that the romantic "I" has previously done for the reader in these college works. Like Wordsworth in "Tintern Abbey" and the *Prelude,* Dos Passos here affirms the transformational value of imagination and memory, but his technique and tone suggest that he has developed stylistically beyond the tendency to allow memory to surpass reality, a romantic flaw Wordsworth cautions against. And the poem's final lines, relating what the boys actually see, reinforce Dos Passos's new facility and sense of ease with realism: "seated on a creaky chair, / A grizzled Italian spells the paper out, / And mutters as he reads" (ll. 19–21). As "Genre" illustrates, Dos Passos's years at Harvard had taught him "to be both engagé and disengagé" ("Interview," 11). The reading, course work, and atmosphere he absorbed there set him to work at developing a literary style that transcended these influences and let him express his own broadening perspective on the world.

While Harvard broadened his academic perspectives, Dos Passos engaged spiritedly and openly with stimulating new ideas the world outside Cambridge offered as well. Frequent excursions to Boston, for instance, fed his work with visual impressions that excited him. After a "tremendously long ramble through Boston" one day in spring 1916, for instance, he wrote excitedly to his friend Rumsey Marvin of the "reflections of the orange and yellow lights . . . on the wet streets" and the "sort of paganism . . . in the cheaper parts of the city," of the "wonderful" market with its "old grizzled . . . flashing eyed Italians buying vegetables," and of the freshness of the "reds and greens and yellows" of the produce "in the rainy atmosphere" (*Fourteenth,* 39). Dos Passos's increasingly acute and subtle sensitivity to color and atmospheric effects produced out of these observations realistic images characteristic of the nascent modernist air of such poems as "Incarnation," "City Twilight," and "Genre," whose vividness obviously grows directly from the Boston scene Dos Passos describes to Marvin. The ability Dos Passos was developing to translate observation directly into literature, even if at this point he did not always know the most expressive form to impose on it, shows clearly in the effect of this single city scene on his visual imagination.

The Armory Show

What a "jolt," then, as Dos Passos himself termed it in retrospect, must the hundreds of paintings in the 1913 Armory Show have been to his sense of color, motion, and form in writing and painting.[38] The Armory Show, as the International Exhibition of Modern Art came to be known, gathered in one place for the first time about 1,600 paintings, sculptures, prints, and drawings representing some of the best of the new in both American and European art. If Dos Passos saw the show in New York, its opening location, during February or March of 1913, he viewed many works by American artists whose methods and themes paralleled or influenced his own writing at Harvard. Among the paintings in the exhibition were plein air, painterly landscapes by impressionists Childe Hassam and Theodore Robinson; the bolder romantic, nascently modernist work of Albert Pinkham Ryder; and many Ashcan city scenes. He saw also many works produced by artists who were just before exploring more radical forms of modernism such as cubism, German expressionism, and precisionism.[39] Perhaps these cityscapes by John Marin and Stuart Davis, still lifes by Marsden Hartley and Joseph Stella, and landscapes by Morton Schamberg and Charles Sheeler seemed to Dos Passos the work of artists who were poised on the brink of new aesthetic directions just as he was. But the quarter of the works that represented European painting provided Americans with their first glimpse of Europe's revolutionary directions in art. Cézanne, Matisse, van Gogh, Gauguin, Seurat, Duchamp, Picasso, Derain, Vlaminck, and Braque were only a few of the innovators whose work startled—in some cases, shocked—Americans into an awareness of fauvism, cubism, and expressionism, and other postimpressionist innovations.

Symbolism

The Armory Show also featured many works by European painters associated with the symbolist movement: Puvis de Chavannes, Bonnard, Vuillard, Denis, and especially Redon, his oils representing the largest group of paintings by a single artist (Rose, 53). The late-nineteenth-century symbolists evolved a kind of hyperromanticism out of the earlier romantics' focus on individual expression and the power of the imagination. With the romantics the symbolists "shared the conviction that only ideas represent that superior reality which art should elect and retain" and concurred in their aim to "transform modern life" by introducing into it expressions of the interior world.[40]

New ways of expressing the individual world, both in literature and in painting, were thus necessary. Gustave Kahn, one of symbolism's spokesmen, expressed this need for "more appropriate words that are not worn out by twenty years of hackneyed usage" and for a new form of prose that was "rhythmic . . . and mobile," adapting itself to the idea, not the "banal prose . . . [of] conversation" (quoted in Rewald 1978, 148). This move toward free verse, a way to "clothe the Idea in a sensitive form" rather than "going straight to the conception of the Idea itself" (J. Moreas, quoted in Rewald 1978, 148), seems close to the aims of Dos Passos's late Harvard works. In them, for instance, he abandoned meter for free verse, sometimes in midpoem. Early in his senior year, he struggled toward an individual style that at times seemed poised between a new realism and the romantic tendencies out of which he and the symbolists developed. During his development, Dos Passos discovered the free-verse, richly imagistic poetry of the Belgian symbolist Emile Verhaeren (Ludington 1980, 65), whose work Redon illustrated. Stimulated by the symbolists' work, Dos Passos advised his friend Rumsey Marvin, who was also a beginning writer, with a quotation from another symbolist poet, Verlaine, revealing that Dos Passos shared some of the symbolists' goals: ". . . never / Choose your words without some

contempt: / Nothing is dearer than the grey song / Where the imprecise
joins the precise" ("Art Poetique," quoted in Ludington 1980, 79).

Literary symbolists such as Verlaine conceived of symbols as consisting of something more than "simply . . . units of language," a departure
from prenineteenth-century allegorical conceptions of symbols both in
literature and painting.[41] In that a symbol's meaning, both in verbal and
visual works, depended on both the reader's perception and the symbol's context, the symbol was thus to some degree autonomous to these
nineteenth-century artists, a concept that called into question the relia-
bility of language as meaning, or, as modern theory would express it,
that divided the signifier from what it signified. Symbolist works only
opened a "little door" for a viewer—or reader—who must then "go further" himself (quoted in Rewald 1978, 178), as Redon himself insisted
of his own work, which dominated the Armory Show.

Although they did not necessarily agree about Redon's artistic mer-
its, literary symbolists of his era did agree that Redon's work and theories constituted the closest analogue to their own. And, broadening the
analogy, literary symbolists, recognizing the impreciseness of the symbol
and striving to evoke or suggest rather than define or depict, felt that
literature had to "become music, since music . . . can evoke better than
words the mystery of life" (Rewald 1978, 150). In his theory, practice,
and interdependence with the other arts for technique, Dos Passos had
much in common with the symbolists by the time he left Harvard. Like
them, he recognized that the word is somehow insufficient or unreliable,
and he too sought a new language, beyond words, that would be ade-
quate to express the new ideas of the revolutionary times he felt he lived
in. These goals he shared with the symbolists emerged in the visual and
aural imagery of his late college works and in *Rosinante to the Road Again,*
the book he began to conceptualize in Spain just after his graduation.

Dos Passos also shared with the symbolists some visual and literary
influences. American painters such as Abbot Thayer and James A.
McNeill Whistler, whose work was espoused by the aesthetes, the symbolists' direct descendants, had developed their "art for art's sake" doctrine out of early exposure to the emphasis on technique of the Barbizon
painters, who had also influenced Dos Passos. In fact, some critics cite
the "French landscape painters" as the origin of the symbolists' "continuous line of development" (Lucie-Smith, 20). Many of the symbolists,
such as Gustave Moreau, developed facets of their exotic, often boldly
colorful styles influenced by the Byzantine mosaics that had also impressed the young Dos Passos. Literarily, he shared with Moreau and

Redon as well an attraction to the "visionary detail" (Lucie-Smith, 66–67) of Flaubert in his *La tentation de Saint Antoine*, a book Dos Passos described as "seething with life and beauty and bitterness" (*Fourteenth*, 68).[42] And, like most of the symbolists in their time, Dos Passos came to believe during his years at Harvard that the existing world social order, so insensitive to what was beautiful, harmonious, and just, needed restructuring.

As his work just before, during, and after World War I illustrates, Dos Passos's political awareness and activism increased sharply as he looked more and more for subjects in the common places and faces of the masses he wrote about during his senior year, as he struggled free of the "stays . . . of us cotton-wool plutocrats" (*Fourteenth*, 40). His war novels show that the conflict obviously constituted for him an abrupt political awakening and a shove to the Left; as much an activist as he came to be through the Sacco-Vanzetti and Spanish Civil War years, however, he never approached the violent anarchism most of the symbolist artists espoused (Rewald 1978, 154–56). Whereas Dos Passos's early work shows affinities with the symbolist paintings he saw at the Armory Show, the direction he took after Harvard departs from these nineteenth-century artists in one vital aspect that helps define Dos Passos's mature work. The symbolists deliberately aimed their highly personal, private, and subjective idiom at a small, select audience who, they felt, could appreciate art for its own sake. But Dos Passos moved away from this hyperromantic and hermetic art of the symbolists and aesthetes toward a greater integration of individual vision and perspective on the world. Increasingly, he engaged with what he judged the more common aspects of realism although striving in his own way for a unique form of expressiveness. The "new language" Dos Passos sought, tentatively at this point, drew its vocabulary, he must have sensed, from the same spatial and temporal forms and ideas that had sparked the modernist works in the Armory Show.

Chapter Four

"Other Sorts of Education": Spanish Art and Culture

Vital to the growth of his visual and literary imagination were the trips Dos Passos took to Spain after his graduation from Harvard in October 1916 to study Spanish and architecture, and after his experiences with the war and his discharge from the army in July 1919. Out of these periods of exposure to the traditions and rituals of Spanish culture, the stark expressionism of its art and landscape, and the fiercely individualistic nature of the Spanish people, he began to move toward the radical aesthetics and politics of his greatest work.

Writing in retrospect about his four years at Harvard, Dos Passos implied that, for all its cultural excitements, the university was a "bellglass" of intellectual regulation scarcely penetrated by the political unrest of the period that saw the beginning of World War I. One of the autobiographical "Camera Eye" sections of *The 42nd Parallel* characterizes his college education as "four years under the ethercone":

> four years I didn't know you could do what you Michelangelo
> wanted say
>> Marx
>>> to all
> the professors with a small Swift break all the Greenoughs in the
> shooting gallery
>> but tossed with eyes smarting all the spring night reading *The Trag-ical History of Doctor Faustus* and went mad listening to the streetcar wheels screech in a rattle of loose trucks round Harvard Square and the trains crying across the saltmarshes and the rumbling siren of a steamboat leaving dock and the blue peter flying and millworkers marching with a red brass band through the streets of Lawrence Massachusetts. . . .
> and I hadn't the nerve

                                    to jump up and walk outofdoors and tell
    them all to go take a flying
        Rimbaud
        at the moon.

                                            (*42nd,* 262–63)

If his Harvard years seemed stultifying to Dos Passos by the time he reached his midtwenties as he judged them against the backdrop of the years of war and cultural upheaval that followed, they nevertheless had exposed him to some central political movements of the day. Labor unrest was brewing, as the "Camera Eye" reflection intimates, and socialism was finding a voice both among workers and on college campuses. At Harvard, students formed a socialist club and organized support for various other causes of the day—women's suffrage, anarchy, Marxism. John Reed visited the campus to speak several times—he was an alumnus and a former protégé of Charles Townsend Copeland—and Dos Passos published in the *Harvard Monthly* reviews of two major works by Reed, *Insurgent Mexico* and *The War in Eastern Europe.* But these reviews dealt primarily with Reed's aesthetics and his reportorial skills; they declined to engage at any depth with Reed's politics.

Such a stance was characteristic of Dos Passos during these years— not disengaged from the issues that were swiftly changing both national and international politics, but carefully considering them and coming to terms with them in his own way. Besides, he was still conscious of his role and responsibilities as the son of John R. Dos Passos, who toward the end of his life opposed most of the social and labor reforms so central to current debate during his son's youth and whose final book, *Commercial Mortmain,* published in 1916, lambasted the Sherman Anti-Trust Act and upheld the social Darwinism that had always characterized his economic beliefs.

Yet John R. and his son were allied in their responses to the events that sparked the war in Europe and eventually dislodged the United States from its isolationist position. At the end of Dos Passos's junior year, the spring of 1915, news reached the campus of the horrific new weapon— poison gas—the Germans had employed at Ypres and of the Zeppelin bombings being inflicted on London. Then, on May 7, 1915, a German submarine torpedoed the liner *Lusitania*; nearly 1,200 passengers, many American and even more British, lost their lives; and the news of this attack galvanized many Harvard students, Dos Passos among them. Thus he was proud when his father published in the *New York Herald* four days later a vehement protest to the Germans attempt to justify the act. "No one, as I understand, seriously contends that the wholesale slaughter of the innocent passengers on the Lusitania can be justified, mitigated, or even explained," John R. wrote. "No rule . . . could justify or excuse inhuman and uncivilized conduct by a belligerent."

Although he jokingly referred to himself as a "pacifist" in a letter to his friend Rumsey Marvin (*Fourteenth,* 44), Dos Passos nevertheless agreed with his father that such an act could not go unanswered. In his senior year, one of his contributions to the *Harvard Monthly,* "The Evangelist and the Volcano," condemned America's "supercilious disapproval" of the war, an attitude he compared to "an Evangelist preaching a sermon to a volcano—from a safe distance."[1] Americans, he wrote, "must realize that we are not isolated onlookers, that our destinies as well as those of the warring nations are being fought out on French and Turkish battlefields . . . and come to understand that such a huge catastrophe is above and apart from all praise and blame" (61). Yet, characteristically, he approached thoughtfully the problem of what kind of response would be appropriate for him. As he wrote to Marvin in August 1916, while he believed that service in the military could be a useful tool to make young people genuinely democratic, he realized that in practice such organizations seldom worked that way. Moreover, he asserted, "when you have an army you immediately want to use it—and a military population in a government like ours would be absolutely at the mercy of any corrupt politician who got into the White House" (*Fourteenth,* 45). His apprehensions about big organizations would extend beyond the military when he addressed larger forces threatening to overwhelm the individual in his mature modernist works.

For the time being, he began to seek a way to involve himself in some nonmilitary role. Besides his contributions of fiction, he published two more pieces in the *Harvard Monthly* addressing the war. In his editorial, "A Conference on Foreign Relations," concerning a conference on international affairs being held at Western Reserve University, he urged its participants to mobilize popular support for America's opposition to "the powers of darkness" through the practice of "constructive pacifism."[2] "A Humble Protest," a long essay, decried the rise of technological culture as an enemy to "thought and art," and implicated "Science" and industrialism in creating "the same civilization [that] had produced . . . the Eroica Symphony and the ruins of Rheims" (120).

Not only his distress about the war in Europe but also personal sorrow broke through the insulation of his life in Cambridge. His mother's health, perhaps strained by the years of secrecy and isolation while she waited to regularize her relationship with John R., had declined since he had been away at college, and in 1914 subsequent strokes had left her enfeebled physically and mentally. Ever solicitous of the mother to whom, in the long absence of a constant father figure earlier in his life, he had grown so close, he spent as much time with her as he could spare from his studies, visiting with her both in their home in Washington and at the farm in Sandy Point. When she died in May at the end of his junior year, despite his years-long consciousness of her frailty, Dos Passos was distraught: in a "Camera Eye" from *1919* he wrote autobiographically that at the news of Lucy's death "the bellglass cracked in a screech of slate pencils" (368).

He proposed postponing his return to college for a year, but although he was reluctant to leave his father alone, John R. encouraged him to return to finish his degree. Out of a characteristic tendency to divert himself in work and travel, he filled his senior year with cultural and intellectual activity that carried over into the summer following his graduation, when he joined his father at Sandy Point. Even his ambitious daily working schedule for that summer, however, could not mitigate his restlessness to travel abroad. Neither his political stance nor his professional goals had crystallized yet, but out of his instinctive sense that he must get some perspective on both his country and the war before he could decide his future, he had applied to work for the Commission for the Relief of Belgium, headed by Herbert Hoover. Understanding his son's need to escape the intellectual restrictions of Harvard and the familial confinements of Sandy Point, John R. was also concerned that his son direct his energies toward discovering a professional direction. As a compromise, he proposed that Dos Passos go to Spain to study architecture and Spanish culture. After hearing from the commission that he was too young to serve, Dos Passos agreed to his father's plan. But he was conscious, even as he undertook his father's plan, that he wanted to be in Europe as much to put himself in a better position to join the war as an ambulance driver as to broaden his intellectual experiences beyond those of Harvard.

Harvard had taught him much, obviously, and had exposed him to ideas and images that formed and changed his work, sometimes by prodding him to react against what he felt was false or pretentious in literature. In his poetry and essays, for instance, he had rebelled against the rarefied aestheticism that set the tone for much that the *Harvard Monthly* published. Eagerly, he had absorbed what was new in all the arts. During his senior year, for instance, Diaghilev's Russian ballet corps performed in Boston the music of such composers as Debussy and Stravinsky against scenery designed by futurist artists such as Nathalie Gontcharova (Ludington 1980, 72). He had come to realize that sometimes "education is nothing but a wall that keeps [one] from seeing the world" by inculcating "the lingo . . . the little habits of speech and action . . . the petty snobberies of one's own class" (*Fourteenth,* 48), as he wrote to Rumsey Marvin just before sailing for Spain. What he sought now were those "many other sorts of education" that would provide him genuine "illumination . . . regardless of garlic or lavender water" (*Fourteenth,* 48). He was ready to leave behind the "lavender water" primness and good taste of classicism, romanticism, and aestheticism that had surrounded him at Cambridge and plunge into the world of experience, not to be put off by the "garlic" of the commonness where, he somewhat naively assumed, reality resided. Living for four months in the cultural and political ambiance of Spain—its village life, its religious tradition, its landscape, and its rich native art—he wrote and painted with a vital freshness and began to gain the perspective on his own country that would be necessary to write his great modernist satires.

Settling in Madrid, where he studied at the Centro de Studios Históricos, Dos Passos immediately and volubly realized essential differences between his own country and Spain, where traditions and culture had developed over the course of centuries. Perceiving these contrasts often in visual terms from the texture of the life around him, he expressed them in letters, journals, poems, and, later, essays through direct and concrete graphic and structural images. He developed the habit of accompanying them with rough sketches in margins, showing both his growing stylistic independence from Harvard influences and his increasing reliance on a visual language. A letter to Marvin, for instance, a few days after Dos Passos arrived in Madrid, encompassed a broad range of elements that constitute early forms of concepts important to his mature style.

The texture of daily Spanish life derives from traditions centuries old, as Dos Passos immediately saw in the common details around him. His letter to Marvin enthuses that Madrid's "streets abound in donkeys & mules with lovely jingly harness inlaid with brass and red enamel . . . and people actually use pottery water bottles of the most divine shape."

The Madrileños of 1916 dressed much as they had for hundreds of years, in woolen mantas of "red and green, purple and yellow" (*Fourteenth*, 50, 51). In the letter, he augmented his verbal description with a sketch, employing a form of illustration describing shapes or details or striking faces or figures, suggesting the central role these visual elements now assumed in his aesthetic vocabulary. He used the manta as an example to Marvin of his realization that daily life in Spain provided evidence of the *"strata* of civilization" that had "passed through Spain and left something there—alive." Always sensitive to the individual figure against the large backdrop, as in the frescoes he liked, Dos Passos saw "in the way a peasant wears his manta, in the queer wooden plows they use, in the way they sacrifice to the dead," the "actuality"—not artifacts—of the cultures that had shaped Spain: "Celt-Iberians, Phoenicians, Greeks, Romans, Moors and French" (*Fourteenth*, 56–57).

The letter catches the essence of the cultures he describes in well-chosen, fresh details that, in comparison to the wistful stasis of his Harvard work, clearly illustrate his growing capacity to characterize with a single deft, colorful stroke, expressionistically. This skill he developed in the poetry Spain inspired him to write. Clearly, Dos Passos was impressed with the richness of Spanish culture, a richness that revealed in comparison all the more pointedly the "rootless," "abstract . . . lack of depth and texture" ("Against," 270) in American culture and literature he had bemoaned in an article written earlier that year and published only a week before his letter to Marvin.

Similarly, Dos Passos was impressed by the centuries-old temporal rhythm of Madrid, a major commercial city, but one where the business schedule was adjusted to human needs, not vice versa. Its leisurely pace amused him: "One has dejeuner a la fourchette—almuerzo—at about one or two then dinner between nine and ten at night. No one seems to get up in the morning and as late as I have ever been up the cafes and things seem to be in full blast" (*Fourteenth*, 51). Madrid's insistence on living by the schedule—late mornings, a three-hour midday rest, and nighttime dinner—and the customs it had observed for centuries must have illustrated to Dos Passos how raw and functional the ways of American cities were. When he came to express the American city's fragmented, pragmatic rhythm, he saw the necessity of originating new forms, modernist techniques, to evoke that rhythm.

But Spain's resistance to change had serious implications for the quality and character of life there as well. The ancient foundation of the nation's culture, the Catholic Church, retained its hold on Spain's reli-

gious practices, as it does today. Especially in the smaller towns and villages, the power of the church is clearly evident in inescapable visual
statements that require no other text. In Toledo or Segovia, where Dos
Passos traveled on short jaunts from Madrid across the landscape whose
starkness and colors pervade the essays, the Romanesque or Gothic
spires of a cathedral almost inevitably dominate the visitor's first impression of these ancient cities. An artist such as Dos Passos studying
architecture would not have missed this visual metaphor for the religious force that shaped Spain's politics and values for centuries.

Journal entries and letters he wrote in the fall and winter of 1916,
when he would sometimes strike out on foot or by train to see more of
the country, often begin descriptions of the towns he visited with a perspective that was initially somewhat distant. Usually, Dos Passos composed the picture carefully, making the cathedral the central element of
the scene. Alicante, for instance, a coastal town near Cartagena, is "a
high cream colored mountain with a castle—two churches with dark
blue domes, pale blue sky, dark blue sea" (quoted in Ludington 1980,
107)—a visual painting. Once inside the cathedral, Dos Passos's artist's
eye and architectural knowledge would assess its aesthetic qualities con-
fidently. The "really handsome plateresque lower story" of the cathedral
at Murcia contained "one of the most beautiful pieces of stained glass
[he had] ever seen, in orange and blue green"; the vaulting of the cathedral at Toledo was "beautifully proportioned," its chapel tombs "carrara
marble with charmingly done kneeling figures," which he sketched
("Diary of Italy").

His writer's eye, always attuned to the details that bespoke individual
lives, met in the interior of the cathedral further evidence of the power
of the church to shape Spanish life. As they do today, villagers who
dressed much as worshippers had done when the structure was new gen-
uflected before retables gilt stunningly with precious metals, stones, and
icons. Priests whose distinctive silhouettes he sketched in his journal
hovered around the treasures and paintings, protecting the church's
property from parishioners. In his awareness of such dire contrasts—
the wealth against the poverty, the ornate architectural excess of the
church's edifice beside the simple tiled roofs of the villagers' dwellings—
lies the philosophical origin of the satiric vision of the social and economic hierarchy Dos Passos saw developing in his own country when he
was writing *Manhattan Transfer* and *U.S.A.,* a hierarchy whose divisive-
ness he saw plainly in the political unrest that plagued Spain and culmi-
nated in its civil war that so passionately involved him.

Politics and landscape, two aspects of Spain that predominate in Dos Passos's letters and journals during that time, are combined in an important third element of Spanish culture that constitutes the aesthetic basis for his writing there: Spanish painting. His journals from 1916 note visits to both the Museum of Modern Art and the Prado within two weeks of his arrival in Madrid, and his entries about the two collections reveal a new authority in his artistic assessments and some major shifts in his tastes since his pre-Harvard visits to European museums. The collection at the modern museum, for instance, he finds "numbing junk," "afflicted with huge historical canvasses of people dying—Lucretia, Seneca, etc." These are the kinds of romantic paintings on classical themes that he had dutifully recorded in his travel journal of 1911 to 1912. Now, the only thing that he liked in the museum was an "interesting sense of swaggering noisy color" ("Journal," 73). Significantly, he conceived of the art there in expressionistic terms, in terms of colors described using a musical adjective—as the symbolists tended to describe painting—and especially in terms of motion.

The Prado, however, made a much deeper impression. This magnificent, wide-ranging collection is housed in a late-eighteenth-century neoclassical landmark in the center of Madrid adjacent to the city's finest parks; its architecture and location alone would have drawn Dos Passos. In keeping with the disparity between nobles and commoners that so intrigued Dos Passos, the Prado had been open to the public fewer than 50 years when he visited it. It had originally been the Royal Art Gallery, first founded in the reign of Ferdinand VII, featuring among its 311 original holdings a preponderance of paintings by Velázquez, court painter for Phillip IV.

It was these paintings, Dos Passos later wrote, that "gave [him] most pleasure" ("Satire," 1), these paintings he "plastered" on the "pink shiny walls" of his room at the Pensión Boston (*Fourteenth*, 56). Little wonder, since the beginning writer and painter was developing in Spain a new sense of how to capture in the most telling detail the essence of the individual and a more complex sense of spatial form, skills he found in Velázquez's mastery. Achieving an almost naturalistic style of portraiture that broke free of Renaissance and baroque ideals to present his subjects sharply characterized by expression and lighting (de la Croix and Tansey, 600), Velázquez exercised his skill not only to produce sumptuous court portraits for his patron but also to capture the strange characters who composed the decadent seventeenth-century court. Phillip IV retained jesters and dwarfs to amuse him, and Velázquez's 10 portraits of them manage to portray the malign grotesqueness of those who were psychologically stunted and the innate human dignity of those who were merely dwarfed physically. The Spanish painter's great skill "moves us more to pity than to amusement" at these characters.[3] In his mature satires, Dos Passos likewise displays his ability to create not only scathing characterizations but also unsentimental portraits that evoke compassion rather than scorn.

His later use of the city's spatiality to create theme also recalls Velázquez's painterly innovations. Velázquez's portraits bespoke his insight into the "essential mystery of the visual world" (de la Croix and Tansey, 602) in his brilliant manipulation of space and the viewer's perception of it, and his use of space to illuminate theme. Perhaps his greatest masterpiece, Las Meninas (The Maids of Honor, 1656), was the Prado's greatest pride when the gallery opened in 1819 and is still so today, meriting a small exhibition room all to itself. The portrait depicts Velázquez himself at his easel painting a subject whom the viewer assumes is the princess Margarita, attended by her two ladies-in-waiting, two of the court dwarfs, and a dog. Velázquez built into the self-referential portrait other reminders of the ambiguity of depicted space and of the work as artifact. Paintings within the painting, an open door, light from undepicted sources, and a mirror image of the king and queen, who are apparently watching the scene from what should be the viewer's point of view, all create an interior world within the frame that nevertheless presents "the image of a whole epoch" (de Pantorba, 165).

Such masterful composition and handling of optical effects and elements surely impressed Dos Passos, whose journals and letters of these months are full of the broad, deep perspectives from various angles that the topography, architecture, and urban spatial arrangements of Spain presented him. In one entry, for instance, he describes a cathedral seen from the mountains; then he offers the reverse shot, the long mountains seen from the cathedral's tower; and finally he descends to the ancient perplexing streets of a town like Toledo "that wander in and out and end in strange unexpected little squares or in old arches or pillared doorways." Such perspectives "fascinated" him ("Journal," 1–2).[4] Velázquez's creation of an independent, self-referential, small interior world that nevertheless opens for the viewer a door on the world of which it is a part constitutes a foreshadowing of modernist techniques. In such painterly accomplishments, one can see mirrored the adult Dos Passos's manipulation of space and compositional elements both verbally and visually to show the relationships among planes of existence.

Whereas Dos Passos found "pleasure" in Velázquez's work, he found himself "scared by the Goyas . . . in the Prado" ("Satire," 1). Given his growing awareness of the war raging not far to the north of his mellow existence in Madrid, as his letters and journal testify, Dos Passos must have found Goya's dark power and unflinching portrayal of the evils of war difficult to assess merely as art. Stylistically, the progression of Goya's work in the Prado constitutes an overview of all the styles in the Spanish royal collection. Goya moves from the "use of the art of earlier masters" to the crystallization of an entirely individual style that isolates him as an artist as surely as the artist and individual in his works is alienated from his world.[5] Indebted to Velázquez for the realism of his portraits, Goya nevertheless catapulted Spanish art—and all painting— headlong toward twentieth-century expressionism. In technique, his work acknowledged what came to be one of the primary concepts of modernist art, that "a frame can no longer enclose a world" that has no coherent order, no absolute truth (Paulson, 294).

This same dark vision that Dos Passos was poised before in 1916 emerges with nightmarish clarity in Goya's depiction of a world in decay and destruction. In the savage grotesquerie of Goya's court portrait *The Family of Charles IV* (1800) lies a harbinger of the brutal realism of Dos Passos's biographies in *U.S.A.,* both groups of characterizations express- ing the artists' detached disgust at the corruption endemic in the ruling class of both periods. In the violent distortions and dissonant colors of *The Third of May* (1808), Goya's cry of outrage at the brutality of Napoleon toward the Spanish commoners, lurk the formal disruptions and abrupt oppositions of *One Man's Initiation* and *Three Soldiers,* Dos Passos's revelation of the atrocities of World War I. Compositionally, the graphic precision and use of space in Goya's early-nineteenth-century series of etchings *Disasters of War* show the same attention to drafting evident in Dos Passos's sketches during the war and to commenting through open form essential to the structure of *Manhattan Transfer* and *U.S.A.*

Dos Passos's satire and pessimism, even at their nadir, never reached the appallingly bitter despair manifest in Goya's horrific late "dark" paintings, images executed in alienated old age—the witches' Sabbath, Saturn devouring one of his children, the dog buried in the sand. But like Goya, the mature writer Dos Passos was to become depicts ragged common people at the mercy of militaristic forces, or of mindless gov- ernments, or of the unthinking mob, or even of their own self-destructive natures. In his revolutionary compositions, Goya foreshadows the attitude and techniques of the adult Dos Passos after the war and just before the depression, who depicts the individual struggling, like Goya's dog engulfed by sand, against dehumanizing social and economic forces. Small wonder that Dos Passos, even in 1916, alludes to Goya often in his writing as a kind of shorthand stroke to characterize the tone or detail of a figure or scene, or that the day after his visit to the Prado he notes in his journal the intention to "compare the civilized savagery of Spain with the savage civilization of America" ("Journal").

Dos Passos's Spanish Poetry

Spain's rich artistic tradition, its centuries-old political and cultural continuity, its spatial perspectives and natural colors so different from America's—little wonder then that Spain "moved [Dos Passos] to write poetry" (Ludington 1980, 103). He hoped to convey a sense of Spain's landscape, of its daily life, and of the relationship among the country's landscape, culture, and history, in the "running series of things on Spain" he began there. Writing to Marvin and enclosing some of the poems, he described them as "very wild and irregular" (Fourteenth, 57)—and, indeed, compared to the formal traditionality of most of his Harvard poetry, they are. But even if "wild" is too extreme a label for these blank-verse poems, the comment shows not only Dos Passos's own awareness that his style was changing, evolving beyond the Harvard influences toward the modern, but also his consciousness of working toward that end. These Spanish poems, eventually published in Dos Passos's only volume of poetry, A Pushcart at the Curb, are not as modernist as the others in the volume written during and just after the war. But their imagery, their versification, and their use of visual elements represent a further step toward modernism from the style of his late Harvard poems.

To recreate the texture of the commoners' life in Spain, for instance, Dos Passos used classical images of the type that had characterized many of his Harvard poems. Instead of imposing the iconography of romanticism on conventionally pastoral material that, especially in his 1912 to 1914 poems, seems entirely removed from the actuality of his own experience, now Dos Passos integrates the classical allusions into material to which they seem organic, juxtaposing the classical images against a realistic setting. The results are more direct, accurate pictures of the culture that surrounds him, giving the reader a sense of immediacy that is entirely missing in the effete and languid Harvard pastorals.

"Beggars" (*Pushcart*, 23 –24) presents vignettes of the waifs and peasants dozing and panhandling "[a]ll day long . . . in the scant sun" (l. 24) beside the fountain in Madrid's Plaza de Cibeles.[6] The poem turns on contrasts. The fountain "some dead king put up / conceived in pompous imageries" (ll. 1–2) is surrounded by the ragged poor in the modern city. The fountain's "mossgreened [P]ans and centaurs" (l. 3) the poet imagines as counterparts to the waifs and peasants. Pan, for instance, is actually "a bearded beggar with blear eyes"(l. 11); "a little barefoot Eros" is merely a dirty child "crouching to scratch his skinny thighs / . . . star[ing] with wide gold eyes aghast / at the yellow shiny trams that clatter past" (ll. 20–24). In his picture of Spain as a country whose pastoral essence manages to survive its modernization, Dos Passos depicts modern urbanized Spaniards as the "last foster-children" of the goddess Cybele, nourished by her now "grey withered dugs" (ll. 29–30).

Using classical imagery to create a detached portrait of the archaisms that characterize Spain, employing hard, realistic diction, Dos Passos undercuts the sentimentality that such romantic iconography would have conveyed in his earlier poems. The coexistence of past and present and the resultant social disparities emerge gently in "X" (*Pushcart*, 32–33), another poem where Dos Passos imagines history but does not idealize it, placing it against the present to let readers view the contrast for themselves. In a garden in Aranjuez by the Tagus, another monument, a fountain built by one of the kings who inhabited the palace there, now "fill[s] silently with leaves / and the moss . . . / [clothes] simpering cupids and fauns" (ll. 13–15). The noise of the river's "speeding dark-green water" (l. 2) flowing by the barred, decaying palace, carries the speaker's thoughts from the "rich brocaded gowns / and the neat silk calves of the halcyon past" (ll. 17–18) to the reality of the present. "[T]hree stooping washerwomen" swirl piles of linen that "gleam" in the green water (ll. 4–5); "three gray mules pulling a cart / loaded with turnips" rumble past the symbol of Spain's archaic nobility, but the driver, "a man in a blue woolen sash / who strides along whistling . . . does not look toward Aranjuez" (ll. 26–27). Dos Passos lets these contrasts speak for themselves. The grandeur and wealth of this palace, built for Phillip II in the sixteenth century and expanded in the eighteenth by the Bourbon kings, is set against the simple poverty of the masses, and the proud if excessive past power of the Spanish nation against the turnip farmer who, absorbed in his own round of work, does not even notice the palace.

These contrasts and the dignity of the Spanish common people existing much as they had for centuries made Spain for Dos Passos "a living museum—a perspective view of Europe," as he noted ("Journal," 90). Similarly, in "XXII" (*Pushcart*, 56), an untitled poem written in Cercedilla, Dos Passos finds unbroken tradition in a picture of a shepherd on a hillside, the kind of image that romantic painting or poetry would sentimentalize and use to suggest a golden arcadian past. But this Spanish pastoral merely depicts the shepherd and his dog at work. The "long flock straggles" (l. 7); lambs bleat; wet yellow wool steams in the sun. Even though the point of view is a romantic "I" who watches in the "intimate silence" (l. 4), the portrait is dispassionate.

Nor does Dos Passos romanticize the city in his sketches of daily life. "I" (*Pushcart*, 14–15), a poem capturing a scene on the Calle de Toledo in Madrid, includes the beggars and the blind, the "penny swigs of wine / [and the] penny gulps of gin" (ll. 24–25), and the "tripe steaming in the corner shop" (l. 28), along with the "pink geraniums" (l. 3) and the caged goldfinch's song. The colors and compositions of these unsentimental though obviously engaged poems are far more realistic than earlier efforts such as "From Simonides" or "The Past." The colors of the Spanish poems are more vivid for being broad, realistic strokes rather than self-conscious patterning after pictorial styles. Their forms—blank verse with line lengths and syntax determined by the needs of the image or effect rather than the requirements of a conventional form—are more modernist because of their openness.

When Dos Passos's color images in these poems recall specific pictorial styles, however, they are techniques of Spanish painters, organic to the material. In the context of his more modernist structures, Dos Passos's stark groups of images evoke from the El Greco- and Goya-like colors and perspectives the expressionism hinted at in the works of these Spanish painters. The landscape that pervades Dos Passos's letters and journals of this period naturally dominates these poems, but, unlike his technique in the imagist-influenced Harvard poems, Dos Passos no longer uses landscape for its own sake.

In "IX" (*Pushcart*, 30–31), a poem written at Toledo that perhaps most effectively paints the Spanish landscape, Dos Passos deliberately evokes El Greco's famous view of the city against an ominous sky, but not sheerly for painterly effect. Rather, he uses the landscape with its livid colors and foreshortened perspective to comment on the church's historical force in Spain's history. Of the "bronze bells of Castile" hanging "[g]reen against the livid sky / in their square dun-colored towers / . . . / jutting from the slopes of hills" (ll. 1–5), he asks if they "remember" what the perspective evokes for the speaker: "stench of burnings, rattled screams / . . . / The crowd, the pile of faggots in the square, the yellow robes"(ll. 22–28).

In these images distinctly reminiscent of El Greco, Dos Passos links Castile's role in the Inquisition with the painter's vision of Toledo, his home city. Dos Passos, in fact, wrote in his journal that El Greco "fascinated" him when he visited the Prado, and his writing about one of his visits to Toledo is filled with his awareness of El Greco's life in that ancient city. The Casa de El Greco, where the painter lived and died, was to Dos Passos a "wonderful" place "where I'd give my hat to live" ("Journal," 2), he wrote excitedly. And perhaps the painter's most famous work, *The Burial of the Count of Orgaz,* painted for and still hanging in Toledo's Church of Santo Tome, made an impression that Dos Passos recalled 20 years later ("Satire," 1). El Greco's juxtaposition of the heavenly and earthly realms in that painting and his deliberate use of different styles to depict them show something of the juxtaposition of romantic and realistic elements Dos Passos used in his late Harvard poems as he worked toward his own style. Certainly El Greco's portrait of Toledo resonates in Dos Passos's own portrait of another city, Getafe, in "XI" (*Pushcart,* 34). In this poem, Dos Passos places the "[s]udden . . . village / roofs" (ll. 3 – 4), the "leaping buttresses" of a church (l. 5), and "a tower utter dark like the heart / of a candleflame" (ll. 7–8) against the "burn[ing] yellow" (l. 2) of the sky.

Dos Passos again captures something of the ominous quality of El Greco's Toledo, interjects the tone of Goya's horrific *Panic,* and uses both to modernist effect in one of his first poems about the war. A poem written at Cuatro Caminos, "XIV" (*Pushcart,* 40 – 42), sets clouds like "mouldered shrouds" over the "crumbling skull of the dead moon" (ll. 13–14). Beneath that spectral light, "Black as old blood on the cold plain / close throngs spread to beyond lead horizons" (ll. 8–9). This dim, undifferentiated throng mills under the visage of its "[h]uge . . . grinning . . . / . . . . / . . . God" (ll. 15–16). The imagery suggests it is death that "drive[s] the pale ones / white limbs scarred and blackened" (ll. 33–34), otherworldly figures distorted as in El Greco's mystical vision, but for a purpose much more consonant with Goya's. The poem reveals in its final lines that the wind that forces the clouds, sweeping away the "dry death-rattle" (l. 12) sound of the horde, "shrills from the cities of the north / Ypres, Lille, Liege, Verdun" (ll. 43 – 44).

In fact, even though he was "mad about Spain—the wonderful mellowness of life, the dignity, the layered ages" (quoted in Ludington 1980, 109–10), as he wrote to his friend Dudley Poore in January 1917—the war occupied more and more of his thinking. Sometimes he still wrote poems, as *Pushcart* (62) shows, in which he imagined himself finding a Beatrice who was not merely "a convention" (3), but, as he admitted to another friend, Arthur McComb, he could not get the war out of his mind. Perhaps one reason for his growing preoccupation with the conflict was that Europe's precipitous self-destruction threatened to obliterate what he had come to love about Spain and to wipe out the culture there and in Europe that "made worthwhile the cruel welter of life" (Ludington 1980, 108).

Spain had shown him the "wonderful mellowness" and the "cruel welter" of life, and it had set the stage for the development of his style into satire, modernism, and an intensive search for a "new language" equal to the task of expressing what he had seen and what he now felt compelled to see—the war. Immersing himself in Spanish culture, Dos Passos had finally gained a vantage point from which to view the strengths and weaknesses of America. He had seen clearly against the backdrop of Spain's "layered ages" the relative paucity of history and cultural precedent that robbed American art and literature of freshness and originality, and his developing style illustrates that he was determined to anchor his own writing in concrete actuality as a result. Spain had given him the color, the noise, and the motion to help him accomplish that, as all of his work from 1917 to 1922 bears out.

But if he had seen America's cultural deficiencies set against Spain's richness, he had also seen America's great social richness and flux against the unchangingness of Spain's traditions and governmental control. The dynamism of American cities, so evident when compared to the antique stillness of a Toledo or a Segovia, became one of Dos Passos's great themes after the war. In the vibrant tones, sweeping landscapes, and passionate native painters of Spain, Dos Passos had found the mixture of unflinching reality and expressionist color that would underlie the development of his literary style in the war novels he would write in the next four years. The colors and culture of Spain would influence as well his pictorial style in the painting and drawing that would increasingly interact with his writing in the coming years.

The realizations about the nature of American culture that Spain had fostered in him during his 1916 to 1917 residence were underscored and amplified by the subsequent two and a half years he spent confronting the mechanisms and costs of the war. As a volunteer in the Norton-Harjes Ambulance Unit, he sailed to France in June 1917 and by August was serving at the front. Later that year, he transferred into the American Red Cross and eventually worked at the Italian front. After a short return to the United States in 1918 for basic training as an army enlistee, he returned to France, where he finished his term of service and was discharged in July 1919. By August he returned to Spain, traveling on foot and by train with an alacrity that suggests both his eagerness to leave the military and the war behind him and his hope that the country that so engaged his artistic and political passions would nurture the writing he had begun about the war.

It was writing that moved toward a new realism of observation, writing that began to evolve the experimental modernism of his best work. That experimental modernism was predicated on the realization that the "old words" and the values of the golden age they represented were no longer viable in the culture the twentieth century was creating. The techniques Dos Passos developed as analogues to this modern culture evolved out of his recognition that a new language was necessary for this purpose, a new language that transcended the limitations of expression inherent in traditional narrative techniques. After his war experiences, as he recognized the inadequacy of both the verbal and visual languages he had used in his Harvard writing, he began to search for a more authentic, immediate mode of expression than his classical and romantic background had taught him. Even the relatively realistic style of his war writing seemed unequal to the civilization he imagined the United States to be during his postwar travels in Spain.

Like the American romantic landscape painters, he began to see his own country and its art more clearly by juxtaposing it against another country's culture. From the Spain of 1920, he saw in Europe a revolutionary spirit similar to the hope engendered by the French Revolution that had inspired the romantics, as he wrote in *Rosinante to the Road Again.*[7] Against the fierce individualism he saw in Spain, against the enthusiasm for reform he saw in postwar Europe, he observed by comparison his own country's great advantages and the responsibilities they conferred. And when he began working his way toward a verbal portrait of America after the war, he did so from the perspective of Spain.

As he wrote about ancient Spanish culture, he began to explore in his style the techniques that later characterized his mature modernism. The resultant collection of essays, *Rosinante to the Road Again,* begun in 1920 but published in 1922, marks Dos Passos's transition from romanticism to modernism. He structured these essays around a quest by characters out of myth, a structure used by T. S. Eliot in *The Waste Land* and James Joyce in *Ulysses,* both also published in 1922. What Dos Passos's two characters, Telemachus and Lyaeus, are searching for is a "gesture"—an immediate tangible sign—that will go beyond the "rubbish" (15) of words to express the essence of their country and culture. That is what Dos Passos was searching for, too. *Rosinante* shows the progress of the writer's quest for a new language that was spatial as well as temporal, nonrepresentational and not subject to the limitations and distortions of language: a visual language that could paint America. The quest in *Rosinante* for the telling "gesture" considers the communicative capabilities of several arts. Not surprisingly for Dos Passos, painting is the medium most often explored for its expressive potential.

The first art considered in the volume, however, is dance, the flamenco of the famous Spanish dancer Pastora Imperio, who had greatly impressed Dos Passos when he saw her perform at the Café Oro del Rhin in 1916.[8] Likewise, his two characters are inspired by her rendition of *lo flamenco* to seek the one gesture that will *be* Spain. Although Dos Passos is obviously limited to the expressive capabilities of his verbal medium, through his characters' quest he conveys the different potentials of other methods of establishing meaning. Pastora Imperio's dance itself is a system of signs involving her body, her face, her "yellow shawl . . . [with] embroidered flowers [making] a splotch of maroon . . . [and] a flecking of green and purple" (15), her finger snapping, and the guitar music. By a process of associative thinking, Telemachus and Lyaeus begin seeking other gestures that also express the essence of Spain. In Charles Pierce's terms, they are looking for more "signs" of the same "referent."[9]

The other gestures they consider bespeak what Spain means to them and to Dos Passos. A guiding principle in their search is that the gesture have the same quality as "the gesture that a medieval knight made when he threw his mailed glove at his enemy's feet or a rose in his lady's window" (17). What they seek is the archetypal, elemental quality of the gesture, and Dos Passos expresses those qualities with characteristically modernist allusions to myth and to the ancient culture that propagated the ideal of the quest. The young men suggest several gestures that qualify: a toreador's turning from a bull and "dragging the red cloak on the ground behind him" (17); "Torquemada" and "Santa Teresa" (235); *zarzuela*, a form of Spanish light opera (176). What these gestures have in common, besides their reference to the soul of Spain, is that quality of "thingness" (Steiner, 17) that the modernists aimed for in a work of art, the same quality that validates the interartistic analogy between the goals of modernist literature and modernist painting.

In fact, the imagery and content of *Rosinante* suggest that for Dos Passos the *most* expressive gesture is visual art. His descriptions of the audience at Pastora Imperio's performance and of her dance as well read like expressionist paintings. For instance, the dancer who precedes Imperio is "a huge woman with a comb that pushed the tip of her mantilla a foot and a half above her head. . . . Her dress was pink . . . ; under it the bulge of breasts and belly and three chins quaked with every thump of her tiny heels on the stage" (15). With these exaggerated lines and proportions, Dos Passos creates a dancer reminiscent of those grotesque performers in the paintings of Toulouse–Lautrec. The landscapes of Spain Dos Passos paints in *Rosinante* vibrate with expressionist color too, their tones and perspectives evoking the Spanish culture in an "inexplicable" (15) way that words cannot. Telemachus and Lyaeus stand "with thumping hearts on a hilltop looking over inexplicable shimmering plains of mist, hemmed by mountains jagged like coals. . . . The light all about them was lemon yellow. The walls of the village behind were fervid primrose color splotched with shadows of sheer cobalt. Above the houses uncurled green spirals of woodsmoke" (72).

These exaggerated colors and distorted lines commonly used by expressionist painters originated in part in the work of the Spanish painters El Greco (actually a Greek who worked and lived in Spain) and Goya. One of the truest gestures of Spain, Dos Passos suggests in his allusions to these artists in *Rosinante*, is their painting. "In painting," he asserts, "the mind of a people is often more tangibly represented than anywhere else" (57). Because of the "intense individualism" that characterizes the Spanish "soul" (77), the "aim" of Spanish artists such as El Greco and Goya is "self-expression," not beauty. "Their image of reality is sharp and clear, but distorted," Dos Passos writes; "Burlesque and satire are never far away." All the greatest Spanish art, thus, borders on "the extravagant, where sublime things skim the thin ice of absurdity" (58). As examples of gestures that capture the soul of Spain, he cites El Greco's "ecstatic figures" (54), especially in a painting such as *The Burial of Cont de Orgaz* (1586).

What constitutes the "thingness" of the gesture to Dos Passos, besides its tangibility as a painting, is its existence in time and space. The meaning of the *Burial,* for instance, resides in the nature of the action: "Remember the infinite gentleness of the saints lowering the Conde de Orgaz into the grave" (75), Lyaeus notes. In fact, all the gestures Dos Passos considers in *Rosinante* are movements in time. To arrest them is to change their nature, as Lyaeus cautions Telemachus when he vows to make the gesture permanent. To find a gesture or a sign that can give perceivers direct, immediate knowledge of the referent is to invite them into the process of experience, to invite them to create reality for themselves. In the same way, for instance, the techniques of montage or cubism, as they fragment and disrupt reality, invite perceivers to assemble those fragments for themselves, thereby making the work of art an experience, not a recreation, of reality, as in traditional mimetic techniques. Ultimately, Dos Passos suggests in *Rosinante,* the ideal gesture is one that "makes the road" or the *way* of approaching knowledge "so significant that one needs no destination" (46): that is, the perception itself becomes the art.

Achieving this dynamism, realizing the potency of the work of art was Dos Passos's goal as a modernist, a goal he articulated in the framework of this pivotal group of essays. In that this dynamism was a modernist goal in general, most modernist artists wrestled in some manner with the central problem inherent in achieving it, the problem Dos Passos is exploring in *Rosinante:* how to create a work that combined the temporal quality of writing with the spatial quality of visual arts but transcended the limitations of both mediums.

For Dos Passos, of course, the work of art was inseparable from its relationship to the cultural context that produced it. But the interartistic analogy implicit in the central quest of *Rosinante* also offers a particularly illuminating way of reading his work that follows that collection. For these reasons, the traditional historicism that has usually been the methodology for exploring Dos Passos's evolution into modernism seems too limited a critical tool. But the "language of gesture" (Steiner, 25)—a broad term for semiotic theory—allows us to integrate all these crucial elements of his aesthetic.

Chapter 5

The End of "Memories" and the Beginnings of Modernism: *Streets of Night*

His visual and political sensibilities quickened by his months of travel in Spain before the war, Dos Passos was loath to return to the United States even after he received word of his father's unexpected death in January 1917. Not that Dos Passos did not grieve at this loss so soon after the loss of his mother in 1915: on the day after he learned John R. had died, he wrote to his friend Rumsey Marvin that he found himself "suddenly alone in the world." Nevertheless, he was grateful that his father had died "suddenly, without the long sordidness of disease," doubtless recalling his mother's slow, sad decline. Characteristically, the 21-year-old Dos Passos dreaded returning home to "all the sentimental flutter that clutters up the great stark events of life." Besides, he continued in his letter to Marvin, he had felt he was "just beginning to fathom [Spain] a little" (*Fourteenth*, 66), and he would have preferred to divert himself from his grief by continuing to travel and write there.

Feeling that in Spain he had finally begun to participate in the world that he had only written wistfully about at Harvard, he also felt "a certain exhilaration about being absolutely untrammeled and having no idea what [he was] going to do next." The colors, the noise, and the generations of culture in Spain had thrown his own country into a new perspective for him. Seeing America now in unflattering comparison, he made the journey home reluctantly, determined to "look at life straight and sincerely without having to dim [his] sight . . . with church windows and shop windows and the old grimy glass of outworn cultures" (*Fourteenth*, 66–68).

Not surprisingly, Dos Passos had little patience with the business of settling his father's estate in New York City. The tedious legal process doomed him to "a terrifically uninteresting and unprofitable existence" (*Fourteenth*, 68), he wrote to Marvin in April 1917. Consequently, as it became apparent that John R. Dos Passos's holdings after probate would afford him only the barest income, he watched with "much amusement . . . the rapid evaporation of The Estate." Such matters seemed to him vastly trivial compared to the "dance of death" he saw consuming the European cultures he valued as the United States finally entered World War I. Watching "all this complicated civilization the European races have labored and murdered and cheated for during so many evolving centuries . . . frittering itself away in this senseless agony of destruction" made him feel "hopeless." But even though the reality of the war induced despair, he was unwilling to allow himself to retreat into the safe removal of the intellectual life or to remain the detached observer any longer. He was conscious that his Harvard years had fostered that tendency in him too much, as his college poems and stories, with their inevitable conflicts between art and life, clearly show. Now he was "very anxious to see things at first hand" (*Fourteenth,* 69–72), he wrote to George St. John, headmaster of Choate when Dos Passos attended the school.

His determination to witness firsthand what he perceived was the formative event of his generation would seem to contradict his growing opposition to the war and to the forms of government and civilization evolving in America. During the spring he spent in New York between his return from Spain and his departure for France and the front, his disillusionment with Woodrow Wilson and his belief in the necessity of a revolutionary reformation of American society grew into vocal radicalism. Initially, although he was too young to vote, he had supported Wilson, applauding his victory in the 1916 presidential election because, as the slogan of the time declared, "He kept us out of war." As Dos Passos recalled in his introduction to the 1969 reissue of *One Man's Initiation: 1917,* his first war novel, Wilson's subsequent reversal of position when he declared war in 1917 was "a bitter disappointment" that caused Dos Passos to begin "listening seriously to the Socialists."[1] Their message— "that all that was needed to abolish war was to abolish capitalism"— made more and more sense to this young man who had come to believe that "war was the greatest evil" (Introduction, *Initiation,* 2). He and his friends found themselves in the thick of the heady radicalism of New York that spring: they protested, signed petitions, read the *Masses,* and lionized the icons of the left such as Max Eastman and Emma Goldman.

Still, as Dos Passos acknowledged half a century later, his "motives were mixed," an attitude he shared "with most of my fellows of that college generation. We were full of righteous indignation but at the same time we were full of curiosity about the world at war" (Introduction,

Initiation, 4). And like many others of that generation who came of age during the Great War, he joined the volunteer services as a way of putting both of those attitudes into action. Given his objection to serving in the military, he also hoped to avoid being drafted by enlisting in an ambulance corps.

Besides expressing his radical views in letters and working on essays he had begun in Spain, Dos Passos spent these months in New York learning the basics of automobile mechanics and emergency medical training while he waited to hear of his acceptance by the all-volunteer Norton-Harjes Ambulance Corps. As antimechanistic as he was, he feared that only with such training would he be allowed to drive at the front, since he was extremely myopic. But once he was accepted, he wrote to Rumsey Marvin and other friends gleeful farewell letters describing humorously the "delightful equipment" he was required to buy—"wonderful big boots and duffle-bag and bed roll and hurricane lantern and pins and needles and a cake of soap and other wonders besides" (*Fourteenth,* 75). A few months at the front would dampen his bravado and crystallize his bitterness about the insanity of the war. But for the moment, he was excitedly engaged in the course of action he had chosen. By the time he sailed for France on June 20, 1917, to drive in the ambulance unit, he believed he was leaving behind his tendency to intellectualize rather than to act. He believed that acting thus on his political beliefs, idealistic as they were, signified an important reversal of his tendency to romanticize life rather than to experience it.

These were the impressions he expressed in a poem he wrote on board the liner *Chicago* during the voyage to France. In the poem, he opposes his former life of romantic imaginings to the realistic life ahead of him. While he attempts to characterize the difference between the two worlds using images of color, sensation, and space, he depicts, despite himself, the romantic life as more vivid and alive than the realistic life he aspires to lead.

In "At Sea June 27th 1917" (*Fourteenth,* 86–87), Dos Passos contrasts his life "Before" with his life "Today" (ll. 2, 10). He creates "Before" as something like a synaesthetic impressionist painting, a landscape of "misty-colored towns, / Full of gleams of halfheard music, / Full of sudden throbbing scents" (ll. 4–6). That its streets are "[v]ague" he intends as a criticism, but then he adds that they are "rainbow glowing" (l. 7), valorizing the painterly impressionistic prettiness of the scene. Moreover, in these streets he is free to "wander" (l. 8), suggesting that the speaker feels latitude and ease in the romantic world of "Before."

"Today," on the other hand, he "stand[s] aghast in a grey world, /
Waiting" (ll. 13–14). Again, he creates the landscape as a canvas, except
that he seems unable even to imagine its details so alien is the world
of reality to him. This time, the picture again is blurred, as in the impressionistic canvas of "Before," but "pale," "smeared" as if by a "gritty
stinking sponge" (ll. 11–12). His creative imagination fails to supply
the necessary sensory details of "Today." In the "real" world of "Today,"
the speaker can merely "stand . . . / Waiting" (ll. 13–14), a stasis
imposed by his inability to participate in the world of action even as an
imaginative exercise.

The poem continues for 54 lines creating this polarity whose imaginative details prove to be at odds with the young writer's bravado for
the here and now. Although its mostly free-verse style is an attempt to
escape the more classically structured meters of his Harvard poetry, "At
Sea" nevertheless falls back into some regular rhyming in its second
half. Although it dwells on the "striving / . . . sweating" stokers, "hard
bodies writhing" (ll. 39–41) in the stokehold below, more often it
relies on melodramatic aesthetic images even as it tries to characterize
the more realistic life Dos Passos longs for. The pain of that life is "a
dagger plunging / . . . [through] the misty veil" (ll. 48–49); its strife is
"a red sword [   ] lunging / . . . out of the pale / Blankness of despair"
(ll. 50–51).

While the young writer's inability to participate even imaginatively
in the world of realities he so eagerly sought may have resulted from his
callowness and his immaturity as a writer, that world did, ironically,
prove to be literally unimaginable in the horrors it thrust upon him. Dos
Passos's experiences in the war would transform him and his writing
over the next two years. But when he noted this poem in his journal in
1917, its style and subtext clearly undermined the dramatic assertion
with which he began the verses: "I have no more memories" (l. 1).

Romantic memories had, in fact, controlled his creative imagination
all through his Harvard years and would exert great influence even in the
writing and sketching he produced during his first assignment in the
war. These memories consisted of the complex of European aesthetic references by which he still measured his own experiences and which still
dominated his artistic responses. The impressions he recorded in "At Sea,"
for instance, became about a year later the perceptions of Martin Howe,
the protagonist of *One Man's Initiation: 1917*. As Howe, like his creator,
crosses the Atlantic toward Bordeaux and active duty, he feels that "the
past is nothing to him." Yet, now that the author had gained enough per-

spective on his own experiences to use them creatively, he admitted through Howe the persistence of these "memories": "very faintly, like music heard across the water in the evening, blurred into strange harmonies, [Howe's] old watchwords echo a little in his mind" (*Initiation*, 45). The imagery with which Dos Passos contrasts his protagonist's past and present is the imagery of the writer's own journal entries. Although "a new white page spread[s] before" Howe, his old romantic dreams, his "old watchwords," still color his perceptions "[l]ike the red flame of the sunset setting fire to opal sea and sky" (*Initiation*, 45–46).

By the time Dos Passos was able to transform his impressions into fiction, albeit heavily autobiographical, he had begun to understand more clearly the ambivalence he felt in his college years and just after about both the rosily impressionistic "Before" and the starkly unknown "Today." Even though he began to graft his war experiences onto his European aesthetics, the writing and sketching he produced in those war years often show the influence of European visual art and of the romantics' preoccupation with memory and the individual's subjective perceptions.

Streets of Night, the first completed novel Dos Passos worked on but the third he published, effectively provides an aesthetic background against which to measure his progress in the war novels away from romantic and European aesthetics and toward an American modernist style. In 1915, he had written for course assignments and for his own amusement a "longish collection of sketches" (*Fourteenth*, 28), an incomplete novella, that exists only in manuscript form under the title "Afterglow." Using some of the same character types as in "Afterglow," he began what became *Streets of Night* in 1916 while at Harvard and worked on it sporadically while in Europe during the war, finally completing it there in 1923. As a result of the span of years its production covered, *Streets of Night* depicts with growing detachment the conflict Dos Passos felt between the overintellectualized, removed existence of the aesthete, whom he associates with "Before" and with premodernist European aesthetics, and the more authentic, immediate life he longed for "Today," which he paints with more realistic or at least postimpressionist images. The novel illustrates Dos Passos's disillusionment with the "buried life"; to friends he later described the novel somewhat disparagingly as "a tragedy of impotence"[2] and "largely concerned with . . . futilitarianism."[3] But it reveals as well his doubt that the more active, realistic life offered a complete answer either, an ambivalence emerging as early as the stories he published in *Harvard Monthly.*

Even the origin of the novel's name establishes the ways in which this conflict that preoccupied Dos Passos during this period became the central dilemma in this first book. Notes for the novel from his 1916 journal label it "Le Grand Roman," an example of Dos Passos's typically self-mocking style, but project an "atmosphere of streets of night Supper table & garish restaurants Youth in the city" (*Fourteenth*, 34). That same spring, his last at Harvard, he wrote to Rumsey Marvin of his exultation in a nighttime "ramble through Boston—I love cities on a rainy night." The letter goes on to describe with obvious relish the sense of life he felt "in the cheaper parts of the city." He polarized the cultural removal of Harvard and its aura of classicism against the more authentically grimy but colorful life in the city. He delighted in the "beautiful . . . ugly gargoyle grotesque" faces he saw in the city (*Fourteenth*, 39), and he returned to Harvard to describe them in writing.

Three years later, after he had been at the French front and had finally gained his release from the military after much bureaucratic entanglement, he used the title's controlling image once more to express the same commitment to experience. Now he was living in Paris, embarking in earnest on a literary career. "V" (*Pushcart*, 147), the poem containing the image, shows the beginnings of modernism in its imagistic basis and free-verse form. The image it devolves upon recalls, in fact, Ezra Pound's "In a Station of the Metro," a landmark of modernism, also predicated on a visual image, published when Dos Passos was still an undergraduate, six years before he wrote "V."[4]

But Dos Passos's controlling image still betrays the remnants of aesthetic/symbolist artistic influences. In "V," the speaker likens himself in an extended simile to a "gardener in a pond / splendid with lotus and Indian nenuphar / wad[ing] to his waist in the warm black water / . . . to cull the snaky stems / of the floating white glittering lilies / . . . [and] the imperious lotus / lifting the huge flowers high / . . . till they droop against the moon" (ll. 1–8). "[T]hrough the streets of night" the speaker wanders, "culling out of the pool / of the spring-reeking, rain-reeking city / gestures and faces" (ll. 10–13).

Style and sentiment show a modernist embrace of the actual. But in its controlling image and its portrayal of the artist as selective gatherer rather than full participant, the poem illustrates Dos Passos's conflict between aesthetic removal and emotional commitment that was emerging, consciously or unconsciously, even after his war experiences. In fact, as late as 1920, a year after he wrote "V" at the Place St. Michel, he was still calling his college novel "Quest of the Core," paradoxically, an abstract phrase intended to express the struggle toward the concrete. Moreover, he still had not broken free of the European aesthetic tradition that he believed kept American writers from evolving an American aesthetic and that he associated with bloodless conventionality always at a remove from reality. In his helpful study of the ways in which Dos Passos's early fiction draws on American literary and intellectual traditions, Michael Clark suggests that the novel demonstrates the author's attempt to resolve the conflict between the aesthete educational environment of his Harvard days and the more pragmatic direction in which he was moving.[5]

In *Streets of Night*, Dos Passos uses artistic allusions as one of his primary means of characterizing the three protagonists who represent this conflict between art and life. Fanshaw Macdougan and Nancibel Taylor cling to academics and art to insulate themselves from their emotions and their environments. Allusions to and images drawn from classical and Renaissance art and some late-nineteenth-century premodernist styles convey these characters' "genteel paralysis of culture," their inability to connect with or participate in the present.[6] David Wendell ("Wenny") struggles to escape the emotional and experiential confinements of his upbringing as a minister's son. The artistic allusions that characterize Wenny are primarily expressionist images, the greater emotional immediacy of expressionist art suggesting that Wenny to some degree succeeds in his attempt to break out of the repressive New England culture that is this novel's setting. Yet through Wenny and his aesthetic associations, Dos Passos shows, as he did in many of his Harvard stories, that unalloyed realism and complete disconnection from the past's moral or aesthetic traditions may be as disabling as complete domination by them. Wenny and Fanshaw are "foils" illustrating the author's "argument with pure aestheticism . . . much to the disadvantage of the latter" (Clark, 12).

Clark asserts that all three protagonists of *Streets* "lack secure identities" (32). But the problem for Fanshaw and Nan particularly seems not to be that they *lack* identities, but that they are, in fact, rigidly defined by identities growing out of their conventional and traditional backgrounds. Dos Passos delineates these backgrounds largely through allusions to the visual aesthetics of the characters' environments.

Immersed in classical and Renaissance art, Fanshaw suffers a kind of anxiety of influence about the quality of his own life that results in his devaluation of the authenticity of modern life and art. Writing on "The Classical Subject in Racine" and on "Florentine sculpture," Donatello,

and "the Ghiberti doors" (*Streets,* 27, 108–9) constitutes his daily work
at college. His aesthetic predilections have been inculcated in him by his
elderly mother, who was "bound [he would] take to the arts." When
Fanshaw imagines her, he sees a "picture of a grey head against a pillow,
heavy despairing wrinkles . . . the mouth . . . a wry peevish twitch of
pain." The mise-en-scène of his mental portrait of her signifies the narrow, obsolete conventions she embodies. In particular he associates her
with a "curio cabinet . . . in the corner of the drawing room with a shepherd á la Watteau painted on the panel" (*Streets,* 74–75).

Invoking Watteau, Dos Passos associates the tone of Fanshaw's upbringing with that neoclassical painter's studied, stylized, and idealized
images, especially of love. From Watteau's most famous work, *Embarkation for Cythera* (1717–1719), Dos Passos borrowed also the title for one
of the poems he wrote in Paris just after the war, while he was working
on *Streets. Embarkation,* a large, florid painting, presents lovers attended
by amorous cupids in a scene of arcadian bliss, a vision of romance that,
as Fanshaw's relations with Nan will illustrate, permeates and dooms
the young man's attempts to connect with a woman. Mrs. Macdougan's
curio cabinet contains other aesthetic signs as well: "a filigree gondola
from Venice, the Sistine Madonna in mosaic . . . the Nuremberg goose
boy." All signify classical or pastoral ideas of love or romance that Fanshaw substitutes for authentic engagement with women. To Wenny, he
rationalizes that he would go abroad to live if he "could only leave
Mother." But in the next breath, he resignedly admits that his mind is
much like his mother's curio cabinet, a closed, fixed system of objéts
d'art: "That's why I am so appropriate to the groves of Academe," he
explains (*Streets,* 72, 76).

His relationships with women attest to his distance from actual experience. Obviously preoccupied with sexual feelings he cannot reconcile with
his ideals of womanhood, Fanshaw's mind strays in the middle of a com-
parative literature exam to a recent encounter with an arranged date. In a
pastoral setting "á la Watteau," he had found himself repelled by the
"rouged lips" (*Streets,* 25), peroxided hair, and commonality of Elise Montmorency. In midexam, however, he begins to fantasize about how he
should have kissed her, blushing at the thought. Yet, recalling that "she
was common and said ain't," he is glad he had not kissed her, thus re-
taining the "spotless armor of Sir Galahad." Creating a romantic scene
more palatable to his refined sensibilities, Fanshaw continues to use the
medieval imagery, as the Pre-Raphaelite painters did, to signify nostalgia
for the Middle Ages' traditions of courtly love and the idealization of

women. Fanshaw imagines himself with his "flower-like girl," "two souls
. . . consumed with a single fire." In "a boat with red . . . lateen sails . . .
she [is] in his arms and her hair [is] fluffy against his cheek" as they sail
away to "wet rose gardens" (*Streets,* 29–30). The stylized woman, the bold
primary colors, the heightening of color, and the transformation of the
"fallen" woman into a spiritually purified icon, all characteristic of Dante
Gabriel Rossetti, recall Dos Passos's brief flirtation with the aesthetic
movement that borrowed at times from elements of the Pre-Raphaelites.

Fanshaw is annoyed by reminders of the physicality of love, and he
distances himself from his own sexual responses by intellectualizing
them into specific aesthetic images. A couple kissing in a dark doorway
seems "vulgar" to him: "Other ages . . . had . . . romance in them; Paola
and Francesca floating cloudy through limbo" (*Streets,* 69–70). He must
even keep himself at one remove from works of art, themselves mere
representations of sexuality, whose sensuality threatens to involve him.
He does not "waste much time on Rubens," for instance, snidely dis-
missing the passion and voluptuousness of the Flemish master as "more
acreage than intensity . . . and all of it smeared with raspberry jam"
(*Streets,* 205). When he does imagine committing himself to a woman,
he casts as his wife someone he has not met yet, "a Titian blond" in a
scene ascetically free of "[w]restling sweaty bodies, hands . . . feeling up.
. . . O, I don't want to think of all that." Instead, he hastily reassures
himself of an "[o]ldfashioned jolly wedding" (*Streets,* 158).

In fact, he finds himself drawn to someone he already knows, but he
is attracted to Nan primarily because he understands her emotional
composition and finds relief in her cool distance. Nan's repressive
upbringing has left her so "elaborately emotionless" (*Streets,* 123) that
Fanshaw's propensity to visualize her in terms of artistic compositions
seems natural. Most frequently, Nan appears to him as a "Renaissance
princess" (*Streets,* 235), an image whose associations would seem to suggest that Fanshaw sees in her that characteristically Renaissance min-
gling of the spiritual and the earthly. But the Renaissance elevated the
formal elements of expressions of love to an art form, the sonnet, for
instance. Fanshaw, then, envisions Nan at the remove of works of art
that subscribe to an aesthetic of stylization and aesthetic distance. To
him, she is always "like a girl by a Lombard painter" (*Streets,* 68).

Nan herself almost always translates her feelings into aesthetic ideas
that insulate her from actual emotion. In her relationship with Fanshaw,
she is safe from feeling because together they create an atmosphere of
safe, smug artistic distance. But Wenny elicits from her more visceral

reactions, and she has to work hard to avoid them. When emotions do threaten to penetrate her remoteness, they occur to her as postimpressionist images that she swiftly counterposes with the tamer classical or preimpressionist aesthetics of idealization.

Walking arm in arm with both men, Nan senses the immediacy of Wenny's response to the foggy night. It makes him think of Wagner, and "Wagner plus fog" makes him feel "like sitting on the curbstone and letting great warm tears flow down [his] cheeks." To this outburst, Fanshaw can only respond, "I say." But Nan responds as much in kind as she is able, with sensory images of the yearning the night engenders in her. Even so, she ends up "talking like a book" (*Streets*, 63–64), as Wenny laughingly points out.

When she tries to close the gap between response and expression, Nan visualizes her sentences in expressionist terms: "Beginnings of sentences flared and sputtered out in her mind like damp fireworks. Slowly the yellow fog . . . that had somehow a rhythm of slow vague swells out at sea sifted in upon her, blurred the focus of herself." In color and dynamic, her animation of her idea faintly suggests a van Gogh composition. But as soon as she attempts to fix the moment—that is, to render her experience in static, objective terms—her perception of it shifts to a classical allusion: "There had been Greeks who had cut the flame of an instant deep on stone in broad letters for centuries to read" (*Streets*, 64). The moving words that she felt she now sees graven in stone in regular script.

Likewise, amidst a tea party, Nan finds herself "imagining . . . the muscles of [Wenny's] arms, the hollow between [his] shoulders, the hard bulge of calves," and her desire takes the form of expressionist exaggerations that upset the aesthetic mise-en-scène she has contrived in her apartment. Wearing "grey jade beads," "reassuring" herself with the "smooth bulge" of the blue teapot that she rests on a "Jacobean table" next to a "Buhl cabinet," she fights her attraction to Wenny by reminding herself, "careful Nancibel" (*Streets*, 37–41).

Nevertheless, when she touches his arm, "writhing hump-backed flares dance[ ] an insane ballet through her body." The star they gaze at together "[bristles] with green horns of light" and "palpitate[s] with slow sucking rhythm" (*Streets*, 37–38). Again, the expressionist colors and motion, suggesting van Gogh's passionate starry nights and vibrating suns, connote immediate feelings that Nan deliberately quashes. She finally controls them by focusing on the "line of grime" around Wenny's collar as he leaves, a manipulation of her responses that leaves her able to think of him distastefully as a "[d]irty little animal," much the same way Fanshaw repressed his desire for the "common" Elise Montmorency. Once more in control of her feelings and alone, Nan can then note "with compressed lips" how "hideous" is the "design in reddish orange on the bright blue curtains" (*Streets,* 40), a warm, immediate color scheme she wishes she could change. This, after all, is a woman who buys "orangered" Japanese persimmons "for the color" (*Streets,* 276), puts them in a blue bowl, and chooses to admire them rather than eat them. Her existence is indeed an aesthetic still life.

Wenny, however, more nearly realizes the authentic existence Dos Passos sought to live and to express. Unlike Nan and Fanshaw, Wenny struggles to allow himself the strong emotions he feels, emotions Dos Passos characterizes through dynamic expressionist images. During an evening's walk through Boston with his two friends, for instance, Wenny sees the "black pavement shiver[ing] in squirms and lozenges of yellow and red and green light." He persuades Nan and Fanshaw to go with him for a minute into a burlesque show, promising that it will be "the most grotesque thing [they] ever saw." Nan responds to the suggestion of adventure, and they cajole Fanshaw to accompany them, although he protests that "[i]t'll smell fearfully" (*Streets,* 91–92).

Once inside, they confront a scene that Dos Passos paints with the colors, movement, and iconography of the German expressionists or the earlier Toulouse-Lautrec: "At the end of a smoky tunnel in front of a curtain the color of arsenic and gangrene five women badly stuffed into pink tights like worn dolls, twitched their legs in time to the accentless jangle of a piano. The light streamed out from them among eager red faces, moist lips, derbies. . . . Now and then a girl dropped out of the wriggling, tired dance" (*Streets,* 93). The same images, colors, and perspectives also characterize one of the watercolors Dos Passos painted sometime during the years he was writing *Streets of Night.* In the painting, however, the buxom, expressionistically rendered dancer is more fully clothed, as his character Fanshaw, who leaves the club in disgust, evidently would have preferred.

Certainly Wenny and Nan's attitudes suggest their profound ambivalence about sexuality, as do the grotesque images from the club. Wenny's responses to Nan are strong and immediate, as the expressionist images that convey them communicate. With her, he feels keenly the atmosphere that surrounds them. Walking beside her he sees a church dome "swell[ ] with purple against a tremendous scarlet flaming sky across which grimy green clouds scud[ ]." Her presence makes "stars bloom[ ] green in the amethyst sky" (*Streets,* 182, 169). And when he vows to stop merely dreaming of Nan and embrace "hard actuality," he immediately imagines the "yama, yama blare of brass bands, red flags waving . . . and Nan," an expressionist image of his excitement. He struggles to reject "the little neatly painted world of his childhood" and feels that he no longer "imagine[s] every man, woman and child . . . part of some absurd romantic vortex." His conventional, religious background is an artificial structure, the resultant romantic view of the world a dangerous force. "I know better now," he assures himself, while the next moment admitting his doubt: "Do I?" (*Streets*, 189, 197, 187).

In fact, as he is honest enough to admit, Wenny's relationships with women do suffer from the "fear" inculcated by his upbringing as the "son of a minister with his collar on backwards" (*Streets*, 138). Moreover, his attraction to Nan makes him sometimes associate his longing for her with the punitive sexual guilt that was standard issue for young men of his cultural milieu: "The social evil, prostitutions of the Canaanites, venereal disease, what every young man should know, convention, duty, God." Yet, at the next moment he forces himself to confront "[w]hat rot" all those Calvinist preachments are. In an effort to free himself of the restrictions of his father's teachings and of what he calls "this sickness of desire" for Nan, Wenny picks up a prostitute. Finally, he is actually confronted by the immediacy he had sought: "She was naked sitting on the edge of the bed under the gasjet . . . ; her breasts hung free as she leaned toward him." In his head he suddenly hears "a ghastly sniggering," the voice, perhaps, of the detached, priggish prurience about sex that is his legacy from the Reverend Wendell. Although he is "fainting with desire for the woman's body naked on the bed under the gasjet," he is "drowning" in the memory of Nan's eyes and "the smell of her hair" (*Streets*, 140–41).

What "sickens" him about his desires is not simply their baseness, with the prostitute, or their intellectualization, with Nan, but his inability to find fulfillment in either extreme. Wenny's polarized reactions, Dos Passos tells the reader with his artistic allusions, result from the false romanticism, aestheticism, and conventions of behavior he receives from his genteel background. In the distorting power of Wenny's memories, Dos Passos conveys the process of his own artistic growth away from tired, secondhand aesthetic techniques that made immediacy and realism impossible. As Fanshaw expresses his classical aesthetic, Dos Passos inveighs against it by couching Fanshaw's perceptions in clichés: "Taught by our ideal of the past, of the Greeks and the people of the Renaissance, we are learning to surround ourselves with beautiful things, to live less ugly, money-grubbing lives," Fanshaw lectures Wenny. Wenny cuts through the clichés to his own truth: "Culture, you mean. Culture's mummifying the corpse with scented preservatives" (*Streets,* 185). Expressing through Fanshaw and Wenny the conflict between romance and realism and between cultural values and actuality, Dos Passos expresses also his realization that neither stance by itself affords much room for individual growth.

As he wrote *Streets of Night,* however, still under the influence, albeit unwillingly, of the cultural milieu at Harvard, Dos Passos evidently felt more familiar with the aesthete's method of experiencing the world, for all the stagnation and spiritual death that method seemed to embody. His greater familiarity with the "safe" course that Fanshaw chooses emerges in the two characters' ultimate fates: Fanshaw at least survives, while Wenny commits suicide, unable to reconcile his longing for basic immediacy, his "libidinal energy" (Clark, 45), with the repressive moral and intellectual values of his genteel American education. Dos Passos's own reluctant knowledge of the more conventional path may help account for his choosing to let the narrative follow Fanshaw. That familiarity would help account also for Dos Passos's choosing to have Wenny self-destruct, an element of the narrative that Michael Clark (40) and Linda Wagner (25) have found only weakly motivated. Certainly Dos Passos's inexperience with the novel form weakens *Streets of Night.* But by contrasts, which Dos Passos favors already in *Streets of Night* as a method of development, he does provide both the background and the aftermath of Wenny's death, reinforcing his theme of the conflict between convention and immediacy.

Indeed, as Wagner points out, the motivation for Wenny's final act builds by repetition of scenes that bring "little . . . new to the themes already presented" (25). The repetition of scenes and motifs works, however, to intensify the forces that ultimately defeat Wenny. For instance, a letter that he receives from his father restates the self-righteous, hypocritical religiosity that engenders guilt and rebellion in him. But hearing Reverend Wendell's own voice speaking from the letter in its sentimentally platitudinous style allows the reader to contrast directly and immediately with it Wenny's own voice as he recalls his childhood church attendance. Whereas Reverend Wendell writes of "the merciful help of the Allknowing and Allforgiving Creator in Whom [he has] never lost faith," Wenny recalls the faithful as "trained seals" who "[settle] back flabbily into their pews in the mustard yellow, mudpurple, niggerpink light from the imitation stained glass windows." His expressionist imagery, previously associated with energy and life, now becomes distorted and grotesque as he approaches his crisis, ever more often recalling his father's conventional expectations of him. He vows, "I will live [my father] down if it kills me" and longs to break free of the expectations, "to climb on a hydrant and . . . to draw people . . . about him and explain all the joy and agony he [feels] in words so simple that they would tear off their masks and tell their lives too" (*Streets*, 170, 172, 183). This impulse toward immediate communication in a new language that transcends the dictates of authority and the image Dos Passos chooses to communicate the impulse foreshadow a theme and image that become central to the three works he undertook during and just after the war.

In *Streets of Night*, however, Dos Passos displays a pessimism about the individual's ability to realize such an impulse and about the person's future if the realization is achieved, a pessimism that, clearly determines Wenny's fate. Wenny continues to struggle toward genuine feeling, as the expressionist images suggest. But as Wenny's ambivalence grows, so do his self-doubts, and as he tries to escape these feelings in a bout of drinking, the expressionist images become concomitantly more distorted. Having failed yet again to express his feelings for Nan, Wenny seeks refuge in the bottle of Orvieto the three friends share at a bar, finally taking his leave of them in a snowstorm. He sees faces bloom "white as plaster casts, red as new steak, yellow and warted like summer squashes, . . . expressionless like canteloupes. Occasionally . . . a wall seemed to bulge to splitting with its denseness" (*Streets*, 193). Space and perception grow more and more subjectively distorted as the passage immediately preceding Wenny's act shifts entirely to his point of view. Dos Passos's concentration on and expression of Wenny's perceptions in this section convey a sense of the expressionist painters' focus on the individual's alienation from a normative "reality." Dos Passos reiterates this alienation and shows how Wenny's conventional background succeeds in separating him from his genuine feelings by interspersing his repeated memories of his father with his perceptions of his surroundings as he sees them reflected in mirrored surfaces.

Leaving his friends, he finds another bar, one with "little mirrors in the ceiling and . . . bottle ends . . . all [radiating] endlessly in dusty looking-glasses on the walls." He orders a martini, and the glass that holds it becomes "the center of a vortex into which were sucked the cutting edges of light, flickering cones of green and red brightness." The image of the destructively spiraling vortex, common in the paintings of the Italian futurists, later becomes a central motif conveying forces overwhelming the characters of *Manhattan Transfer,* just as Wenny's past now overwhelms him. He hears "Fanshaw's voice and his father's voice," the two men representing convention and authority to him, "droning like antiphonal choirs" (*Streets,* 195). Imagining the artificial world of his childhood as if "through the wrong end of a telescope," he looks into the mirror above the bar and suddenly realizes his reflection is no longer his face, but his father's: "I am my father" (*Streets,* 197, 199). Unable to escape his upbringing or to integrate it functionally into his emerging identity, now even unable to find his own face in the mirror, Wenny chooses to die. Before he shoots himself on the East Cambridge Bridge over the Charles River, he imagines death in terms of the erotic connection his "little neatly painted" life will not allow him: "death's all that, sinking into the body of a dark woman, with proud cold thighs, hair dark, dark" (*Streets,* 197, 201).

After this stark, intensely expressionistic treatment of Wenny's death, Dos Passos shifts the narrative point of view to Fanshaw. The dark distorted images that convey the price of Wenny's confrontation with the truth he has sought are succeeded immediately by Fanshaw's visualization of *his* ideals, conveyed in images borrowed from Italian Renaissance painters and the aesthetes.

The chapter following Wenny's death opens, in fact, with Fanshaw's waking the next morning to thoughts of artists he must cover that day in class and aesthetic images of freedom as *he* imagines it. As he prepares to get up, "names of Italian painters [stream] through his head" (*Streets,* 202). He thinks of Lorenzo Monaco, Gozzoli, and Fra Angelico, painters in fifteenth-century Florence whose "whole population . . . [was] permeated with ideas . . . highly intellectual by nature, . . . keen in perception," the kind of culture Fanshaw aspires to.[7] Fra Angelico, in particular, constitutes a resonant reminder of both the values and the limitations inherent in Fanshaw's ideals. Stylistically uninnovative and conservative, although formally accomplished, Fra Angelico subordinated perspective and technical realism to the spiritual impact of his works (de la Croix and Tansey, 450). For instance, in his famous fresco *Annunciation* (1440–1445), painted for the convent of San Marco in Florence and one of the works Dos Passos noted on his youthful grand tour, Fra Angelico framed the kneeling angelic messenger and the demure Madonna seated under the arches of symmetrical cross-barrel vaults. Since the loggia the vaults support do not seem to be sufficiently high to permit the figures to stand erect, however, the painter obviously intends for his composition and techniques to serve his religious meaning above all else, including realism if necessary.

Likewise, when Fanshaw imagines "living always free" of the demands of academe and the world as he perceives it, his visualization, an aesthete's dream, ignores entirely what is actually possible. He fantasizes living "like a Chinese sage in a hut of rice-matting beside a waterfall, . . . [retiring] to an exquisite pavilion ornamented with red and black lacquer. . . . And Wenny for an attendant . . . Wenny, brown from the sun, gleaming with sweat . . . with a piece of scarlet cloth about his loins." The aesthetically precious and the potentially homoerotic combine here in a fantasy that reveals how entirely and successfully Fanshaw substitutes art for realism about himself and his future. When he goes on to fantasize about Nan, his dream is similarly couched in romantically artificial images: "The old dream of love . . . the moon rising out of the dark sea . . . [Nan] playing the violin in a long-raftered hall . . . with the smell of the old incense-drenched tapestries . . . and the smell of jessamine" (*Streets,* 202–3). Clearly, Fanshaw can create an imaginative future only out of elements of artifice. Whether he or his companions could actually exist in such lives is of secondary importance to their aesthetic power to substitute for reality. Implicit in these images are the artificiality and emotional removal that will determine Fanshaw's fate as inexorably as Wenny's internalized guilt and his emotional honesty determined his end.

As Dos Passos uses contrasting images from Wenny's and Fanshaw's imaginations, a technique forecasting the primary technique of *Manhattan Transfer,* he depicts the implacable social forces that overwhelm individuals. The beginnings of his modernist pessimism emerge in the inevitable conclusion, given Wenny's and Fanshaw's destinies, that neither a direct engagement with reality nor a retreat into an aesthetic idealism is sufficient to sustain a meaningful or, in fact, a bearable life. On the other hand, in *Streets of Night,* Dos Passos seems to suggest for the first time that successfully integrating these impulses—successfully coming to terms with the past and making productive, original use of the present—is nearly impossible even for the strongest individuals. This skeptical realization underlies the future Dos Passos creates for Fanshaw: hanging on to romantic dreams of an idealized past world, Fanshaw survives his service in World War I essentially unchanged, an ambiguous accomplishment at best.

In the book's final chapter, in which Fanshaw briefly considers then rejects remaining in Italy to live as Wenny had imagined, Dos Passos once more uses opposing images from the visual arts to characterize the differences between the two options. In a penultimate scene that parallels Wenny's final experiences, Fanshaw, a captain in a Red Cross unit, visits a brothel in Palermo, but mostly because of his unwillingness to offend his more eager companion, the French Captain de la Potiniére. Fanshaw's distaste for the Frenchman's single-minded pursuit of sex is simply the mature version of the priggish sexual inhibition that caused him to deride Wenny for cajoling his two friends to visit the Boston burlesque show. As in the book's opening scene depicting Fanshaw's encounter with the common Elise Montmorency, he is equally attracted and repelled by Tina, a childlike prostitute in a pink dress. He does stay with her, a daring decision for him. But waking beside her the next morning, he feels compelled by his guilt and physical distaste for her to escape as quickly as possible to a bath, clean clothes, and the white stateroom of the ship on which he is scheduled to return to America. Safely there, he recalls a foray with Wenny when he "wanted to pick up a girl." Fanshaw's memory of the night is cast in expressionist colors and exaggerations, Wenny's visual vocabulary. Fanshaw remembers the night's "arclights were pinkish blobs among the shuddering green fringes of elms," and the girls were "[s]tumpy . . . with heavy jowls . . . , swaying from the hips." What Wenny had accepted as life, Fanshaw once again rejects as "ugliness" (*Streets,* 309).

Then, however, in a one-sentence paragraph emphasizing the singular novelty of this perception, Fanshaw remembers that "Tina had been pretty in her pink dress." And when he follows his train of thought to predict the life he is going back to, he sees it as "Venetian Art and Culture in the Eighteenth Century . . . the museum and tea with professors' wives." The asceticism, aesthetic removal, and stasis of the old life that he again faces propel him to realize the emotional sterility of that life. Suddenly, he confronts a vision of what he is leaving, remembering when he had "leaned out . . . over the gold and rusty roofs and the domes and obelisks swaying in the great waves of honeycolored sunlight, and smelt gardens and scorched olive oil, and seen a girl with a brown throat come out of an arbor" (*Streets,* 309–10).

This sensual image of a Mediterranean landscape is immediately striking for its concreteness, simplicity, and dynamism, qualities Fanshaw's previous imaginative worlds have lacked. This image's aesthetic origins also quite obviously differ from the neoclassical, Renaissance, and aesthetic bases of all his other visualizations. Instead, perspective, form, color, and motion here seem to recall the Provençal landscapes of Cézanne. The most influential figure in the transition in European art from the transitory subjectivism of impressionist painting to the modernists' depiction of color as structure, Cézanne created constructions of space and form in landscapes that were precursors to the later cubists' analyses of abstract forms; his conception of the painting itself as a surface on which to arrange the shapes he is using signals the beginning of the shift toward the modernists' conception of the relationship of the work of art to the world.

Fanshaw's recollection of the vista of a Mediterranean village emanating light evokes some of Cézanne's views during the 1880s of his most frequently painted subject—the trees, roads, cottages, villas, and fields around Mont Sainte-Victoire, near his home in Aix-en-Provence. Dividing into planes of color the elements and spaces between foreground and background—the mountain—Cézanne, using light and shade, creates a sense of receding perspective. Nevertheless, the composition, with the Midi sun reflecting off the mountain's white rocky slopes, makes the background seem equally close to the viewer. Cézanne's organization of natural forms approximates the perspective the viewer might actually experience at the site, a kind of "deep focus." That cinematic technique, exploited by innovative American filmmakers in the 1920s and 1930s, manipulates depth of field to present with equal clarity objects that are both near and distant from the camera. Likewise, in these paintings of the mountain, Cézanne maintains over his entire perspective such uniformly intense color and light that gradations of distance are largely undifferentiated. These landscapes "[lack] the resolution associated with a spatial hierarchy."[8] A similar composition, the 1887 *View of the Domaine Saint-Joseph,* an estate near Le Tholonet, uses a wide chromatic range and a minimum of details to create a composition of basic colors. The hillside estate at the center of the canvas seems to grow organically from the upward-rising brush strokes representing the pines characteristic of this region. The unity of the elements and colors forces the viewer to seek any compositional resolution, since Cézanne does not follow the "usual visual rules" that offer the viewer a conventional direction into the painting (Shiff, 123).

Confronted by a canvas such as the *View of the Domaine Saint-Joseph,* as Dos Passos may have been when it appeared in the 1913 Armory Show, the viewer is challenged to open his or her perceptions to new concepts of order in the immediate scene. Confronted by the new perspective and the vitality of the scene he overlooks, Fanshaw likewise realizes that he must decide for himself what his experiences in Europe and his experience of Wenny's death will mean to him. The "honeycolored sunlight" and the sensuous brown throat of a girl, overarching effects and small details, seem equally as persistent and immediate; they represent transformations in concept and perspective as potentially revolutionary in

Fanshaw's life as Cézanne's innovations were to the course of modernist painting. The two primary narrative elements Dos Passos uses to underscore this moment are essential to Cézanne's practice as well: the insistence on the truth of concreteness as opposed to what Cézanne called "intangible speculations" (quoted in Shiff, 186); and the belief in composition by "contrasts" communicated not by black and white but "by the sensation of color" (quoted in Shiff, 123).

Certainly, Fanshaw's momentary insight, whether an overt allusion to Cézanne or not, embodies the same possibilities for Fanshaw's life that Cézanne's art created for impressionism and art in general at the turn of the century. In the challenge of this fresh perception lies Fanshaw's chance to forge an original identity, one that is not borrowed from moribund cultural conventions or expressed in secondhand terms of the artifices of previous centuries.

But this vision of the new and the immediate is itself a memory, as Dos Passos reminds the reader on the final page of this apprentice novel. Even the vitality of this recent memory proves too threatening to the aesthetic distance Fanshaw has chosen, and he forcibly offsets the warm, strong, seductive colors of this Cézanne-like image with a more distant, more comfortable memory, one that embodies the future he has inevitably chosen. He opts to return to the vicariously experienced life of lectures and walks in Boston, knowing that he can pretend Nan and Wenny are beside him "and that [they] are young, leansouled people out of the Renaissance, ready to divide life like a cake" (*Streets*, 311). His refusal to confront his sexual feelings for Nan, like his inability to accept Wenny's struggle for emotional authenticity, is a product of the same restrictive, genteel acculturation that ultimately destroys Wenny. These conventions are no less harmful, in another way, to Fanshaw, as Dos Passos affirms by ending the novel with these potent contrasting artistic images, the concrete and sensual reminder of Cézanne against the twice-removed memory of the formulations of the Renaissance. Fanshaw, aboard the ship back to America, chooses the memory over the actuality.

Visual Impressions of Paris

Arriving in France in 1917 just weeks before he was to join an ambulance corps at the front east of Paris at the end of July, Dos Passos, too, seems to have clung to a romantic, aesthetic vision. Although he was determined to "break with everything past"—"conventions, social ordinances, the lies of a civilization" (*Fourteenth*, 88, 119)—and declared that he had "no more memories," his highly pictorial informal writing about France, like his actual visual records of the time, retained an impressionist prettiness that seemed to belie his later horrific literary images of the war. Despite the debris from a recently torpedoed steamer that floated around the *Chicago* as it docked in Bordeaux, there was little to remind Dos Passos that his beloved France was now under siege. During the journey to Paris, he reveled in the landscape, where to him each "village with its steeple and mossy tiles was a picture out of a book of old fairy tales" (*Best,* 48). Even when he tried to capture something of his sense of the contrast between what he was seeing and what he knew he would be facing, the resulting poem was much more accomplished in its lovely visual imagery than in its confrontation with war. "Poitiers—July 2nd" (*Fourteenth,* 87–88) likens the poppies of the "old sad fields" to "the blood of battles" (ll. 4, 7), a general metaphor familiar in the British war poems written earlier in the conflict. The image of the landscape, however, specifically recalls the broad perspectives and saturated colors of Monet in such compositions as *A Field of Flowers in France* (1891) or *Path in the Île Saint-Martin, Vetheuil* (1881). "Wide grey-green fields, / Dappled with swaying vermillion" is the poem's predominant image (ll. 1–2).

Waiting in Paris to be sent to the training camp at Sandricourt with his Norton-Harjes unit, Dos Passos delighted in revisiting the places he had seen and loved as a child. Now, to get a glimpse of the enormous stained-glass windows of Sainte-Chapelle, one of the greatest of the cultural refinements that marked the midthirteenth-century court of Louis IX, Dos Passos had to peer through the gaps between piled sandbags. Even so, his memories of the city in 1917 focused impressionistically on its pictorial beauty. From the "vague hint of moonlight overhead," he wrote later in *The Best Times,* the buildings he had "known as a child loomed out of the faint blue lights at streetcorners" (49).

The delicate shades and artistically blurred outlines of these images pervaded his impressions of Paris as late as 1918, even after he had endured the major offensive of late summer 1917 at Verdun. The small sketchbooks he filled with serene pastel cityscapes during July and August 1918 contrast in tone with the bitter disillusionment his journals and letters of the same period show. Perhaps, like Fanshaw Macdougan in *Streets of Night,* Dos Passos clung to aesthetic conventions to avoid confronting realities. The realizations Fanshaw dodges are potentially painful, to be sure—his friend's suicide, his own failure of will, the emotional handicaps from his lifetime of cultural conditioning. But in the summer of 1918, Dos Passos, having already confronted battle and the dehumanizing brutalities of military discipline, was facing dishonorable discharge from the Red Cross for pacifistic and antimilitaristic comments he had made in a letter to José Giner, a Spanish friend, in the early spring of 1918 (*Fourteenth,* 149–53). His sketches and poetry of that period concentrate on the harmonious compositions of the Parisian buildings and streets and on the atmospheric effects on the city of rain and sun, techniques that may have been his way of escaping momentarily what he had seen of the war and the "complete lack of human decency people exhibit at times" (*Fourteenth,* 194).

In this sketchbook, Dos Passos combines his architectural knowledge with an impressionist rendering of transitory light and weather to produce 20 five-by-eight-inch pastel crayon scenes of Paris. He chooses the perspective carefully, varying the focal distance and angle of perception in almost every sketch. His selection of point of view helps determine the dynamic of the composition and the placement of its central element. He is conscious also of the placement of the whole image on the page, using empty space as a structural element, rarely defining the background and often creating open forms by bleeding an element off the page. His obvious discrimination in these compositional choices, despite the fact that he probably executed the sketches on site, suggests an active awareness of relationships among all the disparate compositional elements he is using. This Paris journal illustrates his learning to manipulate these relationships and exploit the potential of unconventional points of view, skills that later became crucial to his modernist narrative techniques. For all their impressionist prettiness and skilled draftsmanship, these crayon compositions show the beginnings of a modernist conception of the work of art as the arrangement of forms in space rather than as a mimetic representation.

Still, in the midst of the difficulties of this summer in Paris, Dos Passos most often chose to sketch places with aesthetic or emotional resonance for him or scenes that reminded him of his past. The first picture in the book, "Quai d'Anjou, July 9–1918," depicts the view across the Seine from the place where he lived during this summer, in a small room over the Rendezvous des Mariniers, a "little plain restaurant" on the Île St.-Louis (*Best,* 58). That charming island in the Seine, "a beautifully old seedy part of Paris" that Dos Passos loved, was removed enough from both the more cosmopolitan part of the city and the bohemian fascinations of Montmartre to provide him with the calm working atmosphere he had lacked while on active duty. He took advantage of that repose to "spend [his] spare time writing and sketching up and down the river," as he wrote happily to Rumsey Marvin (*Fourteenth,* 194). In this opening sketch, he frames the Seine with two trees balanced by a lamppost in the middle foreground. Water, trees, and the foreground sidewalk are all merely suggested by impressionistic, incomplete patches of color.

The day after creating this introductory sketch from his island haven, he set about once again "eating the lotos" (*Fourteenth* 100), as he termed his wartime interludes in Paris, times he spent "quite forgetting war and discipline and duty" (*Fourteenth,* 88). On July 10, this day's sketch records, he executed a view of the Institut de France, "for years [his] favorite building in the world" (*Best,* 50). Perhaps it was the pleasure of his long-standing recollections of the structure that resulted in one of the most complete sketches in the journal. He depicts in it "the slender dome that soared above the arches linking [its] pedimented wings" (50), although his memory of the place in *The Best Times* captures more of its grace than his portrait did nearly 50 years earlier. Competent, pretty, and fairly conventional, his mostly charcoal sketch of the Institut is notable more for its draftsmanship than for its innovation.

While many of the 20 sketches capture sites familiar even to tourists, some of the later entries experiment a bit artistically. A view of the Place des Voges he drew on August 3, for instance, places the base of the column of a building's arch squarely in the middle foreground, so that the viewer seems to be seated under a colonnade looking out around the column at the garden and fountain at some distance. On August 7, Dos Passos completed three different views of the Cathedral of Notre Dame. One is from the front, as in Monet's painting of the cathedral, and uses shades of blue, again like Monet, on gray paper to create the paradoxical delicacy of the giant facade. Another view, the most familiar, is of the east end of the cathedral apse with its graceful flying buttresses. The third, however, is of the north flank toward the right bank, a side that seldom appears in the countless artistic renderings of the structure. In this view, Dos Passos arranges the airy spire of the cathedral on the far left of the composition, the transept roof hiding all but the very tops of the facade towers, the transept wing comprising the biggest block in the center of the space. Unlike in his sketch of the Institut, which he outlined with charcoal, here he uses color to suggest shape, but only enough to establish the forms. The crayon work is impressionistically minimal, in royal blues for the building and dark greens for the surrounding foliage. Yellow highlights suggest the sun's reflection. It is an unconventional perspective executed in skillful modeling and delicate impressionist shading.

His painterly images of Paris and his frequent returns to the city during his 1917 to 1918 service in France seem to have constituted for Dos Passos a welcome immersion in the personal and artistic memories its scenes embodied for him. His journals bear out the sense of escape he felt there—the hours he spent "wandering through autumn gardens and down grey misty colonaded streets," as he wrote to Rumsey Marvin during his late 1917 stay there. In the pastimes he relished browsing through bookshops, eating at cafes, and attending concerts, he rediscovered the ancient refinements of European culture that represented the accomplishments of long generations. After what he had seen of the war, he appreciated these French aesthetic conventions "[a]ll in a constant sensual drowse at the mellow beauty of the colors & forms of Paris, of old houses overhanging the Seine and damp streets smelling of the dead and old half-forgotten histories" (*Fourteenth*, 102).

Precursors of Modernism in Poetry

As the descriptive imagery of this 1917 letter to Marvin intimates, however, Dos Passos had begun to realize that those cultural and personal memories he cherished and sought refuge in bespoke an order of life that was irrevocably past. His crayon sketches from this stay in Paris, drawings he self-deprecatingly but somewhat proudly characterized to Marvin as "exhibit[ing] . . . improvement" (*Fourteenth*, 194), may have expressed a romantically nostalgic view of the city. But his journals and the poems he wrote during this period acknowledged the passing of that aesthetic traditional order. In these poems, eventually published in *A Pushcart at the Curb*, Dos Passos's visual imagery portrays the aestheticism and classicism of Europe's past as decayed and moribund. A poem such as "VI" (*Pushcart*, 148), subtitled "To A. K. McC." (Arthur McComb), imagines the Tuileries gardens as haunted by the "exquisite Augustans" (l. 1) and seems by its images to charge the neoclassicists with the precious artificiality that had permeated the kind of poetry the young aesthetes had produced. The garden is autumnal, a "russet mist of clustered trees / and strewn November leaves" (ll. 2–3), impressionist diction but not the vibrant summer views of the impressionists. The Augustans' "ancient vermillion" shoes "crunch . . . / the dry dead of spent summer's greens," their "mincing" (ll. 5–7) steps punctuated by the sounds of their snapping snuffboxes and their epigrams. Dos Passos suggests visually that such literary and artistic antecedents are not only outmoded but also faintly ridiculous.

The poems often suggest also the enervating power of the romantic past to thwart life in the present, a central theme in *Streets of Night*. "La Rue du Temps Passé" (*Pushcart*, 153–54), for instance, uses impressionist imagery, but to sinister effect, in a series of vignettes depicting lonely individuals immobilized by memories or by fear of reality. The third vignette, in the fourth of five six-line stanzas, presents a "pale boy" looking out a window "at the vast grey violet dusk" (ll. 19–20). A book lies open in his lap, and the boy trembles "[w]ith cold choked fear [at] the thronging lives / That lurk in the shadows and fill the dusk" (ll. 22–23). The image juxtaposes the removed realm of literature, here a twilight world, with the "thronging" activity of a more immediate existence. The poem's final stanza introduces a symbol of that immediacy: a tram whose "clattering drone" breaks the "breathless . . . silence" of the hushed and static preceding scenes, leaving the houses "listening" (ll. 27–30). Into the romantically vague, archaic world of the aesthetic past, Dos Passos seems to say, the harsh dynamism of the present, of the coming industrial age that the electric streetcar suggests, must inevitably intrude. And this awakening, the poem's imagery argues, not only will dominate but also can rejuvenate culture.

In fact, the poem following "La Rue du Temps Passé" in *Pushcart* bears out that argument in its own images and dynamics. This poem, titled only "X" (155–57), appears in draft form on the inside back cover of the 1918 sketchbook that celebrates visually the ancient harmony of Paris. Paradoxically, the poem shows the beginnings in Dos Passos's writing of a new realism whose aesthetics can recall the work of the Ashcan painters or even look forward to the cityscapes of Georgia O'Keeffe, not backward to the impressionists, as the sketches do.

"X" progresses by following the course of tugboats and barges along the Seine, painting city scenes along the quais. Interspersed with these images is a refrain that opens and closes the poem: "O douce Sainte Geneviève / ramène moi a ta ville, Paris" (ll. 1–2) ("O sweet Saint Genevieve, take me home to your city, Paris"). The wistfulness of the appeal to the patron saint of Paris and the use of French instead of English distinguish the refrain entirely from the rest of the poem. Dos Passos thus integrates into this poem the contrast between past and present stylistically and graphically, rather than by overt and more obvious imagery. He animates his urban and industrial images, moreover, but refuses to romanticize them. Instead of a misty twilight, he now paints the "smoke" and "orangy sunshine" (ll. 3–4) of the morning. Instead of open books or faded roses, the icons of the past in "La Rue du Temps

Passé," he now depicts tugboats and "black barges" plying the Seine, "[b]ending their black smokestacks . . . / muddling themselves in their spiralling smoke" (ll. 5 – 6).

Of course, a few years after this poem, tugboats and ferries along with other methods of conveyance became for Dos Passos symbols of American industrialization in *Manhattan Transfer,* and symbols of the blunt reality of New York City itself that helped recreate the rhythms of the city's commerce and social flux. In this lively hymn to St. Genevieve, the images of river traffic, along with the counterpointing styles and languages, convey a sense of transition from a romantic to a realistic view of the city, and of motion through space and time. This dynamic spatiality, so different from the stasis of his earlier work, was obviously one of the narrative goals he was consciously developing as his style evolved during the war.

He now seemed to find in the forms, motion, and space of Paris embodiments of the changes he was working toward—from the impressionist sketches of the romantically aesthetic icons of the old city to the realistic, unadorned verbal images of the present-day traffic of life. The idea of such a transition seems to be embodied in the title of the section of *Pushcart* containing these poems about Paris—"Quai de la Tournelle." This is one of the wharves adjoining the bridge that connects the tiny Île St. Louis to the west end of the Blvd. St. Germaine, the central thoroughfare that runs parallel to the Seine. The fashionable couturiers, exclusive antique shops, and renowned hotels and cafes along the boulevard create constant mercantile traffic. At its west end, it borders the fifth arrondissement, where the Sorbonne and other institutions constitute the lively center of Paris's student district.

In leaving daily the slumberous traditional remove of the Île St. Louis and crossing the Pont de la Tournelle to the constant activity of the Left Bank, Dos Passos must have perceived an actual spatial sense of the differences in the two worlds he was poised between. He knew that the conventionally linear narrative techniques he had been schooled in could not convey the forces and the dynamics of life as it had been transformed by the war. And as he looked at America from across the ocean, beginning to perceive that his own country's "mechanical civilization" ("Humble," 116) was the theme he needed to develop, he began also to work at creating a style equal to his theme. The direction of his writing about Paris during the war reveals the germ of his transition toward that style, one in which the painterly techniques of color, spatiality, and simultaneity were integral facets of the narrative structure.

Chapter Six

"Mechanical Civilization" and the Images of War: The "Great Novel"

Dos Passos had voiced his profound misgivings about the "mechanical civilization" he saw America becoming even before he witnessed the ramifications of that new social order in the workings of the American military system. "A Humble Protest," his final essay for the *Harvard Monthly*, questioned "the goal of this mechanical, splendidly inventive civilization of ours" under the "rule of science" (116). Industrialism had not, as one might have expected, provided humans with more freedom or impetus for "producing great art, . . . certainly one of the touchstones, if not *the* touchstone of a civilization." Indeed, "Under industrialism . . . [t]hree-fourths of the world are bound in economic slavery that the other fourth may in turn be enslaved by the tentacular inessentials of civilization, for the production of which the lower classes have ground out their lives." The "immense machine" of industrialism, he perceived, doomed millions of laborers to "stultifying" lives "without ever a chance of self-expression." Worse, science and industry had bred the war, Dos Passos generalized. He offered as an example Germany, the "one modern nation" with the most fully developed industrial system as well as "a really great living art." Germany had "slipped back into barbarism," he charged: "The same civilization has produced . . . the Eroica Symphony and the ruins of Rheims" ("Humble," 118–20).

Mechanical civilization, Dos Passos protested in 1916, threatened to obliterate the powers and freedoms of the very individuals it had ostensibly been evolved to benefit. The primacy of the individual was a theme he would consider at more length in *Rosinante to the Road Again* (1920), the collection of essays he began conceptualizing during the war in which he considers Spanish individualism but with an eye toward the American character. The individual's powerlessness against the systems, the magnitude, the materialism, and the repressiveness of mechanical civilization became a central theme in his war novels, a theme that matured and intensified in *Manhattan Transfer*.

Responding thematically in his work to the modern juggernaut of industrialism and governmental control, he recognized that he must also respond stylistically. In "Against American Literature," his first paid publication, he had evaluated the national literature of his own country and found it lacking because it failed to respond specifically to its own places, peoples, and accomplishments. The "hybrid" quality of American literature, "its lack of depth and texture . . . [and] dramatic actuality," he asserted, resulted from its "dependence on the past" and on European aesthetic traditions for its context and origin. Obviously, a culture that was becoming a mechanical civilization, floundering . . . in the sea of modern life," had outgrown its European cultural antecedents and needed to recognize its own *"âme nationale,"* as he ironically labeled the missing spirit. For better or for worse, he presciently declared, "An all-enveloping industrialism, a new mode of life preparing, has broken down the old bridges leading to the past, has cut off the possibility of retreat. Our only course," he predicted, "is to press on" ("Against," 269–71).

And, in fact, the essay he had provocatively titled "Against American Literature" was actually a case *for* American arts and a kind of preliminary manifesto of his own goals within the context of that aesthetic. While he deplored the effects on the individual of America's developing cult of science and industry, he believed nonetheless that "in America lies the future" (*Fourteenth,* 122). An essay he began in Spain in 1916, just after "Against American Literature" appeared in the *New Republic,* searched at more length for the distinctive American character that could shape the nation's arts in the future. The half-satiric "Art and Baseball," never published, cited architecture as the only example of indigenous American art he could find and the one art form in which American aesthetics depended on the future not on the past. The "skyscraper," the "beauty of Manhattan," were the only aesthetic artifacts American arts had produced that were not mere "imitation of French painting, of French sculpture, of British literature."[1]

Less than 10 years after Dos Passos played with the idea of the skyscraper as the lone pure product of American aesthetics and ingenuity, he returned to the same concept in *Manhattan Transfer.* That mature modernist work, published in 1925, looks at this idea in the context of the intervening years, however. During those postwar years, America had enjoyed peace and prosperity that should have fostered the democratic goals of the founding fathers. Instead, as Jimmy Herf discovers, the nation had betrayed all those promises of "Pursuit of happiness, unalienable pursuit . . . right to life liberty" (*Manhattan,* 365). The new mechanical civilization had distorted the definitions of those terms in the process of creating a superficial materialism predicated on the victimization of the individual by corrupt, superpowerful systems of business and government. Dos Passos uses the skyscraper as a "symbolic objectification" of the betrayal of the original promises of the nation.[2]

No longer is the skyscraper even "the accidental result of straight lines and great mass" ("Art and Baseball," 5), as Dos Passos envisioned it from the less subjective perspective of 1916. The structure has become a threatening bulk that looms over Herf with the cold perfection and sometimes sinister, anonymous vitality of precisionist paintings: "a grooved building jutting up with uncountable bright windows falling onto [Herf] out of a scudding sky" (*Manhattan*, 365). The building into which Herf cannot find a door bristles with lights, like *Brooklyn Bridge*, a painting done between 1917 and 1918 by Joseph Stella, whom E. E. Cummings introduced to Dos Passos while he was writing *Manhattan Transfer*. Dos Passos's "humming tinselwindowed skyscraper" (*Manhattan*, 366) intimates hidden, separate lives behind each square of light, the sense of anonymity conveyed by the cityscapes produced from 1926 to 1929 by Georgia O'Keeffe, whose work Dos Passos reviewed during that period. In its clear identification with American industrialism and all that it had wrought, the skyscraper served for Dos Passos as a symbol of the betrayed promises of America. Herf, also a young writer, wanders confusedly among the towering buildings, "[h]is mind reeling phrases," coming to the realization that none of the "old words" on which the nation was founded have any meaning any more (*Occasions*, 14). For Dos Passos, the skyscraper that once embodied America's artistic and social potential has become merely "a temple to the false words" that now disallow belief in that promise (Vanderwerken, 264).

Yet, *Manhattan Transfer* ends on what may be construed as an optimistic note: Herf keeps searching for a new version of the "old words" as he leaves New York. Dos Passos's search for a new language continued, too, during the years between 1916 and 1925, with the conviction that he must respond truly and directly to his own time and to focus not on "the name of the thing" but "on the thing itself" ("What," 30), a stylistic goal he reiterated as late as 1968, two years before he died.

"Seven Times Round the Walls of Jericho": New Themes, New Structures

Dos Passos's goals did not alter, but his means of achieving them were irrevocably altered by his exposure to the fate of the individual under mechanical civilization and in the world war it had caused. After just a few months in the midst of the fighting, he had come to believe that his "business was to tell the tale" (Introduction, *Initiation,* 5). In "A Humble Protest" in 1916, he had predicted that the war would act as "an acid to sear away the old complacency" (117) of the nineteenth century, that people would be forced to reexamine old beliefs and try new ones. After a year in the war, he wrote in his journal flatly, with none of the metaphoric gilding of his college essay, "The idea of individual liberty does not exist any where— . . . it is an unended and unending battle that of man to free himself from the monsters of his own creation" (*Fourteenth,* 208).

Impelled by this disillusionment, by his determination to exorcise private "memories" of the Harvard glass bell and outworn aesthetic traditions, and by his conviction that he must speak out against what he had seen in the war, Dos Passos began "forming gradually in [his] mind" a "great war novel," part of which would eventually become *One Man's Initiation: 1917* (10). In his original conception of the magnum opus that his journals and letters of 1917 reveal, the novel was to have accomplished all these goals. In fact, the ideas and manuscripts this undertaking generated became the basis for five major works eventually completed before he undertook *Manhattan Transfer* in 1923: *Streets of Night,* published in 1923; "Seven Times Round the Walls of Jericho," never published; *One Man's Initiation: 1917,* published in 1920; *Three Soldiers,* published in 1921; and his play *The Garbage Man,* produced in 1925 as *The Moon Is a Gong* and published in 1926. Central to all these works is Dos Passos's concern with the primacy of the individual and with his chances for freedom, self-expression, and ultimately simple survival under the convention and faceless authority of mechanical civilization. Even a brief overview of the history and techniques of the "Great Novel" (*Best,* 71), as Dos Passos later called the mass of work, illustrates how his war experiences transformed these themes and their expression.

Although Dos Passos conceived of his great novel as a way to expose the repressive affectations of American upper-class culture and to protest the cant by which governments justify war, he noted in his journal in August 1917 that he had actually begun writing the novel as a way of "amusing [himself]." Between trips to the front to transport the wounded to field hospitals, he and the rest of his Norton-Harjes unit endured long bouts of the "waiting [that] is the main thing one does in the war," as he wrote to Rumsey Marvin. He was delighted to discover in his unit a Harvard classmate, Robert Hillyer, who wrote poetry, and they began alternating chapters of what Dos Passos tentatively named "The Walls of Jericho" (*Fourteenth*, 91, 113, 185). His earliest general outline of the work, sketched out in his journal in August 1917 as his unit made its way to the front at Verdun, projected "the Streets at Night" as the novel's first part (*Initiation*, 12). The outline of part I follows the plan of what was later published as *Streets of Night*, but it illustrates that he originally intended a connection between the protagonists of *Streets* and those of what he calls "Part II The war . . . the philosophy of scorn." To this entry he appended a quotation from the symbolist poet Verlaine: "De trop de délicatesse / J'ai perdu la vie" ("From too much fastidiousness / I lost my life") (*Initiation*, 12).

He seems to have realized quickly that the "Cantibridgian atmosphere" (*Initiation*, 12) of part I did not advance the narrative decisively enough toward what he had to say about the war and American government. Then, he focused in his notes on "Part II The War." The art-life polarity that Fanshaw and Wenny represent in *Streets* carries over into the new work, but in "Jericho" the characterizations are a bit less schematic. The central character, Martin Howe, is more sympathetic and more integrated than Fanshaw, although Wenny's rebellion against genteel conformity and his quest for authenticity find expression in "Jericho" in the character of James Clough, Martin's young uncle. Once Hillyer and Dos Passos began developing these characters and themes, Dos Passos envisioned the emerging work as consisting of four parts in itself: Martin's childhood, education, young adulthood, and war experiences.

But in September 1917, Hillyer "had to go home [to America] on pressing family business," and his and Dos Passos's "collaboration on the G. N." ended with Martin "barely out of prepschool" (*Best*, 56). Soon thereafter, when the Norton-Harjes ambulance unit was to be integrated into the regular army, Dos Passos joined the Red Cross as a way of staying in Europe. But he was prevented from renewing his enlistment when Red Cross authorities intercepted letters he had written to friends criticizing the war—condemning all wars; the authorities brought charges of disloyalty and ordered him to return to the United States. Once there, Dos Passos continued the bildungsroman, completing a draft in late 1918 at Camp Crane in Pennsylvania, where he was awaiting enlistment in the Army Medical Corps so he could return to Europe and the war's aftermath. By that time, his regular army initiation into rank-and-file soldiering and his ongoing confrontations with the cant and dogma of America's wartime spirit had impelled him to begin *Three Soldiers*. Representing another step closer to a fully modernist style, this novel focuses completely on the war and uses a minor character from "Seven Times," Martin's musician friend John Andrews, as the protagonist. Andrews has much in common with Fanshaw/ Wenny and Martin/James—and, as do all these characters, with Dos Passos himself—but is still more integrated a character than any of the protagonists so far. This more skillful integration results from the greater objectivity of Dos Passos's style as he developed more perspective on his own experiences and literary goals.

That new perspective motivated him to revise completely the manuscript of "Seven Times" in 1919 amid the "artistic ferment" of postwar Paris. Officially, he was studying anthropology at the Sorbonne under the auspices of the Army Overseas Educational Commission. Actually, he was hungrily absorbing all that was new in the arts at that time, as he remembered in 1968: "les Fauves, the Cubists, Modigliani, Juan Gris, Picasso," Satie, Les Six, Poulenc, Milhaud, Stravinsky, and the "Diaghilev ballet [that was] . . . a synthesis of all the arts" ("What," 30). Responding to all the artistic stimuli, he continued his own sketching, drawing human figures in a small class. These charcoal sketches of nudes show the influence of the modern painters, especially the early Picasso, he cited later as important in that era. Although Dos Passos, in a letter to Rumsey Marvin, disparaged his "attempts" as "strangely celluloid-looking" (*Fourteenth*, 247), they may only have seemed strange to him because they *are* fairly avant-garde. While they are not cubist, neither are they strictly representational. In them, he sketches women almost as overlapping circles, with exaggerated breasts, midsections, and thighs, giving a sense of the African influence on Picasso's early cubist nudes. In one sketch, Dos Passos focuses on the body from neck to knees, treating the figure as an amalgam of abstract shapes with almost no human identity.

All these new artistic influences certainly began to have their effect on his emerging narrative style. He evidently felt the style of his revisions of "Seven Times" different enough from the original to omit Hillyer's name from the manuscript when he began trying to publish it in 1919, even though he had revised only parts I and II. There were even more profound influences at work on his thinking, however, and they too shaped the course of all the work he was conceptualizing. It became clear that the uprising of citizens and workers against oppressive regimes that was to have occurred on the first of May would not come about, much to the disillusionment of Dos Passos and his fellow survivors of the war.

As he realized that the status quo was entrenched and as he gained some distance from his own war experiences, his detestation of the "patriotic cant" and the "lies" (*Fourteenth*, 134, 152) of "greedy nations . . . drunk on commercialism" that led to war crystallized into action. Merely protesting in general terms about "the machinery of government" (Dos Passos, quoted in Ludington 1980, 176) would not effect the changes he saw clearly were imperative for the survival of "the finest human things . . . [t]he things that give life an added dimension" (*Fourteenth*, 152–53), as he wrote to José Giner in the letter that earned Dos Passos the charge of disloyalty. From Paris, Dos Passos held forth to Rumsey Marvin on the urgency of the state of the world: "[I]t is no time for similes when someone is sitting on your necks. A false idea, a false system, and a set of tyrants, conscious or unconscious, is sitting on the world's neck at present and has so far succeeded in destroying a good half of the worthwhile things in the world. . . . [We must] save what we can of the things worthwhile and . . . decide damn quick what things are worthwhile and what are not. . . . [T]he machinery of government means a set of people, individuals, with individual greeds and stupidities" (*Fourteenth*, 176).

While this new urgency transformed what Dos Passos had to say, the artistic revolution in postwar Paris was transforming the way he said it. The beginnings of modernism around him offered new means of expressing his bitterness at the destructive power of systems over culture. From his circle of friends during the spring of 1919, he gained reinforcement of his political ideals and literary advice on how best to express them. He read his manuscript to old friends such as John Howard Lawson, whose socialistic activism along with Dos Passos's, would later shape the New Playwrights Theater, and to new ones such as Griffin Barry, then a radical journalist, and Robert Minor, cartoonist for the *Masses*. All these factors and his own increasingly discriminating sense of the relationship between style and theme were rapidly developing his work past the inchoate romantic longing for experience and connection that had predominated even through Martin Howe's story.

Now, in the context of his new, more decisively active direction, he perceived that the first three parts of "Seven Times" to some degree articulated different themes than the fourth part. Parts I, II, and III dealt more with his prewar experiences and thus related the formation of the impulse toward meaningful action in the world, as Martin Howe—nicknamed "Fibbie" for his tendency to exaggerate and boast—came of age. Part IV, however, showed Martin actually acting on those impulses by going to war, and so, as a text, it constituted a decisive action in itself, revealing what Dos Passos had learned about the war and its attendant policies. Suddenly, in May 1919, Dos Passos interjected this declaration into a letter to Dudley Poore, a Harvard friend and fellow ambulance volunteer: "The fourth part of Fibbie never was part of him at all. I merely pretended that it was, and as soon as it was read aloud my pretense collapsed. . . . I'm going to enlarge it and put in steam heat and enameled bath tubs and call it France 1917 or something of the sort and try to publish it that way" (*Fourteenth*, 251).

What he called it, eventually, was *One Man's Initiation: 1917*, and he did, in fact, publish it without too much alteration. In that war novel are the beginnings of the satiric vision engendered by the artistic, political, and military forces Dos Passos encountered from 1917 through 1919. *Initiation* moves closer toward expressing the "freedom from the past" (*Initiation*, 157) that its protagonist claims is the meaning of America and that was one of Dos Passos's artistic goals in this work. His master plan for the Great Novel—*Streets*, "Seven Times," and *Initiation*—and his editorial choices in ultimately fragmenting the manuscript illustrate that by 1919 he had finally managed to exorcise the aesthetic and personal "memories" that had impelled him to begin writing. Only in the writing of the apprentice works, however, did he become able to relinquish these memories and to move stylistically beyond the romantic aesthetic that had pervaded his early work.

That part of the manuscript he titled "Seven Times" represents his working through and understanding the antiauthoritarian impulses created by his upbringing and conventional education so that he could cast his themes in a more objective, effective style. In this manuscript are the origins of two central themes in the works that grew out of this effort: the necessity of the individual's speaking out against oppression in all its forms and the paradoxical vitality and machinelike force of the city. Each theme is connected to a primary image that once again implies Dos Passos's background in the visual arts, and both images and themes reappear in major works of the following five years. The increasing subtlety and skill with which Dos Passos uses the visual images, however, indicate the growing complexity of the themes and of the narrative techniques he employs to delineate them. Even in "Seven Times," which he was never able to place with a publisher, that progress toward modernism emerges.

Perhaps the most frequently repeated image in his work up to 1919, an image Dos Passos used integrally for several years more, is one in which a boy or a man envisions the moon as a gong or drum on which to strike and be heard universally. That fantasy bespeaks the individual's struggle, in Dos Passos's early fiction, to transcend conventional methods or patterns of communication, which inevitably lend themselves to the societal lies he inveighed against. The image appears as early as in the poems eventually published in 1917 in *Eight Harvard Poets,* although in "Memory" from that collection, it is in a highly romanticized form recalling the visual preoccupations of the aesthetes. At the end of "Memory," the speaker merely *sees* the moon "like a golden gong" waiting for a priest to strike it "into throbbing song" (57–61). The image is associated with unrequited love for a fleetingly glimpsed girl.

The same image opens "Seven Times" and recurs frequently in variations that signal the growth of Martin and of Dos Passos's theme.[3] In the beginning of the manuscript, Dos Passos quotes the passage from the sixth chapter of Joshua in which the prophet brings down the walls of Jericho with the sounds of shouting and trumpets. To tumble the bastions of stultifying conventions and customs is Martin's dream in this novel, a dream fed by and partly modeled on the efforts of his visionary artist uncle, James Clough. That hope finds nascent expression even when Martin is a child tended by his nanny, Marie. Questioning the common assertion that the moon is made of green cheese, Martin observes the moon for himself and concludes that it is more like a "toy balloon," a child's storybook visualization. Inspecting the night scene from the perspective of his bedroom window, Martin sees the moon rise "easily above the complicated roofs of the town" ("Seven Times" I, 5). Implicit in the image's diction and composition are the fullness, the lightness, and the inaccessible nature of the moon, and the complexity and weightiness of the city below. These relative values grow more explicit in later uses of the image as the moon becomes identified with Martin's and James's need to be heard—the hope of communication—and the city becomes identified with the realistic perplexities and dangers of modern civilization.

The child Martin, however, merely knows that he wants to be able to *reach* the moon. When he makes the analogy between the moon and an Indian drum in the library, another fanciful storybook image, he plans to escape the repressive remonstrations of his mother, Marie, or even the police or the bogeyman: "[W]hen he grew up big and strong he'd go up in a balloon and get on the edge of the moon and beat it and beat it" like the Indian drum ("Seven Times" I, 5). But he is impatient to begin making his voice heard. He tells Suzanne, Marie's daughter, that he actually *did* strike the moon, and it is she who then sticks him with the appropriate nickname "Fibbie." Petulantly, Martin nurses his "exhilarating hatred of everybody" when Suzanne tattles to his mother ("Seven Times" I, 6). Everyone *else* tells fibs, he reasons; why are his any worse? With this image of the moon, Dos Passos thus establishes the childhood origins of Martin's quarrel with the world, whose hypocrisy and falsehood instill in him a firm mistrust of "conventional wisdom." In his obdurate search for the truth and the way to tell it, he finds an ally in his black-sheep uncle, James. The brother of Martin's widowed mother, James has rejected the trappings and values of his wealthy, elite Boston family and, as a result, is unwelcome by his sister, who is trying to raise her son as a proper member of his class. James *is* allowed into the Howe residence, however, for the funeral of his and Mrs. Howe's mother. He takes that opportunity to visit Martin in his nursery in a scene that establishes James's connection to Martin's romantic dreams and his vow to strike the moon and be heard.

Telling the child Viking sagas, James clearly associates these adventures with a nobler, freer culture than the narrow one that encloses him and Martin. With his vivid stories, he excites Martin's imagination further, then augments the stories with impromptu charcoal illustrations right on the nursery walls. Creating art, daring to impose on the staid Beacon Hill walls these images of a mythic untrammeled existence, James makes himself heard just as Martin dreams he will. James expresses himself and his rebellion against class and cultural conventions by creating "something to keep the shadows [on the nursery walls] from getting creepy" ("Seven Times" I, 14). Thus, Dos Passos uses visual art at the outset of the novel to link these two main characters' antiauthoritarian impulses, with Martin's as the child's version of James's more considered nonconformity.

James's outcry against all the various forms of false values and hypocrisy he has encountered finds fuller artistic expression in the play he produces. The plot of *The Dreamer Wakes* is not revealed in the typescript Dos Passos eventually tried to publish. But the treatment of the play that appears in the University of Virginia manuscript reveals that in theme and structural conception it is actually a precursor of *The Moon Is a Gong,* whose title more obviously signals the parallel between the later play and the play-within-the-novel. Dos Passos visualized both dramas in expressionist visual images. Linda Wagner notes the "charged, recurring image and quasi-surreal event pattern" (73) that constitute Dos Passos's method in *The Moon,* and both the manuscript outline of *The Dreamer Wakes* and the outline Fibbie provides in the typescript of "Seven Times" confirm that Dos Passos's method in James's play is similar.

In "Seven Times," Fibbie provides the reader's only look at the play through fairly heavy-handed exposition. In the first act, "There had been a coffin with a dead woman in it on the stage. . . . And moving flame-like against the distorted background of stiff funeral attitudes, the figures of a boy and girl, passionately living, their words rising in a crescendo of revolt against mumbled platitudes of aunts and uncles and great-aunts and great-uncles. . . . They ran away at last, in search of glamour of life, gorgeousness of color" ("Seven Times" I, 149–50). Subsequent acts attack the "smallness and convention" of every institution or group that Dos Passos takes to task in the novel as a whole: "the old aristocracy, the genteel people . . . the artists, the would-be free . . . working people, slaves of strange old superstitions" ("Seven Times" I, 150). Dos Passos chooses only one passage for Martin to quote at length, a speech in which the play's protagonist appeals to the other characters "to tilt at windmills . . . to take drums and trumpets . . . and shout down the tottering walls of Jericho, so that the wind should blow through the stinking streets and the idols should fall into the putrifying heaps of their victims" ("Seven Times" I, 151).

In James's play, the opening metaphor of Dos Passos's novel, Martin's story, recurs; the plot of the play resembles the plot of Dos Passos's later, more polished drama, *The Moon Is a Gong;* and that play's central image for striking out against convention begins in "Seven Times" as the symbol for Martin's dream. This maze of self-reflexive and metafictional uses of central visual images reveals Dos Passos's strong identification with both Martin and James and the persistence of these images and this theme in Dos Passos's mind as he revised these manuscripts.

Part III of "Seven Times" introduces the second recurrent image and theme in this group of related works. The city, "an enslaving machine" ("Seven Times" III, 115), appears in vividly visual set pieces; and these often-discrete scenes are interspersed with only tangentially related scenes in techniques that look forward to *Manhattan Transfer* and even *U.S.A.* Dos Passos creates cityscapes that recall Ashcan school paintings or predict the work of the precisionists. The greater visual sophistication of part III along with its far more experimental narrative techniques show how significantly Dos Passos had progressed toward the modernist style of his best work by the time he was revising part II in 1919 and 1920.

Although Martin is still the protagonist in part III, he has now lost a good deal of the romantic angst that kept him longing to beat on the moon in part I. Having begun a sexual relationship with Suzanne, whose work in the theater places her beyond the pale of good society, he feels he has conquered somewhat the priggishness and guilt that are the legacy of his upbringing. The text is concomitantly freer of protracted musings about how "Puritanism has distorted all our ideas of love and life" ("Seven Times" II, 26). He has seen firsthand what society does to dreamers: James has died from a recurrent illness after his play is closed and suppressed. Thus, when Martin's friends begin volunteering for the war that America has now entered, Martin has a more objective target for his protests than he had earlier in the novel. It is almost as if Dos Passos had finally rid his system of his grievances against his proper upbringing and education. Certainly, the works that come after "Seven Times" abandon the stylistic trademarks of that romantic stance—the first-person point of view, the introspection, and the nineteenth-century aesthetic allusions. Even part III of "Seven Times" has far fewer explicit artistic allusions than part I, where Dos Passos occasionally falls back into the aesthetics' visual symbolism.

Ashcan and precisionist urban scenes in part III are more successfully integrated into the narrative structure than are the visual elements in previous works. These scenes are juxtaposed against fragments of action and pieces of dialogue not placed into a context, with narrative relationships indicated by large spaces between segments and sometimes by roman numeral chapter headings. Although Dos Passos uses this technique more often as part III progresses, one particularly effective example occurs about halfway through it.

Section IX encompasses several political discussions about America's entry into the war. Martin has come to the conclusion that "the capitalists have made a mess of America" and feels "an unconscious malignance" behind the voices of people (III, 78–79). To clear their minds, he and his musician friend John Andrews take a walk through the city, seeing in the faces of the people they pass "all the joy, all the disillusion of the lives they had long used away to the dry husk" (III, 81). Yet the variety of the city fascinates them as they wander into an ethnic café portrayed in livid expressionist images. They encounter a self-professed anarchist who proclaims, with "an accent," that "Governments is the police-like that keep the people that's robbed from from gettin' their goods away from the robbers" (III, 87). Yet, he subsides; it is no use speaking out: "[I]t's all talk, talk . . . what good?" (III, 88)

So Dos Passos uses Martin to express his own ambivalence about whether an individual can, in fact, make anyone listen to the truth and to express his perception of New York City as the emblem of the multiplicity of life. As in *Streets*, true intimacy between humans and the sexual connection between them provide one possibility for emotional authenticity in the face of convention, repression, and anonymity, a sentiment that is suggested as Martin leaves the café with the sudden need to see Suzanne.

Section X then presents in one paragraph the faceless flowing of the city, its bright emptiness emerging from images that anticipate the work of the precisionist painters a few years hence: "Fifth Avenue gleamed like a canal. Along its wet pavements a thin stream of motors and taxis speeded uptown. There were few lights in the houses and shops, but the double row of bright lamps cast a constant shimmer on the pavements. The high houses stretching endlessly on either side were white and lifeless, like architects' drawings" (90). The sense of flattened facades in this passage and the play of "the filigree spotting of . . . lights" (Davidson, 206) likewise characterize Georgia O'Keeffe's *New York—Night* (1928–1929) and *Radiator Building—Night, New York* (1927). Although these paintings were not produced until nearly a decade after Dos Passos worked on "Seven Times," they share with the manuscript the characteristic precisionist impersonality of presentation in their views of the city and focus on American scenes.

The "powerful shapes and crisp detailing" (Davidson, 184) of the products of American technology—factories, mills, smokestacks, skyscrapers, machines—attracted these postwar painters, who sought images to express what they felt to be the characteristic directness of the American character. In the finely poised ambivalence of his images, Dos Passos foreshadowed this modernist movement, which included such artists as Charles Demuth, Charles Sheeler, Preston Dickinson, and Gerald Murphy, who later became a close friend of Dos Passos. During the 1920s, when he was refining his use of this visual aesthetic and enlarging his themes, precisionist painting produced its greatest achievements. Anticipating these painters in "Seven Times," Dos Passos was interacting with them by the time he was writing *Manhattan Transfer* in the early 1920s. Besides the precisionist visual elements in that work and later in *U.S.A.,* the aesthetic emerges also in his paintings from that period. And both his literary and painterly works express and augment the ideology of Americanness the precisionists espoused.

Following the precisionist image in section X, section XI returns to the personal specificity of section IX. Martin arrives at Suzanne's apartment eager to forget the anarchist's despair. He tries to lose his feeling of enslavement at the hands of society in the sensuality and intimacy of his relationship with her; but he is reminded of the supremacy of materialism when she, who is becoming a successful theatrical designer, crows that she will "soon be drowned in money." To her, the daughter of a domestic, money *is* freedom. When Martin insists on seeing the two of them romantically, as passionately noble souls against the world, Suzanne pragmatically reminds him that "it's stronger than you are of course" and that, essentially, living well is the best revenge. Martin is able to quell his idealism long enough to go to bed and fall asleep, but his urge to change the world returns when he wakes up, gets out of bed, and stands at the window looking down at the city. His view of it captures the elegant emptiness of the precisionists' cityscapes: "pinkish white buildings with their endless lines of windows and their blue veils of smoke. It seemed more some sterile rock formation than a city. . . . There was nowhere any sign of life" (III, 92, 95).

Dos Passos neither vilifies nor glorifies the city, nor does he valorize either Martin's or Suzanne's way of acting in it. Instead, by means of juxtaposed scenes, he presents fairly objectively the city's variety, the cost it can exact, and the way individuals try to survive in the culture it represents. James's life and his expressionistic work seem to represent a positive option for action in the world, even though he dies. Martin seems to carry on James's ideals, yet he perceives the threat of the city as it appears in precisionist images. And Suzanne, who survives happily, has sold out to a commercialized form of the drama James risked so much for. Dos Passos develops these themes by juxtaposition in part III. In discrete sections that often consist of a single narrative technique— action, dialogue, or description—Dos Passos disengages himself from the text, opens out the subjective, romantic point of view that had pervaded his fiction up to this point, and begins to make his statement by showing rather than telling. Narrative impact begins to depend on the relationships of parts to wholes, the formal quality he admired most in the Italian mosaics and frescoes that had impressed him as a youth, and the central distinguishing characteristic of his best modernist works. As he discovered his own narrative methods, he began to put into action the primary theme of his "Great Novel": the necessity of translating into reality the idealistic desire to alert the world to its peril by striking on the moon, the desire to bring down the walls of Jericho.

One Man's Initiation: 1917
and the Beginning of Montage

Abandoning the metaphors of fairy tales, myths, and the Bible, Dos Passos tried to translate his idealism into action by publishing separately part IV of "Seven Times." That part of the manuscript, which takes Martin Howe into the war, was eventually placed with Allen and Unwin late in 1919. It appeared in print in October 1920 under a new name, *One Man's Initiation: 1917,* after some expurgations of passages the publishers felt were offensive on moral and religious grounds.

In terms of narrative technique, however, *Initiation* is a much more conventional novel than part III of "Seven Times" turned out to be. The war story adheres closely to Martin Howe's point of view, still a relatively romantic perspective until the end of the novel. The focus on the individual's perceptions carries through to the prevalent visual aesthetic as well. Descriptive passages are often impressionistic, but the novel signals a definitive move toward objective realism in the power of its images of war. They usually involve the actions of Martin and his fellow soldiers waiting for battle or in its aftermath, and the images' horrific power in these passages is achieved by a new minimalism, a new freedom from overt or implicit aesthetic allusions.

Perceiving the seeming disjunction between these two narrative elements, both contemporary and current critics of the novel have charged that its episodic structure undermines its effectiveness. Two recent critics, however, agree that there *is* a structural method to the novel, and both identify the principle as the opposition of vignettes. Michael Clark finds the most meaningful pattern of opposition in the alternation of Martin's war experiences with his perceptions of "elemental nature" (65) in the landscape and gardens of France. Linda Wagner locates the organizational pattern in "opposing views of war" (12). Against the "unrelieved horror of physical war," she writes, Dos Passos sets "the propagandist version of that war," creating a "graphic montage to duplicate the effect the sights of war have on Martin Howe's awareness" (12). The patterns that these critics discover in fact are both established in part by the alternating visual aesthetics Dos Passos uses in *Initiation*—the impressionist, and the realistic or sometimes expressionist image.

Martin's consciousness deepens as he grows out of his romantic idealism and confronts harsh reality. This growth is conveyed by these images and their relationships in a style that signals the growth of Dos Passos's own consciousness of narrative technique. In earlier works, such as the *Harvard Monthly* stories and *Streets,* Dos Passos at times seemed as dependent on literary and artistic allusions in establishing tone and character as his artist-figure protagonists were on their academic backgrounds for their identities. As a result, these earlier works seemed to borrow *their* identities from nineteenth-century European aesthetics. In the same way, American visual artists had begun as self-conscious imitators of European styles and subjects.

But as Dos Passos had explored in his 1917 to 1918 essays what would constitute an American art, he was ready to progress beyond uses of the past in his writing. Martin, too, is eager to shed the restrictions of the past—the limitations and lies of genteel society. By the time *Initiation* opens, with Martin on board ship crossing the Atlantic, he believes that his going to France to fight means that "a new white page [is] spread before him" (45). His life, he is convinced, is his to write; "an unopened book" (45) lies beside him on the deck. Michael Clark suggests that his "condition—his mind a tabula rasa—predisposes him to a direct pragmatic appreciation of the succeeding events" and thus makes of him an "American Adam" (62–63).

Certainly, Dos Passos was attempting in *Initiation* to pioneer a style that did not take its form from European aesthetics; but in the process of evolving that style, he recreated the aesthetic perceptions that earlier had made him aware that such a style was now necessary. These perceptions had come to him from the vantage point of France and Spain as he had compared European values, experiences, and aesthetics to those of his own country, seen the more clearly for his distance from them. Consequently, these oppositions are integral to the style of *Initiation;* and to establish the bases of these comparisons, Dos Passos shows that while Martin may believe his life "a new white page," his mind a "tabula rasa," as Clark suggests, he is in many ways still acting on the same romantic ideals that shaped all his previous experiences. Immediately after Martin articulates his independence, Dos Passos makes clear that Martin is not free of the old illusions. To link Martin to the past, Dos Passos returns to the impressionist visual images that in his earlier works were the primary vehicles for the subjective point of view. That aesthetic and that narrative stance recall the preoccupations of the romantic poets and painters and the impressionists' concerns that in some ways developed from the romantic focus on individual vision and how it registers the transience of time.

The persistence of Martin's subjective romanticism is underscored by the visual images the reader sees through Martin's eyes in the first chapter of the novel. From the deck of the *Chicago,* as he anticipates his new life, Martin watches the sunset "setting fire to opal sea and sky," then, as evening falls, watches them "growing claret colour, darkened to a cold bluish-green" (*Initiation,* 46). Here, Dos Passos depicts light as color and uses the changes in atmosphere to foreshadow the sad, inevitable changes in Martin's perceptions that the passing of time will soon bring about. With its high-key colors suggesting temporal concepts, the passage recalls the work of J. M. W. Turner in such paintings as *Fighting Temeraire* (1839). Romantic in concept, this seascape illustrates in its techniques how Turner "foreshadowed Impressionism" (de la Croix and Tansey, 684).

The *Temeraire* was second ship of the line in the English fleet that defeated the French and Spanish fleets at the battle of Trafalgar in 1805. By the time Turner painted the ship in 1836, steam technology had made such large, stately sailing vessels obsolete. Turner mourns the passing of the ship's era by showing the graceful ship, its tall sails furled, being towed out of service by a squat, grimy, steam-powered tugboat belching smut and cinders from its ugly, obtrusive smokestack. Balancing the composition's focus on the ships in the left-middle foreground, the sun descends in the right-middle foreground. Its warm opalescent light dissolves near the water into the claret color Dos Passos used in his description, then becomes a "cold bluish-green" (*Initiation,* 46) as sky and sea merge. Both narrative and painting signal the passing of one age to another, and in both images, the point of view romantically invests the lost age with a nobility utterly lacking in its technologically superior successor.

Usually, Dos Passos suggests the transitions in the world and in Martin's consciousness by juxtaposing a romantic or impressionist image against an expressionist one or an horrifically real vignette. In the journals he kept during the war and even much later in his 1968 introduction to the new edition of *Initiation,* he often discussed the impossibility of expressing the experience of war. He quickly realized that "talk" was "useless," that the "utter goddamned ridiculousness of things" left one with "no other recourse than the lame one of profanity" (*Fourteenth,* 94–98). This frustration is a common theme in the writings of war veterans. As he continued to try to articulate his impressions, Dos Passos obviously was determined to express what seemed inexpressible, an intention commonly stated by romantic theorists and writers as well. Faced with this narrative problem, Dos Passos once again turned to the visual arts for a method, taking pictorial techniques and creating tension between them and the war scenes he wrote down.

The technique is pervasive in *Initiation.* After the single opening example in which Dos Passos uses by itself the resonant Turneresque view of the twilight over the sea, he never again paints an impressionist image without an opposing realistic or expressionist image. Usually, and at their most effective, these paired images help the reader measure the progress of Martin's initiation. Sometimes, corresponding images in Dos Passos's own painting and drawing of the same period reinforce the sense of how close to his own consciousness were the effects of the experiences he writes about. Yet, because Dos Passos has discovered in the method of opposing images a technique more powerful than subjective revelation, readers of *Initiation* never feel as uncomfortably voyeuristic as they do reading *Streets*. In that earlier apprentice novel, Dos Passos had not yet developed the narrative skill to offset the distortions of characterization that often result from an inexperienced writer's lack of objectivity about the people and events on which his or her fiction is based.

Yet, even though his visual works of this period show how immediate were the experiences he was writing about, in *Initiation* the opposing visual images in the narrative create by themselves a powerful sense of Martin's experience without the need for Dos Passos to tell the reader how to react. In one of the best examples of these paired images, one of Martin's first days in Paris serves to open his mind. The first of two successive paragraphs containing these images depicts a scene of Paris café life typical of the impressionists' renditions of bourgeois Parisian society. Also typically impressionist or at least romantic is the emphasis in the passage on the individual consciousness of the moment. Martin sits at a sidewalk cafe reveling in the sensations of the city: "Opposite in the last topaz-clear rays of the sun, the foliage of the Jardin du Luxembourg shone bright green above deep alleys of bluish shadow. From the pavements in front of the mauve-colored houses rose little kiosks with advertisements in bright orange and vermilion and blue. In the middle of the triangle formed by the streets and the garden was a round pool of jade water. Martin leaned back in his chair looking dreamily out through half-closed eyes, breathing deep now and then of the musty scent of Paris" (*Initiation*, 54).

Suddenly, however, the war intrudes on his consciousness when a young veteran arrives at the next table. The second image abandons entirely the play of color and light and instead recounts in mechanically blunt details the sobering reality of wartime France: "As he stared in front of him two figures crossed his field of vision. A woman swathed in black crepe veils was helping a soldier to a seat at the next table. He found himself staring in a face, a face that still had some of the chubbiness of boyhood. Between the pale-brown frightened eyes, where the nose should have been, was a triangular black patch that ended in some mechanical contrivance with shiny little black metal rods that took the place of the jaw. He could not take his eyes from the soldier's eyes, that were like those of a hurt animal, full of meek dismay" (*Initiation,* 54). Although the narrative's focus is still on the individual consciousness, that consciousness now must begin to admit the reality of war. The progress of the narrative will be the process by which Martin's idealism is replaced by anger at the lies and exploitation perpetrated by his country and his pessimism about humanity's fate under enslaving institutions. Moreover, the idea that soldiers become machines, here expressed literally in the image of the soldier's prosthetic jaw, becomes a central theme in Dos Passos's next novel, *Three Soldiers.*

Two of Dos Passos's visual compositions from the same period that produced *Initiation,* 1917 to 1918, have much the same impact when compared to each other. Both undated but probably produced within the same year, one is a bright watercolor of a sidewalk cafe painted in an impressionist style. Green foliage surrounds lilac-shaded houses, trees and roofs rising just above the glowing yellow- and plum-colored awnings. It is a bright cosmopolitan scene reminiscent of Renoir in which color communicates lightness and forms the pleasing round shapes that constitute the picture's compositional dynamic. From the tone of gaiety it conveys, one can sense the feeling about Paris that Martin enjoys in the first image of the two paragraphs.

Equally in keeping with the tone of the second image is a pastel sketch from one of Dos Passos's wartime sketchbooks. In pastel crayon on taupe paper, Dos Passos depicts what seems to be a large, round electric-light fixture pouring yellow beams diagonally down upon the bent head and shoulders of a soldier. Both figures are only roughed in, so that it is difficult to be certain of Dos Passos's intentions in the sketch. But the light fixture looks more like a huge eyeball, with a blue center, connected by those diagonal beams to the soldier. The head of the man, wearing what looks like a military cap, seems in its quick outlines to be a skull. The eyes beneath the cap brim are merely empty holes, and the nose and mouth dark indentions. Visually, the figure of the soldier is linked to the eyeball-like light not only by the diagonal beams, which envelop him in a cone of yellow rays, but also by the bright blue suggestion of his shirt. It is a grim, expressionist image inviting a modernist reading. Perhaps the eye is the artist's, or merely an individual's consciousness opening wide to the unrelenting awareness of human mortality that was inescapable in those years in France. This is the visual shorthand, the shocking expressionist image, of an individual who has witnessed Verdun.

Occasionally, the romantic half of the paired images recalls a particular painter's work, perhaps not only in the painterly narrative technique but also in the subject matter. For instance, Martin's perception of the Cathedral of Notre Dame inevitably suggests Monet's images of the cathedral at Rouen in the changing light of morning or evening. One night, Martin ends up sleeping on the lawn facing Notre Dame after he refuses to spend the night with one of the girls his friends have picked up at a cafe. He is again clinging to his romantic ideals, rejecting the heavily rouged woman to dream instead "of the woman he would like to love tonight" (*Initiation*, 97). Roaming the dark streets, he lies down in front of the cathedral to look at the stars, an apt setting and pastime for a man who persists in idealizing love. When he wakes, a "pearly lavender mist [is] all about him, through which loom[ ] the square towers of Notre Dame and the row of kings across the facade and the sculpture about the darkness of the doorways" (*Initiation*, 99). Its iridescent colors, the indistinctness of its facade, and the sense of its protean quality in the changing light are also the visual elements of Monet's series of views of Rouen's cathedral (c. 1894).

But Dos Passos does not allow Martin or the reader to delight for very long in such beauty. Realistic images crowd out of Martin's mind the symbol of religious faith and cultural achievement before him: "He remembered the man he had once helped to pick up in whose pocket a grenade had exploded. Before that he had not realized that torn flesh was such a black red, like sausage meat" (*Initiation*, 99). As the narrative leaps from the impressionist "pearly lavender" of the cathedral to the stark "black red" of the mutilated soldier, the visual images by themselves communicate the impact of the war on Martin's awareness and how the process of that change actually occurs. Dos Passos thus has begun to achieve his narrative goal of creating "the thing itself" rather than "the name of the thing" ("What," 32).

He shows the reader in the remainder of the passage how jolting to Martin's humanism is his experience of battle. Martin pulls his thoughts back to the facade before him: "with nothing distinct yet to be seen, [there] were two square towers and the tracery between them and the row of kings on the façade and the long series of flying buttresses of the flank gleaming through the mist, and, barely visible, the dark slender spire soaring above the crossing" (*Initiation*, 100). The passage reminds the reader of Dos Passos's paintings of Notre Dame, as well as of Monet's views of Rouen's cathedral.

The sight reminds Martin of an abbey he had seen in the forest of the Argonne, "gleam[ing] tall in the misty moonlight; like mist, only drab and dense, the dust had risen above the tall apse as the shells tore it to pieces" (*Initiation,* 100). The juxtaposition shocks the reader as Dos Passos implies it shocked Martin. The tall, spectral ruin in the moonlight suggests the almost morbidly romantic *Cloister Graveyard in the Snow* (1810), by Caspar David Friedrich. Friedrich's unexpected applications of romantic ideas, techniques, and motifs produce in this painting an obsessive reminder of the omnipresence of death in the ruined Gothic cathedral, the hooded mourners, the tombstones. Dos Passos's image, while romantic in concept and impressionist in execution, introduces such a jarring element of reality that its impact communicates precisely the violence this perception does to Martin's consciousness.

Dos Passos still incorporates a few specific literary allusions into this work, but he integrates them into characterization and action much more successfully than in *Streets.* Martin is a bookish sort, just as Fanshaw was, but the few times Dos Passos allows Martin to recall particular authors' work, the reader is compelled to register the difference between Martin's former genteel life and his present existence in the war. For instance, at one point Martin recites William Blake's "Ah, Sunflower" to try to calm himself during a long bombardment. Dos Passos alternates stanzas with details of the shelling, another form of the montage technique he had begun to develop with visual images. And the poem; recounting how "the youth pined away with desire" and aspired to follow the sunflower's journey to a "far yellow clime" (3–5, quoted in *Initiation,* 121), serves the same purpose as the romantic visual images in their contrast with the realities of war.

Sometimes the images of war are themselves allusive. Dos Passos uses expressionistic colors or iconography in some instances to evoke the emotions of the soldiers. The intense emotion and baroque, unearthly uses of light and color in El Greco's fervent depictions of the Crucifixion (c. 1584–1594) inform some of Dos Passos's views of the battlefield, although Dos Passos undercuts the element of belief even as he invokes the image. In one passage, Martin passes in a ruined village a fallen crucifix "propped up . . . so that it tilted dark despairing arms against the sunset sky where the sun gleamed like a huge copper kettle lost in its own steam. The rain made bright yellowish stripes against the sky and dripped from the cracked feet of the old wooden Christ, whose gaunt, scarred figure hung out from the tilted cross." Martin notes the Christ's "cavernous eyes," meant by its "country sculptor ages ago" to represent "the utterest agony of pain." Suddenly, Martin sees that the traditional crown of thorns has been replaced by a circle of barbed wire, one of the war's most ubiquitous signs. Martin asks the figure, "What do You think of it, old boy? How do You like Your followers? Not so romantic as thorns, is it, that barbed wire?" (*Initiation,* 110, 111)

In this powerful scene, which Allen and Unwin cut from the first edition of the book on the grounds that it was irreligious, Dos Passos paints the suffering Christ against the livid sky to evoke a sense of the passion of belief, just as El Greco did. Dos Passos then uses the image with its barbed-wire crown to illustrate the hypocrisy of civilizations capable of professing such belief at the same time that they are perpetrating such an unthinkable war. He goes on to draw a parallel between the Christ image and the real sacrifices of the war, the passing soldiers, "faces drooped under the helmets, tilted to one side or the other, distorted and wooden like the face of the figure that dangled from the cross." Humanizing Christ, Dos Passos implies in the contrasting images of war just how little humankind benefited from his example and sacrifice as taught by the church. Through the ideas of Lully, one of the French soldiers whom Martin admires, Dos Passos expresses his view of the church as merely another of the "multitudinous tyrannies" that serve to control civilization (*Initiation,* 111, 161).

Late in the novel, Martin sums up much of the change that has taken place in his perspective: "All my life I've struggled for my own liberty in my small way. Now I hardly know if the thing exists." He is specifically terrified at the power of America's patriotic cant, religious rationalization, and the press to control the the thoughts of its citizens. In America, he asserts, "the darkness is using the light for its own purposes" to make of the people "slaves of bought intellect" (*Initiation* 158, 159). By the time the novel closes, with a dying soldier telling Martin that all his friends among the French soldiers have been killed, Dos Passos has created an experience of the war's impact on Martin's thinking.

Dos Passos's opposing visual images, the romantic-impressionist against the realistic-expressionist, convey implicitly the shock and disillusionment that Martin feels. For all its apprentice qualities, the first of Dos Passos's war novels manages to convey through its visual qualities the reasons for the writer's statement in his 1917 journal that he had begun to "think in gargoyles." These small horrific grotesques were included in the facades of medieval cathedrals to remind worshippers of the coming Apocalypse, of the unspeakable tortures and demons of the hell they risk at this Judgment if their faith should falter. Typical of Dos Passos's method of visual shorthand in the new narrative style he was evolving, this image of the gargoyle conveys his sense of how apocalyptic the war was, with "horror . . . so piled on horror that there can be no more" (*Fourteenth*, 89). For Dos Passos, as well as for Martin, the grotesque inhumanity of the war rendered trivial and obsolete all the methods he previously had used to "strike the moon" and make himself heard. In his efforts toward montage in *One Man's Initiation: 1917,* Dos Passos had discovered a modernist technique that he would refine and exploit to even greater effect in the two novels he would write within the next five years, *Three Soldiers* and *Manhattan Transfer.*

Chapter Seven

The Fragmented Consciousness in the Modernist World: *Three Soldiers*

The Part and the Whole

Paradoxically, Dos Passos based *Three Soldiers,* his most skillful evocation of World War I, largely on other soldiers' experiences, not on the personal impressions he had relied upon in *One Man's Initiation: 1917.* Once he had drained off into that apprentice novel the subjective intensity of the horrors of the war, he found the resulting objective distance a more effective narrative stance for the larger picture of the war he undertook next. Under circumstances radically different from the hellish immediacy of battle amid which he had begun *Initiation,* Dos Passos began *Three Soldiers* late in 1918 partly as a response to the regimented monotony of army life at Camp Crane, near Allentown, Pennsylvania, where he was stationed for training before returning to France as a member of the regular Army Medical Corps.

Now, however, after his experiences in the Norton-Harjes corps at the French front and the process of writing "Seven Times Round the Walls of Jericho" and *Initiation,* he knew what he wanted to say about the war, about the systems it represented to him, and about the individual's chances against those forces. But, as the increasing reliance on visual techniques in his "Great Novel" illustrated, he doubted the efficacy of words, of any of the narrative directions he had attempted, to voice his passionate concerns about individual liberty and meaningful action in the world as it had become.

Finally, in *Three Soldiers,* Dos Passos externalized the romantic, subjective quest of the artist figures whose consciousnesses controlled his earlier narratives. The protagonist's inchoate desire to strike the moon as a gong is now focused into conscious action with defined goals. The forces that threaten to obliterate the identity and voice of the individual are clearly embodied in and represented by the war. Defining these mechanistic forces and recognizing that the only defense against them is individual action, Dos Passos shifts the locus of meaning in the novel from the protagonist's consciousness to the construction of the novel and, by doing so, not only attempts his own meaningful gesture but also necessitates thoughtful action on the part of the reader.

In this first of his modernist novels, Dos Passos lets function dictate form: the novel's technical structure, dependent for its significance on the relation of parts to the whole, reflects the theme of the individual's relationship to the system he faces. And that system—the world and America transformed by the "technological revolution" of the modernist age—dictates the novel's very structure.[1] Only by demonstrating how machines—systems and ideologies—could manipulate human beings could Dos Passos hope to stir them to control the machines. To encompass and convey these complex interrelationships, he looked not to the debased language the systems themselves exploited, but to the visual vocabulary and iconography that more accurately reflected the problems and promise of the new world. In the gestural quality of the visual, the medium he felt came closest to uniting the sign and what it signified, he discovered his form. That form and its underlying visual aesthetic were modernist.

The War and the Individual

As recent and comprehensive social histories by Stephen Kern and Cecelia Tichi explain in engaging detail, the technological and cultural innovations that took place in the years between the turn of the century and the end of the war transformed "the dimensions of life and thought" in America and Europe.[2] Events and phenomena resulting from technological revolutions became bywords of daily life not only because the innovations ultimately affected the way the common person lived but also because the very technologies that caused such upheavals also created the means to communicate them quickly to the masses. When the *Titanic* sank in 1912, for instance, the tremendous loss of life resulted in part from the supreme confidence of its builders that the new technologies employed in its construction made it unsinkable. Yet despite the tragedy of the wreck, the media of the day commented frequently and with fascination on the fact that modern communications technology had not only made possible what rescue there was—10 ships had heard the *Titanic*'s wireless distress signal in the midnight ice fields of the North Atlantic—but also that the wireless system had told the whole world of the tragedy six hours after the collision.[3] The speed with which technologies interacted and had an impact on daily life resulted in a wholehearted and naive trust that the impact would be positive. Even a seemingly benign application of an innovation such as the motion-picture camera in the study of worker efficiency seemed to bespeak the subordination of human values to technological systems. By using the camera and electric lights to create "chronocyclegraphs" of the movements of bricklayers, Frank B. Gilbreth applied the mechanistic methods of efficiency engineer Frederick Winslow Taylor not only to prescribe procedures that could triple the workers' efficiency but also to build into the efficiency study an allowance for a set number of "Happiness Minutes" in the workers' monotonous routines (Kern, 116–17). Once again, the celebration of the technology that made such efficiency possible ignored the fact that such an application necessitated a formal allotment of minutes for the worker to spend being "happy."

Of course, the supreme test and application of the new technology was World War I. It seemed the definition of all the early-twentieth-century transformations in human conceptions of time and space and of the place of human beings in time and space. Perhaps the fervor of American religions and the patriotic support of the war, mirrored in the cant that Dos Passos so abhorred, was in part a defensive reaction against the ultimate dismantling of the cozy harmony among the individual, the world, the language, and God, a breakdown begun in the Victorian period.[4] This post–Victorian recognition that "each man is locked in the prison of his consciousness" caused early literary modernists to respond by acknowledging in their subjective narrative points of view that "man must start with the inner experience of the isolated self" (Miller, 8).

Dos Passos's apprentice fiction certainly acknowledges these realizations, but, as Cecelia Tichi points out, he strove also to expand that consciousness in his fully modernist works by introducing fragmentary glimpses of intersecting realities in the forms of his narrative devices. As he began to develop these techniques in *Three Soldiers,* however, he seemed to be searching for a way to expand the consciousness of the reader to arrive at the perceptions of culture and reality that the novel's narrative form reflects and creates. The *way* he achieved his purpose was, as Tichi concludes, by finding his "new omniscient design for fiction . . . in contemporary technology" (197) in *Manhattan Transfer* and *U.S.A.* But what he actually achieved, even in *Three Soldiers,* was to imbed theme so integrally in structure and style that the novel itself becomes the machine controlling the reader's consciousness in the same way that the military and social machines in the novel appropriate to their own purposes the individuals who compose the parts of the machines.

The systems producing the war seemed to Dos Passos the ultimate machine, as the chapter titles of *Soldiers* indicate. He suggests the machine's deadly power over the men who serve by constructing his chapters as a progression from "Making the Mould" (part I) that forms the soldiers, to the "Rust" (part IV) that corrodes them in the system, to their ultimate destruction "Under the Wheels" (part VI) of the powerful source. The war embodied for Dos Passos, as for so many other modernist artists, all the dislocations of time, space, and identity that the early twentieth century had wrought in human lives and the way these dislocations seemed to invalidate the significance of the individual.

The war provided a concrete marker between "Time Before," "the prewar idyll," and "Time After," "the wartime nastiness."[5] This gross temporal division reflects the way the war obliterated the prewar concept of "private time," of time as a function of individual perception so delicately portrayed by Proust or defined by Bergson. A single human definition of time had no place in an undertaking such as the Battle of the Somme, which depended for its success on the synchronization of thousands of British soldiers who, at precisely 7:30 on the morning of July 1, 1916, climbed out of their trenches and advanced en masse into no-man's-land (Kern, 288). The concept of public time, an issue to which in 1912 the Paris International Conference on Time had been devoted (Kern, 13), impinged on individual time: during the war, to effect synchronized mass movement, wristwatches were standard military equipment; and thereafter they replaced pocket watches almost entirely. The war "imposed homogenous time" on the individual consciousness (Kern, 288).

Just as the machine of war attempted to impose homogenous definitions of time, so it redefined concepts of space in terms of its own reductive ideologies. The temporal demarcations of "Time Before" and "Time After" had their spatial equivalents on the field of battle in the "gross dichotomy" (Fussell, 79) between safe territory and no-man's-land.[6] In *Initiation*, Martin Howe often describes the war zone in terms that originate in Dos Passos's own perceptions of it. In a 1917 letter to Rumsey Marvin, for instance, Dos Passos tries to characterize the indescribable monstrosity of battle itself by conveying a sense of its aftermath. He writes from somewhere near Verdun after the successful offensive there in August 1917, from a fantastic wood, once part of the forests of Argonne . . . smelling of poison gas, tangled with broken telephone wires, with ripped pieces of camouflage . . . , filled in every hollow with guns that crouch and spit like the poisonous toads of the fairytales. In the early dawn after a night's bombardment, it is the weirdest thing imaginable to drive through the woodland roads, with the guns of the batteries tomtomming about you. . . . A great labor it is to get through, too, through the smashed artillery trains, past piles of splintered camions and commissariat wagons. The wood before and since the attack . . . has been one vast battery—a constant succession of ranks of guns hidden in foliage, and dugouts, from which people crawl like gnomes when the firing ceases and to which you scoot when you hear a shell. (*Fourteenth*, 98)

Despite the "habit of simple distinction" (Fussell, 79) the war imposed about some matters, it did embody the ways in which technology had dismantled prewar conceptions of space and time, as the last few sentences of Dos Passos's picture demonstrate. The borders of no-man's-land, while they separated "a world . . . highly polarized," were nevertheless "constantly reforming" as territory was gained or lost from hour to hour (Kern, 302). Within that polarized world as well, once-established demarcations blurred: national or ethnic identities, religious affiliations, and social hierarchies broke down under the immediate exigencies of danger. Revolutions in communications technology and weaponry made it possible for commanders to order attacks on several different fronts simultaneously without ever being near any of them. The use of long-range weapons necessitated reconceptions of distance and time lapse and enabled armies to wage war without ever seeing the individual consequences. And bombs dropping from airplanes forced soldiers and civilians alike to rethink the dimensions of safety. For the first time in any war, attack was possible not only from land and sea but also from the air. Likewise, from the airplane itself, the war took on an entirely new perspective that included views of different fronts and separate movements all existing simultaneously.

The Cubist Aesthetic and the War

All of these new perceptions and conceptions of time and space, of the individual's relationship to the world, that the war embodied changed the very dimensions of ordinary life. Naturally, artistic expressions had to find a shape to fit them, to encompass somehow the world in "Time After." Nineteenth-century aesthetics, mimetic in basis, and even the impressionist aesthetic, allowing as it did for the transience of time, had not the scope or the complexity. As a paradigm of all these dislocations, the war constituted for many modernist artists the point of origin in their search for a new aesthetic. Even those who did not experience the war recognized its role in defining their time and direction. Looking back on the war in 1938, Gertrude Stein saw how it had both summarized and generated the spirit of her age and how that spirit in turn had engendered modernist art: "Really the composition of this war, 1914–1918, was not the composition of all previous wars, the composition was not a composition in which there was one man in the centre surrounded by a lot of other men but a composition that had neither a beginning nor an end, a composition of which one corner was as important as another corner, in fact the composition of cubism."[7]

The techniques of cubism were a creative response to the destruction of all the prewar traditional forms of thinking, ways of seeing, and structures of society. Artistically, the compositions of cubism had originated primarily out of Cézanne's attempts to redefine pictorial space. Since the Renaissance, painters had usually tried to create the illusion of space in a single plane as it exists in front of the fixed viewer in light and air. Following Cézanne's innovations of form, however, cubists based their compositions on the manner in which the human eye actually sees— with many discrete eye movements, from many different angles over the course of separate instants—and, thus, on the manner in which one actually perceives. Cubist pictorial space recognizes the interrelationship of time and space that Einstein had revealed to the world in 1905, a rethinking reflected in the technological revolutions of the modernist age and the war. In their attempt to "present the total essential reality of forms in space, and since objects appear not only as they are seen from one viewpoint at one time," cubists had to "introduce multiple angles of vision and simultaneous presentation of discontinuous planes" (de la Croix and Tansey, 729). The entire concept of subjective reality was splintered into a reconception of multiple, fragmented perceptions, a shift that reflects a changed view of the relationship between the individual and reality.

Indeed, cubism was defined by multiplicity and "simultaneity," as Dos Passos himself characterized the style he was developing during the war and just after, while in Paris in 1919 and 1920.[8] Although in the spring of 1919 he was still revising what became *Initiation,* by May he had already written three chapters of what he was then calling the "Sack of Corinth." As he began this new work, he conceived of it as a bildungsroman structured something like "Seven Times" (Ludington 1980, 179), whose title, with its mythical-historical implications for his intended theme, suggests the close connection in his mind between the two works in progress. But by early spring of 1920, after the artistic and political ferment of Paris in 1919 and his reacquaintance with the fierce individualism of Spain when he visited there from 1919 to 1920, he fragmented the narrative consciousness of the new work into three characters. He also developed a new narrative structure that completely abandoned the traditional pattern of the bildungsroman; and he chose a new title, *Three Soldiers,* that reflected something of the multiplicity and simultaneity he tried to achieve in the novel.

Although Dos Passos's new form had not yet developed the fully modernist, cubist structure of *Manhattan Transfer* and *U.S.A., Three Soldiers* did use some of the basic techniques of cubism and, in its descriptive aesthetic, often acknowledges the applicability of cubist fragmentation, multiplicity, and simultaneity. Journal entries from around the time of the novel's inception at Camp Crane show that even in 1918 he was beginning to see places and scenes in images far more similar to a cubist aesthetic than to the impressionist or expressionist aesthetics that had been primary visual directions in "Seven Times" and *Initiation.* During his first week at Camp Crane, Dos Passos pictured a Sunday afternoon activity, the camp band playing in an oak grove for the soldiers and their visitors, in pictorial terms of fragmented forms of color, light, and intersecting lives: "The instruments glitter—silver facets of sun—in the mottled varying shadow of the tall oak-trees and men and women walk to and fro—and soldiers—mostly soldiers—changing patterns like the bits of a picture puzzle cut into scraps by the alternation of sun and shade—shifting and forming into pictures—purple and blue, drab yellow and lilac against a background of khaki—mostly khaki—Questing faces of homely young women—questing faces of reddish healthy youth" (*Fourteenth,* 212).

This is the pictorial sense that infused *Three Soldiers* also, a cubist aesthetic built of juxtaposed planes, dependent for its effect on the actual process of seeing. Dos Passos uses such descriptive techniques often to convey the intensity of battle as it both focuses the soldiers' consciousnesses on the moment and fragments them into simultaneous perceptions of all that impinges in that instant. For example, chapter 2 of "Machines" opens on Chrisfield, one of the soldiers, alone in woods "ringing with a sound like hail" as "batteries 'pong, pong, pong' in the distance":

As far as he could see in every direction were the grey trunks of beeches
bright green with moss on one side. . . . In front of him his eyes followed
other patches of olive-drab moving among the tree trunks. Overhead,
through the mottled light and dark green of the leaves he could see now
and then a patch of heavy grey sky, greyer than the silvery trunks that
moved about him in every direction as he walked. He strained his eyes
down each alley until they were dazzled by the reiteration of mottled
grey and green. Now and then the rustling stopped ahead of him, and
the olive-drab patches were still.[9]

In such descriptions, Dos Passos overlays intersecting realities, such as
Chrisfield's minute-by-minute processing of danger and the incongruent
stillness of the forest, in compositions whose modernist visual quality
underscores their modernist wartime sensibility.

In *Three Soldiers,* the organic world has been invaded by the machine
and so no longer unequivocally represents "a basis for . . . faith in man"
or "an ideal state of wholeness," as Clark asserts (87). While nature does
at times constitute a healing escape for Andrews, the artist figure to
whom Dos Passos devotes the greatest attention, in the end not even the
pastoral village in the Loire valley to which Andrews escapes as a
deserter is free from the insidious military machine. It is there, at Poissac, where lindens blossom beside the "blue and silver and slate-colored"
river (*Three,* 432), that he is betrayed to the military police. His last
sight as he is taken away under arrest is the windmill "turning, turning"
against the sky (433), the machine in the garden. Unlike the presentation of nature as a state of "wholeness" in the earlier works (Clark, 87),
in *Three Soldiers* nature becomes merely one more fragmentary element
in the composition of a war landscape.

Indeed, as perceptions such as Chrisfield's earlier illustrate, the very
colors and structures of nature were subsumed into and synthesized by
the modernist aesthetic. As Gertrude Stein exclaims in her memoir
about Picasso, the war adopted and helped generate the forms of
cubism. She came to this realization when she and Picasso first saw a
camouflaged truck on the Boulevard Raspail in Paris: "It was at night,
we had heard of camouflage but we had not yet seen it and Picasso
amazed looked at it and then cried out, yes it is we who made it, that is
cubism" (11).

Certainly cubism was one of those movements that was "in the air"
("What," 30) of Paris in 1919 while Dos Passos was writing *Three Soldiers.* The work of painters such as Picasso, Modigliani, and Gris stimu-

lated Dos Passos's "interest in experimentation" ("Contemporary," 26). But he had been exposed to examples of cubism even earlier, during college, at the 1913 Armory Show. In Marcel Duchamp's 1912 *Nude Descending a Staircase,* the most controversial work in the show, he had seen a paradigm of the central concepts of cubism in the French artist's "sophisticated union of the phenomenon of movement and the immobile surface of a canvas on which it is portrayed."[10] As an artistic response to the twentieth-century reconception of time and mobility, cubism was related to futurism, another European modernist movement.

Futurism

In fact, Dos Passos had probably seen more of futurist art and absorbed more of its sensibility than he had of cubist art at the time he was writing *Three Soldiers.* In the autumn of 1917, he had traveled south through France into Italy and down the Mediterranean coast with a Norton-Harjes ambulance convoy dispatched to aid the wounded of the Italian forces who had just been defeated by the Austrians. The ambulance volunteers on the long, slow drive had to deal with the mechanical vagaries of their worn Ford and Fiat vehicles, the British disdain for the Italians, and the "simplemindedness and ignorance of the Italians" (*Fourteenth,* 116), an opinion Dos Passos ruefully admitted, in addition to the usual frustrating routine of long waits punctuated by short bursts of frantic duty. Dos Passos took advantage of the idle periods to immerse himself once again in the Italian Renaissance art whose variety and forms had caught his imagination when he was a young teenager on his grand tour. But the futurists, early-twentieth-century Italian modernists, had introduced a revolutionary, new artistic spirit into Italy, and he was "much enlivened" by these artists, whose works he bought "in a bookshop in the Galleria in Milan on [his] way to the Piave and the Brenta" ("What," 29).

In its artistic philosophy and practice, futurism anticipated much of what Dos Passos was attempting in his fiction by the time he undertook *Three Soldiers* in 1917. In general, futurism aimed "to transform the mentality of an anachronistic society" by "revitalizing . . . the traditional arts of painting, sculpture, poetry, music, architecture" (Tisdall and Bozzolla, 7), and especially prose. True to its revolutionary spirit, the chief purveyor of the movement had published "The Founding and Manifesto of Futurism," an article that set out its goals, on the front page of the

major newspaper *Le Figaro* in February 1909. Excited by the way modern technology was revolutionizing and expanding the world, the futurists attempted to reform art and society as a response to "the complete
renewal of human sensibility brought about by the great discoveries of
science" (quoted in Tisdall and Bozzolla, 8). That the artist figure must
act and speak meaningfully in the world rather than ineffectually wish
to strike at the moon, Dos Passos's recurrent metaphor for keeping the
immediacy of life at a safe emotional distance, had been a developing
imperative in his fiction ever since *Streets of Night*. The fates of Wenny in
that novel and of James Clough in "Seven Times" expressed Dos Passos's
pessimism about whether art could have any impact on life. Now, in the
work of the futurists, he found exuberant reinforcement for his idealism
about politicizing art.

   Moreover, the futurists' techniques both in the visual and the literary
arts were consonant with his own goals. The futurists' visual aesthetic
drew on symbolism and divisionism, a technique that, like cubism, depended on the viewer's eye to assimilate disparate dots of pure color
that represented light, hue, and form and that yielded the heightened
sense of color the futurists sought. Some futurist painters adopted cubist
techniques of fragmentation to achieve the sense of simultaneous
motion they tried to express. Responding to the new perception of the
world as "a flux of movement and interpenetration" (Tisdall and Bozzolla, 32) made possible by modern photography and scientific techniques, the futurists, again like the cubists, worked to convey the sense
that "all things move, all things run, all things are rapidly changing"
("Technical Manifesto of Futurist Painting," quoted in Tisdall and Bozzolla, 33). In keeping with the futurists' glorification of urban life, technology, and speed, and their conviction that society could only be transformed through violence, their paintings often employed urban scenes
with masses of people in violent, apocalyptic motion. Thus, a common
dynamic in these paintings is the vortex. Paintings such as Umberto
Boccioni's *The City Rises* (1910), *Riot in the Galleria* (1910), and *Raid*
(1911) use divisionist brush strokes to create the motion of the swirl of
light and human movement composing an anarchic force sweeping
through the city. Dynamic and subject combine in them to "place the
spectator in the centre of the picture" (Tisdall and Bozzolla, 8), as the
futurist painters intended, positing an interactive art akin to the cubists'
but with a far more overtly political purpose.

   In subject, purpose, and dynamic as well, Dos Passos's fully modernist work suggests the futurists' influence. The whirl of activity and

the sometimes aimless circularity of life in New York City emerge in the spatial image of the vortex that recurs in *Manhattan Transfer,* as Clark notes (104). Like the futurists, Dos Passos intended for his modernist techniques to involve the viewer or the reader, on whose responses to the diverse narrative elements the work's meaning depends. Likewise, the sense of simultaneous interpenetrating lives in *Three Soldiers* as well as in the later modernist works shows affinities with the futurist painters' declaration: "The sixteen people around you in a rolling motor bus are in turn and at the same time one, ten, four, three; they are motionless and they change places. . . . The motor bus rushes into the house it passes, and in their turn the houses throw themselves upon the motor bus and are blended with it" ("Technical Manifesto of Futurist Painting," quoted in Tisdall and Bozzolla, 33–34).

The literary goals of the futurists seemed also to anticipate Dos Passos's direction. Futurist writers such as Marinetti drew from the same sources that had influenced Dos Passos: "Zola's earthy naturalism, Walt Whitman's songs of life, Emile Verhaeren's exultant faith in the science of the future," and the symbolist poets. To expand the boundaries of culture to encompass "the dawning century of speed, mobility and unprecedented scientific advance," the futurists felt that they must invent "a new dimension of language" (Tisdall and Bozzolla, 89, 7). Their desire to expand the conventional capabilities of language was an early modernist version of Dos Passos's avowed attempt, in his later modernist works, to make the words "stand up off the page" ("What," 31), to create, as one futurist manifesto declared as the movement's goal, "Words-in-Freedom" (Tisdall and Bozzolla, 95).

To accomplish this goal, futurist writers destroyed conventional syntax, created dynamic rhythms, explored the possibilities of onomatopoeia, and exploited the signifying potential of graphic arrangements and typefaces on the page. Calling attention in these ways to the arbitrary relationship between signifier and signified in language, using language in new ways to involve the reader interactively with the text, they were attempting much the same kind of experimentation that Dos Passos developed into his characteristic modernist style in *Manhattan Transfer* and, especially, *U.S.A.* Futurist writers, such as Marinetti in *Zang Tumb Tuum* (1914) and Francesco Cangiullo in *Free-word Painting* (1915), tried as Dos Passos did to express the thing itself, not just the name of the thing, combining visual representation and verbal signifiers to create something akin to what the late-twentieth-century avant-garde would call performance art. Such experiments provided the basis for later avant-garde movements such as dadaism and surrealism that developed during the modernist explosion in the arts. The gestural quality of the futurists' art foreshadows the recurrent image in Dos Passos's work of the moon as a gong to strike and be heard. The futurists' insistence on pushing art past academic barriers to reach and seize the masses is mirrored in the impulses of Wenny and James Clough and Martin Howe to "abandon . . . shallow bohemian aestheticism and to agitate against a complacent culture," as Ludington notes of futurism's appeal for Dos Passos (Ludington 1980, 145).

Perhaps the primary commonality between Dos Passos and the futurists was their synthesis of all the arts, particularly the literary and the visual. As a primary example of such futurist synthesis, Marjorie Perloff cites and discusses extensively *La Prose du Transsiberien et de la Petite Jehanne de France,* a 1913 text created by Blaise Cendrars and Sonia Delaunay.[11] Cendrars, a Swiss poet who adopted France as his homeland, advertised the text containing his poem and Delaunay's illustrations as "le Premier livre simultané"—the first simultaneous book ("Bulletin de Souscription," quoted in Perloff, 7). To reinforce the idea of simultaneity, the abstract, brightly colored, rhythmic discs and shapes of Delaunay's "coulours simultanées" share with Cendrars's poem the volume's one long, continuous page, over $6^1/_2$-feet long and 2-feet wide.[12] The pure, intense color and rhythm of her synchromist style and that of her husband, Robert Delaunay, may have influenced Dos Passos's illustrations for his 1927 book of essays, *Orient Express* (Knox, 27).

The poem itself suggests why Dos Passos responded to Cendrars's work, so much so, in fact, that he later painted a series of watercolor illustrations for his translation of Cendrars's 1931 volume *Le Panama et mes sept oncles,* in which *La Prose* appears. Simultaneity is not only the poem's "structural principle" (Perloff, 14) but also its theme.[13] The "Transsiberien" of the title is the railway whose completion in 1905 linked Russia to the Pacific, and "Jehanne" is a prostitute in Montmartre. The narrative recounts a journey from Moscow to Harbin on the train, but it is presented in a series of vignettes like "successive camera shots" so that spatial and temporal dislocations result in "slippage, [an] erasing of contours . . . on the level of narrative or imagery or syntax" (Perloff, 14).

Ultimately, although the poem celebrates technology, it depicts unflinchingly the horrors of the war. The same kind of ambivalence about the new age of technology marks Dos Passos's great modernist works, although by 1925 in *Manhattan Transfer,* Dos Passos is somewhat more pessimistic than the exuberant Cendrars. Only a year after publishing *La Prose,* Cendrars himself lost his right arm fighting for the French Foreign Legion. Yet he believed fervently in the cause of his adopted homeland even when he and Dos Passos met in the late 1920s, a time when Dos Passos was constructing his chronicles of his own nation. Always political in intent, futurism in fact became an extremely nationalistic movement late in the war. Marinetti later became a staunch supporter of Mussolini, a political direction not unlike that of Ezra Pound, whose manifesto "Vortex" (1916) in the periodical *BLAST* helped introduce futurist ideas in England.

Dos Passos and the "Writerly" Text

The value of futurism for modernist art, however, and specifically for Dos Passos's development was in its revolutionary techniques, its synthesis of the arts, its involvement of the audience, and its "freeing the word" in ways that anticipated postmodern critical theories. More than a half-century after Marinetti published his first futurist manifesto, Roland Barthes in his book *S/Z* reiterated many of the same notions in late-twentieth-century theoretical language, but, like the futurists, focusing ultimately on the role of art in culture and politics.

Barthes divides texts into two categories, the "readerly" and the "writerly."[14] Readerly writing prefers "all of the values implicit in the paradigmatic classic text—unity, realism, and transparency" (Silverman, 242). Because the readerly or classic text purports to depict a reality that preexisted and of which the text is only a portion and image, readerly writing is bound to observe the traditionally agreed-upon relationship between signifier and signified, to propel the reader necessarily upon a linear course that the author determines. As Barthes observes, "the *direction* of meaning determines the . . . management functions of the classic text: the author [goes] . . . from signifier to signified" (174). In such a classic order, then, existing cultural values are reinforced. The author implicitly insists that words, or signifiers, have a "true" or "literal" meaning (Silverman, 240), or signified, an enforcement of meaning that invests the author with the power of a god (Barthes, 174). The readerly text pretends to be a picture of reality, thus "attempt[ing] to conceal all traces of itself as a factory within which a particular social reality is produced through standard representations and dominant signifying practices" (Silverman, 244).

Dos Passos's texts before *Three Soldiers* illustrate most of these characteristics of the classic text, especially the controlling "private conscious-

ness" of the narrator as a determinant of reality, a narrative framework
Silverman (244) attributes also to *Künstlerromane* such as James Joyce's
Portrait of the Artist As a Young Man. Within the private consciousness of
the protagonist in Dos Passos's early apprentice novels, however, there is
always a search for some way of transcending the traditional limits of
language as defined by the readerly text, a search that is a paradigm of
the character's impulse to obliterate the boundaries of conventional culture that the readerly text prescribes. After all the facets of his war experience, however, after Paris in 1919 and Spain the next year, and after
sufficient distance to process all that he saw, Dos Passos began to find
the methods—usually in the practices of the visual arts—to realize his
characters' clearly autobiographical quests for a new way of speaking, a
new way of understanding, and a new meaning. And as he became more
adept at integrating his purposes into his style, he expanded the quest
beyond his characters' consciousnesses into the structures of the text
itself, relinquishing to a great degree the traditional godlike role of the
author and placing the responsibility for meaning on the reader. The
result, beginning in *Three Soldiers* but reaching full development in
U.S.A., was what Barthes later labeled the "writerly" text.

  As Barthes defines it, the writerly text depends for its meaning on the
"infinite play of signification" (Silverman, 246), that is, on the multiple
possibilities inherent in the relationships among its parts. It disengages
the signifier from any necessary meaning; in place of the linear movement from signifier to signified prescribed by the classic text, the writerly
text creates "units of meaning" that are "cut up into a series of brief,
contiguous fragments" (Barthes, 13). Because it is segmented, it draws
the reader's attention "not only to the seams which join together the
pieces which make up the whole, but to the ways in which the former
exceed the latter." Thus, the writerly text "denies the possibility of closure," requiring of the reader participation "in an on-going manufacture
of meaning" (Silverman 246–47).

  This definition describes exactly the structural principle of Dos Passos's fully achieved modernist style, particularly that of *U.S.A.,* a trilogy
to which, as Barthes says of the ideal writerly text, "we can gain access
. . . by several entrances, none of which can be authoritatively declared
to be the main one" (5–6). Although *Three Soldiers* is far closer to the
readerly norm than is *U.S.A.,* its structural principle of segmentation—
the fragmentation of the narrative consciousness and the concomitant
writerly distance from the text—is a distinct departure from the classical linear narrative techniques of all the earlier apprentice works. The

semiotic, segmented structure of *Three Soldiers* constitutes a sensitive technical response to all the intersecting political, cultural, technological, and artistic dimensions of the modernist world: the ambiguities of the war, the paradoxes of the new technology, and the impact of it all on the artists who answered with futurist and cubist innovations.

The Film Aesthetic

Like those artists, Dos Passos sought to capture the essence of the age and, characteristically, found his new narrative direction in the aesthetic that seemed most accurately to embody the multiplicity and simultaneity of the world as it had become—in the techniques of the cinema. He realized quickly the potential of the medium that, in the short time between its inception in the late 1890s and its widespread commercialization in the early 1900s, incorporated the highest achievements of photographic technology, as filmmakers learned to manipulate "real time and real space" through editing techniques.[15] The new medium was not "subject to the laws of empirical reality" (Cook, 14), a quality that made it the perfect vehicle to communicate the "sense of simultaneity and omnipresence" necessary to offer "a fleeting synthesis of life in the world" ("The Futurist Cinema," quoted in Kern, 72), as the futurists themselves apotheosized film in a 1916 manifesto. For the futurists, it was "a romance made in heaven" (Kern, 72).

The techniques of the cinema also seemed made to order for Dos Passos's new writerly direction, as both he and the critics have acknowledged. In 1968, very late in his life, Dos Passos still credited film technique as a stylistic influence, as he had in memoirs and interviews previously. During his time in Paris during the postwar explosion in the arts, he wrote in the *National Review,* he came to believe that he must "record the fleeting world the way the motion picture film recorded it," using "contrast, juxtaposition, montage" ("What," 31). Literary critics tracing the evolution of Dos Passos's style have routinely cited montage as one of the primary structuring elements of both *Manhattan Transfer* and *U.S.A.*[16] Most proceed from Dos Passos's own assertion that he had become "interested in Eisenstein's montage while . . . working on *Manhattan Transfer,*" though he goes on to concede that he did not remember the circumstances "exactly."[17] Perhaps the most accurate and detailed recent discussion of Dos Passos's use of montage appears in an unpublished manuscript by Thomas Evans.[18] In it, Evans sorts out the varieties of montage developed by its early practitioners and demonstrates that

Dos Passos's memory was indeed faulty. In 1981, Michael Spindler came to the same conclusion. Since Eisenstein's first film did not premiere until 1925 in Russia and was never shown in America, and since his articles on his methods were not published in America until 1927, his work could not have influenced the writing of *Manhattan Transfer* in 1923 and 1924 (402–3). In fact, Evans concludes, the filmmaker whose work Dos Passos would have had the greatest opportunity to see before 1925 was the American D. W. Griffith.

Griffith's innovations in film editing anticipated those of Eisenstein, Vertov, and Pudovkin, Russians whose work did most likely help shape the devices of *U.S.A.* In terms of Dos Passos's earlier work, however, Griffith's first two feature-length films, *Birth of a Nation* (1915) and *Intolerance* (1916), set two important precedents. First, in these films, Griffith developed almost all of the montage effects that would become technical commonplaces in American film through the 1930s (Evans, 4). Particularly applicable to Dos Passos's style are the techniques of continuity editing and of dramatic crosscutting. Continuity editing juxtaposes discontinuous images of "shots" to create the sense of ongoing motion over a period of time, thereby collapsing space and time and freeing the narrative from real time in its chronology. Dramatic crosscutting further exploits the juxtaposition of shots not only to drive the narrative forward temporally and spatially but also to suggest meaning through the relationships between each of the successive images. The second achievement of significance to Dos Passos's style was that Griffith used his techniques to create what he intended as epics of the American nation (Cook, 78).

The controversy surrounding the release of *Birth of a Nation* revealed for the first time some compelling and ambiguous truths about the medium that would come to be America's most popular and, to the world, almost a metaphor for American civilization. The techniques Griffith had developed had tremendous manipulative potential and would constitute a powerful political force over the masses. Moreover, these editing techniques communicated the illusion of objectivity because, to most viewers, there was no obvious authorial presence. The problems of objectivity and the ideological force inherent in artistic structure would come to be central concerns for Dos Passos as he became a more skilled artist and a more political one as well, beginning with *Three Soldiers* and continuing through his great modernist works.

In *Three Soldiers,* he searched for a form equal to his themes. His knowledge of the military and of his country's reasons for entering the war, and his experience of the war itself, had compelled him to conclude "that human society has been always that, and perhaps will be always that: organizations growing and stifling individuals, and individuals revolting helplessly against them, and at last forming new societies to crush the old societies and becoming slaves again in their turn" (*Three*, 421). This was the despairing outcry against social determinism that Dos Passos expressed through John Andrews, the character in *Three Soldiers* most like himself. Besides defining for the first time the theme of systems overpowering individuals that would become the focus of his greatest works, *Three Soldiers* is the first of his novels in which he seeks a method to depict America's diversity. His technique here is to abandon for the most part the "private consciousness" of the central character and, instead, to create three protagonists. Each is from a different region of the United States and from a different social class: Dan Fuselli, a clerk in an optical-goods store, is a working-class man from San Francisco; Chris Chrisfield is an uneducated farm boy from Indiana; and John Andrews comes from declining Virginia aristocracy, grew up in a rural "dilapidated mansion" (31), finished college, and has been living in New York City trying to establish himself as a musician and composer.[19]

Andrews bears all the earmarks of the typical Dos Passos protagonist in the earlier novels—the upper-class background, the impulse to escape the stifling bell glass of his education and upbringing, and the ambition to express himself in some lasting way. Once again, Dos Passos uses artistic allusions as a means of characterization but far less often than in his previous novels, and, unlike those in earlier works, the allusions never seem gratuitous. Although Andrews occasionally sees landscapes in descriptions (275, 281, 298, 351) that bring reminders of the impressionist paintings Dos Passos was executing around this time, he attributes explicit allusions to Andrews to suggest the shock of military regimentation to his enlightened individualism and to delineate his artistic goals.

When he is wounded in France, for instance, he is hospitalized in a converted Renaissance hall whose ceiling is decorated with carvings of satyrs and warriors and village scenes. Andrews's impressions of them as he lies in bed looking up at the ceiling recall the sense of vitality and diversity that attracted Dos Passos to the Italian Renaissance frescoes and paintings he discussed in his 1912 journals and again when he returned to Italy during the war. To Andrews, the carvings seem a bit grotesque, almost like gargoyles. They suggest to him "the incarnation of old rich lusts, of clear fires that had sunk to dust ages since" (201), the quality of existence being obliterated by the massive impersonality of twentieth-century mechanical civilization. Lying there among the "wounded men [who are] discarded automatons, broken toys laid away in rows" (201), Andrews finally comes to feel that "people enjoy[ ] hating" and that "civilization [is] nothing but a vast edifice of sham, and the war . . . its fullest and most ultimate expression" (210). He makes up his mind to take whatever action he can against these dehumanizing forces, to desert as soon as possible. Once he has reached this decision, the Renaissance carvings no longer seem "grimacing" (201), but instead seem to be "wriggling out of their contorted positions and smiling encouragement to him" (211).

Andrews's artistic goals before his decision to desert reflect the cloistered aesthetic sensibility that Dos Passos himself had finally rejected as inadequate to the artist's responsibilities in the world. The musical composition Andrews had been working on before his induction is titled "The Queen of Sheba." The title and what the reader learns about the work when Andrews plays part of it for his aesthete female friend Geneviève Rod reveal its connection to symbolist art. The composition, Andrews tells her, is based on the episode in Flaubert's *La Tentation de Saint Antoine* in which the Queen of Sheba visits the saint to test once again his much-assailed virtue. As the discussion in chapter 3 noted of Dos Passos's artistic influences during his Harvard days, the legend of St. Anthony fascinated him, as it had the symbolists and the aesthetes, and indeed artists and writers for centuries. The saint's trials "cast a spell upon popular imagination" (Seznec, 88) partly because of their archetypal nature, but probably also because the guises his demons assumed offered such fantastic imaginative possibilities for artistic interpretations. Artists as diverse in time and orientation as Matthias Grunewald and Hieronymous Bosch in the sixteenth century, Cézanne in the nineteenth century, and Louis Guglielmi and Salvador Dali in the twentieth century have depicted St. Anthony's demons in the iconography of their own times. Symbolists such as Odilon Redon and Puvis de Chavannes were attracted by the rich descriptive qualities of Flaubert's adaptation of the legend.

Andrews's use of the story not only connects his prewar aesthetic with those effete artists but also suggests that they share the goal of letting the work speak for itself, of creating the work as a self-sufficient world. The preciousness of some of their methods aside, the symbolists did lay "the foundations of Modernist attitudes towards the arts" (Lucie-Smith, 55, 54). Like Dos Passos, Andrews seeks to articulate his individual vision of the increasingly mechanistic world by a method that will transcend the limitations of conventional forms of communication. For Andrews, the method is his music, at first associated with the symbolist and modernist qualities of the work of Debussy (374), changing later to an explicitly American political theme, the death of the abolitionist John Brown. Dos Passos himself, attracted by Debussy's synthesis of music and poetry (Ludington 1980, 180), had returned several times to his 1902 avant-garde opera *Pelléas and Melisande* while he was writing *Three Soldiers.*[20]

The method Dos Passos chose in *Three Soldiers,* however, was cinematic. In fact, throughout the novel, the only artistic allusions besides those that help characterize Andrews refer to film. The very first part, "Making the Mould," establishes the significance of film as both a structural principle and a thematic pointer in the novel.

Structurally, part 1 uses cinema and cinematic techniques to draw the reader's attention to the importance of the relationship of parts to the whole. Chapters 1 through 3 introduce the three protagonists and zoom in and out on them, a series of cinematic cuts from character to character that achieves a narrative unity when the three soldiers end up seated next to each other at a movie shown for the camp. After mutual introductions, Chrisfield comments to Fuselli on the fact that they represent a spectrum of America: "You're from the Coast, this feller's from New York, and Ah'm from ole Indiana, right in the middle" (26). Obviously, Dos Passos has not yet full confidence either in his reader or in his narrative structure's ability to speak for itself. Yet, having presented his characters in fairly economically edited establishing shots, he uses the circumstances under which he now brings them together to allow the language of cinema to articulate his themes.

The power of film as propaganda serves as a synecdoche for the overwhelming force of the military system. Dos Passos had written in his journal at Camp Crane that the biggest event in camp life besides "mess time" was the movies—"every night out in the open air in the grand stand." He judged the "pathetic state" that the ennui and regimentation of Army routine had reduced him to by the undiscriminating "delight" with which he fell under the spell of these films (*Fourteenth,* 220). The tremendous power of film to manipulate emotions that he perceived in his own reactions he depicts with sinister accuracy when his three soldiers watch what is evidently a film laden with propaganda. It presents a vision of war as slanted and sentimentalized as Griffith's view of the old South in *Birth of a Nation.* As the three watch, the movie "unfold[s] scenes of soldiers in spiked helmets marching into Belgian cities full of little milk carts drawn by dogs and old women in peasant costume" (27). Even such contrived scenes inspire the soldiers to "hate the Huns" (26) viciously—and, for the Army, usefully. "I'd give a lot to rape some of those goddam German women" (27), one soldier declares. Another agrees, mouthing the party lines and jingoistic diction of the American military in the Great War: "They're . . . full of the lust for power like their rulers are, to let themselves be governed by a bunch of warlords like that" (27).

Dos Passos reiterates the dangers of the collective mentality in the reactions of Andrews, who ultimately becomes the novel's conscience: "Andrews felt blind hatred stirring like something that had a life of its own in the young men about him. He was lost in it, carried away in it, as in a stampede of wild cattle" (27). Presciently, Dos Passos demonstrates the leveling effects of what became a "uniquely democratic art form" (Kern 208), suggesting again in this scene the huge force exploiting the potential of film. When Andrews looks about him in the darkened movie hut, he sees not individuals but "one organism" united in "common slavery" (26). Film, Dos Passos suggests, is one more form of modern technology that the systems of government will use to obliterate individual will and power. It is a particularly insidious weapon, he demonstrates here.

Nor is the impact of film on the soldiers' consciousnesses limited to this instance. Fuselli, the working-class representative, is depicted as especially susceptible to the simplistic, emotional exploitations of the movies. Even before the crosscutting unites these characters at the movies, shots of Fuselli illustrate that he already thinks in images shaped by what he has seen at the movies. To him, promotion constitutes the apex of achievement; he "picture[s] himself [in] long movie reels of heroism" (17) attaining his goal. Dos Passos thus equates in somewhat elitist terms the unsophisticated soldier's acquiescence to the system and his unquestioning acceptance of the values and iconography constructed by the movies. In fact, Fuselli often uses the movies as a touchstone for evaluating his own experiences and ambitions. Incited to patriotic frenzy by news of mobilization and by "The Star-Spangled Banner," he pictures being "over there": "He was in a place like the Exposition ground, full of old men and women in peasant costume. . . . Men in spiked helmets who looked like firemen kept charging through, like the Ku-Klux Klan in the movies. . . . Those were the Huns" (37). Fuselli seems to have been impressed by Griffith's racially inflammatory epic, so powerful in its technical brilliance; perhaps he had also seen *The Life of an American Fireman,* Edwin S. Porter's 1903 film that established the "illusion of separate but simultaneous and parallel actions [as a] basic structural element of cinematic narrative" (Cook, 20).

When Fuselli asks, as early as the first chapter, "Goin' to the movies . . . ?" of a minor character named, ironically, "Mr. Eisenstein,"[21] the soldier is acknowledging in his inarticulate way that the men at the camp, Americans who will fight in the war, have learned the common vocabulary of the "new language form [that] came into being at the turn of the twentieth century, an audio-visual language form which first took the shape of cinema" (Cook, xv). Yet, naive and uneducated both about the power of the new language to shape ideas and actions and about the lack of scruples with which systems will exploit the language, Fuselli will become a victim of the system's indifference. Having "got in wrong" with his superiors and having contracted a venereal disease, he ends up "on permanent K.P." (302–3). Not only is Fuselli easy prey to the visual language of the cinema but also he buys easily into the military's distortions of verbal language as well. Words such as "entrainment" and "order of march" fill him with a "strange excitement" that evokes "[m]emories of movies" (35). Such an explicit linking of the two languages leads inescapably to the recognition that, to Dos Passos, both languages are debased and corrupt.

Acknowledging the inadequacies of any single language, Dos Passos in *Three Soldiers* intensifies his search for a synthesis of techniques that will compensate for these deficiencies. Beginning in this novel, he allows structure both to capitalize on the communicative possibilities inherent in twentieth-century art forms and to reveal their falsities as well. Here, he establishes the cinematic techniques that he will develop to greater advantage in *Manhattan Transfer* and then to their fullest potential in *U.S.A.* His goals are already in place in *Three Soldiers.* He wants to "make an epoch . . . come alive . . . by telling a certain number of individual stories" (80), the aim of *U.S.A.,* as Claude-Edmunde Magny states. Of course, in *Three Soldiers* he has not quite mastered the techniques necessary to fulfill such a goal. Despite the multiple story lines, Andrews does ultimately become the novel's controlling consciousness. But to declare, as Blanche Gelfant does in her seminal work on the American "city novel," that Andrews is "the only character through whose sensibility the outer world [takes] on aesthetic meaning" is to ignore the important fact that Dos Passos in this novel acknowledges aesthetic meanings different from the fine-arts aesthetics that have predominated in his earlier works.[22] This novel acknowledges the aesthetic of the modernist age as well—the film aesthetic—and if Fuselli's victimization and the novel's section names suggest the dangers of the technology that generated the new aesthetic, then the novel's innovative structure suggests strongly some constructive applications of the new way of thinking as well.

Indeed, even in *Three Soldiers,* Dos Passos is attempting the stylistic innovations Magny attributes to *U.S.A.* By refracting his characterizations of the soldiers into different angles of vision using varying focal distances, Dos Passos communicates a sense of the fragmentation of twentieth-century existence and suggests the relative insignificance of the individual part to the subsuming whole of mechanical civilization. He creates a limited montage in *Three Soldiers* by juxtaposing episodes and moods, "beauty and sordidness, elation and depression" (Knox, 28), omitting transitions, advancing multiple parallel stories, and depending on a thematic rather than a chronological unity. He even begins the practice of intercalating popular songs into the narrative as discrete signs of mass culture (59, 60, 64–65, 73–74, 79, 293–94), a practice that he develops into the "Newsreel" device employed in *U.S.A.*

What Dos Passos seeks to achieve in the cinematic techniques in *Three Soldiers* is a narrative structure that attains the essential quality of "gesture." Earlier, chapter 4 discussed the quest for the gesture that unifies the essays in *Rosinante to the Road Again,* which he wrote immediately after *Three Soldiers.* The characters in *Rosinante* search for a "gesture" (*Rosinante,* 15)—an immediate, tangible sign—that will transcend the inadequacies of language to express the essence of their culture. In the text of *Three Soldiers,* the narrator frequently uses the word *gesture* "to describe actions by diverse characters, to suggest an essential truth, the moment at which concrete action and the spiritual life of a character are melded inextricably" (Clark, 91). Dos Passos's focus on the gesture in *Three Soldiers* anticipates in spirit the imperative the narrators of *Rosinante* feel to find the gesture that will express the essence of Spain. It was this uncompromising individuality that attracted Dos Passos to Spanish culture when he returned there in the summer of 1919. And it was this same trait, the ability to act on individual beliefs, that Dos Passos gave to Andrews as he continued working on the novel during his postwar months in Spain.

In Andrews's quest, Dos Passos expresses something of his own search for meaning beyond words. With the painterly and cinematic techniques of *Three Soldiers,* he was beginning to develop a style that approached the quality of gesture. Nearly 20 years after Dos Passos published *Three Soldiers,* R. P. Blackmur discussed in terms that echo Dos Passos's the same potential of narrative that Dos Passos had been working toward in his apprentice novels and that he begins to realize in *Three Soldiers.* Gesture, Blackmur writes, "is what happens to a form when it becomes identical with its subject."[23] As Dos Passos wrote in 1968 summarizing his earlier narrative goals, to be able to express "the thing itself" rather than merely "the name of the thing" ("What," 32) is to make language realize the quality of gesture. These are definitions that not only predict the stylistic achievements of *Manhattan Transfer* and *U.S.A.* but also anticipate the modern aesthetic theories articulated by critics such as Barthes and the semioticians. Dos Passos incorporated the techniques of the visual arts of his day into his style in an effort to integrate completely style and theme, to make them indistinguishable. As he articulates through the characters in *Rosinante,* he believes that the gesture, the individual action that becomes identical with what it expresses, is the only way individuals in modern culture can voice their thoughts and feelings.

Throughout his apprentice works, his characters try but fail to establish identities and to construct meaningful lives. Their quests usually take the form of searches for works of art or for more authentic existences than they see around them; invariably, these efforts are frustrated or destroyed by systems—of belief, of behavior, or of government— much larger than they. In *Three Soldiers,* Andrews undertakes such a quest, and the nature of it identifies it clearly with Dos Passos's own stylistic search. Andrews frets that he has "no outlet, no gesture of expression" (341) for what he feels, but he attempts through his music to find and voice "much more of life than life can give" (329). Thus, like Dos Passos, he recognizes the limiting qualities of twentieth-century life that almost certainly will doom his quest.

Yet he seeks beyond language in another art form—music—to make the gesture, as Dos Passos does in his structural innovations. At the moment in the makeshift hospital when Andrews decides to take action against the system by deserting, even the remnants of art in the hall the army has commandeered escape their static boundaries, escape cultural limitations, and come to life. Once Andrews himself has escaped, an act that embodies his beliefs, he sets himself the goal of expressing to the world the meaning of that individual action. He abandons the formulations of symbolist art, understanding that, removed as they are from essential, pragmatic action, they are ineffectual against the "world of dead machines" (425) that the military embodies to him. He begins a new work, "The Soul and Body of John Brown" (423), whose title suggests his intuitive understanding that the only significant gestures necessarily integrate idea and pragmatic action completely.

Yet, like earlier protagonists in Dos Passos's fiction, Andrews is aware of the tremendous odds against his efforts. When he tells Geneviève Rod that John Brown was "a madman who wanted to free people" (423), he seems to speak of himself as well, for he realizes that, against the systems he opposes, he is like a "toad hopping across the road in front of a steam roller" (425). Typical of the tempered pessimism of Dos Passos's apprentice novels, Andrews expresses himself even in the face of almost certain failure. And, again typical of the early novels, the failure results from small inhumanities, such as the perfidy of Andrews's landlady at Poissac when she betrays him to the military police, as well as from the inhumanity of the world at large.

Andrews himself believes he has failed by not trying "long ago to act, to make a gesture, however feeble, . . . for other people's freedom" (431). Even so, he continues until the day he is arrested to work at his symphony. Clark views Andrews's gesture as a "moral triumph" even if a "material failure" (95). The sheer existence of the symphony, even as the wind scatters it out the window, Clark cites as evidence that the novel affirms the significance of life "even if the world is too crass to notice" (95). And if, as Clark suggests, Andrews should be judged by his own aesthetic standards, then his effort seems the more significant in that those standards are to some degree Dos Passos's own. Andrews has begun a work that promises to try to integrate subject and style, a goal Dos Passos has begun to achieve in *Three Soldiers*. Moreover, Andrews's gesture depends for its form and meaning not on the borrowed aesthetics of European culture or the traditional themes of classical painting and literature, but on a distinctly and significantly American concept— the individual freedom promised by the "old words" of America's founding—and on a thoroughly American subject as well—a radical individualist opposing a powerful, oppressive institution. His symphony grows out of American forms as well. In the same way that American composers such as Charles Ives and Aaron Copland in the 1930s and 1940s would draw on American subjects and characters for their works, so Andrews bases his composition on the folk tune immortalizing John Brown's struggle. Even though Brown lost his life for his beliefs, the gesture by which he expresses them, the work he did, had permanent effects.

Constructing *Three Soldiers,* Dos Passos had discovered the basis of the techniques that would enable him to make style and substance so inseparable that its art would be, as Sartre declared of Dos Passos's style, completely "hidden" (89). At the same time, writing in the aftermath of the war and realizing his nation's complex, self-justifying culpability in it, he discovered that the thing he had to say was multifaceted and difficult, and that in saying it he would be opposing machines even more powerful than the ones portrayed by the style and theme of *Three Soldiers.* The times that produced this novel had shown him that "Organization kills" (*Fourteenth,* 231), as he wrote in his journal at Camp Crane. He saw that to make his gesture against the organizations of the mechanical civilization of the twentieth century, he must evolve his own powerful organization; and that if it were to have lasting meaning, it must aspire to equal the force of the systems it would oppose. Consequently, he built his organization, his novels' techniques, out of the very components of the organizations the novels would speak about.

In so doing, he became "one of the few American writers of his generation . . . [to take] from technology the rhythms, images, and above all the headlong energy that would express the complexity of the human environment in the twentieth century," as Alfred Kazin observed in his introduction to an edition of *U.S.A.*[24] Beginning with *Three Soldiers,* Dos Passos's novels became machines themselves, not merely representations of the machines. *Three Soldiers* was the first of those innovative works by Dos Passos that revealed their workings and that sought to become identical with the astounding and appalling mechanisms that constituted the American culture that was his theme. Like much of the literature, painting, and cinema of the modernist era, the focus on form and particularly on machine technology in Dos Passos's novels that began with *Three Soldiers* was a response to the possibilities and the threat that early-twentieth-century technology presented to the world and particularly to America, the pure distillation of all that technology signified. But Dos Passos was more than a "novelist-engineer." His modernist novels were responses to the impact of this machine age on the life of the individual American. They became his quest to capture the "national consciousness, [the] sociocultural totality of America" and to make a gesture against the machine (Tichi, 201, 197).

Chapter Eight

The Colors of America: *Manhattan Transfer*

In March and April of 1920, just two months before Dos Passos declared *Three Soldiers* "irredeemably finished" (*Fourteenth*, 294) and submitted it to Allen and Unwin for consideration, he began to return north from his postwar jaunt through Spain. In the company of his good friend Kate Drain, who was John Howard Lawson's wife, and Lawson's sister, Adelaide, he spent a few days in Mallorca. Adelaide Lawson was a painter and became a close friend with whom he exchanged ideas and works for many years after. She was one of the artists with whom he exhibited works in his first public showing, at the Whitney Studio Club in 1923.

If the paintings generated by the trip to Mallorca are any indication of the quality of the stay, it must have been a serene and productive time. There, Dos Passos produced several technically accomplished, beautiful watercolors, some of the best examples of his impressionist style, with their indistinct, glancing renderings of villages above the sea. The thin paint produces delicate blues shading into gray and lavender for the ocean and sky, warm yellows with lemon, cream, and gold tones for the sunny villages. Perhaps the most ambitious and accomplished of these is a view of a village with a sloping field of flowers and grass in the foreground. The village rises from the background on a hill and consists of flat copper-colored roofs over sandy and ochre square structures whose colors convey the perspective and the forms. The highest building looks like an ancient ruined fortress. Over the whole scene, a bright, undifferentiated Mediterranean light washes the tones and flattens perspective in an effect reminiscent of Cézanne's Provençal landscapes.

Leaving Mallorca, Dos Passos made his way north to France, stopping first at the ancient fortified city of Carcassonne, where he was joined by John Howard Lawson. Dos Passos' friendship with Lawson would become stronger in the mid-1920s as a result of their common artistic goals in their work for the New Playwrights Theater, an expressionist, politically active school of dramatists. Dos Passos participated both as a playwright and a stage designer. In 1925, Dos Passos's "experimental drama" (Ludington 1980, 243) *The Moon Is a Gong* was produced in Boston and then in New York, with Lawson handling arrangements. The controlling image of the play was the one through which Dos Passos so frequently in the past had expressed his central theme of the necessity for individual action. The play's experimental form, along with the expressionist, vividly colorful sets he designed for Lawson's play *Processional* and for Paul Sifton's *The Belt* in 1927, reflected the degree of his progression toward full modernism since his earliest poem about the moon as a "golden gong" (36), the wistfully romantic "Memory" in the 1917 *Eight Harvard Poets*.

The paintings Dos Passos produced on this 1920 walking trip with Lawson were far removed also from the naive romanticism of just three years earlier. From Carcassonne, they hiked along the Mediterranean coast to Nîmes, Arles, and Les Baux, another fortified town perched on a steep, rocky peak. There, he captured the craggy, romantic mystery of the stronghold, a ruin since the seventeenth century, in watercolors whose swirling brushstrokes depict the site almost abstractly. In effects recalling Turner's seascapes, Dos Passos painted the city, mountain, and sky as irregular, almost undifferentiated patches of blue gray mottled by the white yellow of the rock, as if mist and rain swathed the promontory, allowing only a glimpse of the wet, shining bauxite. The 6-by-10-inch compositions are dramatically romantic in style, but their forms hint at the techniques of abstract expressionism. By the end of July, Dos Passos had made arrangements to return to the United States. Just before he departed, he wrote to his friend Germaine Lucas-Championnière that he felt it was time he left France: "French life is a beautiful ceremony in which every movement is made according to a ritual established generations ago. . . . Elsewhere life, brutal and cruel, plunges toward new forms of organization. . . . [Life is] a death struggle against the vast mechanisms which are the slavery of tomorrow" (quoted in Ludington 1980, 197).

In short, he was finally ready to contend directly with his own nation in his fiction, and the techniques of *Three Soldiers* illustrate that he now had in mind the stylistic innovations necessary to capture the "vast mechanisms," as well as the individual American struggling against them. Back in the United States in August 1920, he settled into a flat overlooking Greenwich Village. After a month, he wrote again to Mlle Lucas-Championnière. New York, he found, was "magnificent . . . a city of cavedwellers, with a frightful, brutal ugliness about it, full of thunderous voices of metal grinding on metal and of an eternal sound of wheels which turn, turn on heavy stones. People swarm meekly like ants . . . crushed by the disdainful and pitiless things around them. . . . O for the sound of a brazen trumpet which, like the voice of the Baptist in the desert, will sing again about the immensity of man in this nothingness of iron, steel, marble, and rock" (quoted in Ludington 1980, 200–201).

In this painterly language, Dos Passos summarizes perfectly, as Ludington points out, the image of the city he would portray in *Manhattan Transfer*, the novel he began making notes for that year. In the next few years, his paintings likewise began to reflect his new aesthetic. Abandoning completely the washed colors and impressionist effects of the 1920 paintings of Mallorca and Les Baux, he painted the city now using thickly applied watercolors in heavy metallic tones. Square, empty-windowed skyscrapers tower over squat, vertical warehouses. The lines of the buildings are precise, creating implacable vertical and horizontal dynamics. These paintings from the early to mid-1920s create an anonymous brute city whose impersonality and mechanical quality recall the works of the precisionist painters in the early 1920s.

These artists employed machine and urban imagery in stylized, geometric arrangements of objects. They attempted to find "epic material" in urban and industrial subjects and, in fact, created a quintessentially American style by translating "the language of cubism into local usage" (Rose, 86–89). Many artists who employed the precisionist aesthetic attempted to depict the city and American technology as heroic, permanent phenomena. The pristine clarity of Charles Demuth's *Machinery* (1920), for instance, or his witty *Aucassin and Nicolette* (1921) immortalize and mythologize the crisp lines and slick surfaces of the cityscape. But some precisionists depicted the force of the city more ambivalently. George Ault, for instance, paints, in *Brooklyn Ice House* (1926), a "low, squat, gargantuan . . . [,] prison-like" (Davidson, 212) structure locked in winter. And despite the great linear beauty of Charles Sheeler's industrial and urban scenes, paintings such as *Church Street El* (1920), an inner-city view down into a small space separating bulking planar buildings, depict a city composed only of surfaces and structures, with no human activity evident.

The idea of the American city as a powerful cultural force preoccupied painters in the early 1920s, as it did Dos Passos. *Manhattan Transfer* (1925), the product of these years, was critically acclaimed immediately upon its publication as capturing the "sense, smell, sound, soul of New York," as Sinclair Lewis declared.[1] As the synaesthetic quality of Lewis's comment demonstrates, critics quickly recognized that Dos Passos had achieved this portrait of the city by incorporating into his style techniques from other arts. Not surprisingly, the aesthetic that has continued to draw the most extensive critical comment is the novel's visual aspect.

Critics have found in *Manhattan Transfer* characteristics of expressionism, synchromism, futurism, cubism, and, most frequently, the aesthetics of film.[2] These visual styles with which Dos Passos creates the rhythms, multiplicity, and modernity of the city in the novel encompass almost all the primary movements that informed his development as a modernist. Dos Passos absorbed and sometimes anticipated in his writing these visual movements out of which modernism grew once he progressed beyond the self-conscious employment of European classical and romantic visual elements in his earliest writings during his grand tour in 1912 and at Harvard. Once he had defined for himself his aesthetic goals by the time he wrote *Three Soldiers,* he sought in the various visual manifestations of modernism a technique that would synthesize the visual and the narrative to yield a direct sense of American life caught up in the new technological revolution. His use of American subjects and the aesthetics of the machine age in *Manhattan Transfer* constitutes the purest expression of his American modernist style, in that *U.S.A.* will mark the beginning of a new narrative direction for Dos Passos.

As in *Three Soldiers,* Dos Passos in *Manhattan Transfer* is still concerned with the theme of the individual's relationship to the system—in this new novel, the force of the city and the culture it represents. Dos Passos is still working, in both theme and form, with the relation of the parts to the whole. But in *Manhattan Transfer,* the parts have no organic center to imply a whole; instead, they work only in mechanical combination—like a machine in continuous motion. Some critics have perceived this novel as reflecting only chaos: Lionel Trilling called it "an epic of disintegration."[3] If it is concerned with disintegration, it is the dissolution of the human, the organic, the holistic; but it is also the construction of a powerful machine. The structure of the novel once more reflects the culture Dos Passos is portraying. His form—the constant motion of the narrative, its dynamic swirl mixing and propelling characters deterministically—is once again the message.

Such a conception creates a problem, of course: how to portray a culture that no longer possesses any organic structure in an art form that demands concessions to order to be intelligible. Once again, the answer lies in the search for a new language equal to that problem, and once again the vocabulary comes from the "gestures," the signs—the aesthetics—of the new culture.

The forms and dynamics of the culture of the machine pervaded American writing and painting after the war and in the early 1920s. In *Rush Hour New York* (1914), Max Weber visually recreated the sensations of speeding down a New York street in an open vehicle. In his *Eggbeater* series of paintings (1927–1928), Stuart Davis used the forms and motions of ordinary kitchen utensils and machines. Photographers, too, found their subjects in machines and industry: Paul Strand focused portraits on parts of a new motion-picture camera, and Edward Weston produced a series of pictures of the Armco steel plant in Ohio.

Manhattan Transfer's use of machine aesthetics—"the rhythms, images, and above all the headlong energy" of industry and technology (Kazin, x) —gave Dos Passos a structure that would enable him to depict the fragmentations of life in a modern industrial city. He created in *Manhattan Transfer* a machine composed of the parts of the city—people, skyscrapers, trains, subways, songs, and newspaper clippings, the phenomena of popular culture—functioning as mere cogs in an inexorable urban structure. As cogs, he suggests, they are entirely at the mercy of the sociocultural forces that fragment their lives and identities, and the structures of his novel provide the reader with a way of perceiving connections among and humanity in characters who are stripped of community or individuality by the city. Thus, although Donald Pizer maintains that one reads *Manhattan Transfer* "not for its 'subject' but for its 'shape,' " its subject and its shape are in fact inseparable.[4]

The structures of the novel are drawn from another of the pure products of the American machine age—the motion picture. Dos Passos was still exploring the potential of the techniques of continuity editing and dramatic crosscutting he had used in a basic way to drive the narrative in *Three Soldiers*, techniques D. W. Griffith had employed in his first two feature-length dramas of American history. Dos Passos's introduction to the Russian film innovators would not occur until after 1925, the year *Manhattan Transfer* was published. The literary-montage style he had pioneered in the war novel he now refined in *Manhattan Transfer*. Whereas the earlier novel had depended primarily on juxtaposition and multiple parallel stories for its form, the new novel becomes an active machine by the varying kinds of motion created by continuity editing. Crosscutting communicates three patterns of motion in the novel, as Evans points out. There is linear movement—transportation or motion across the city, often rapid transit from one site to another by public conveyance. There is circular motion—whirling machinery such as revolving doors or the steamroller, images that are captured in the titles of two of the novel's chapters; or repetitive circularity expressing confusion or helplessness, communicated by imagery of a vortex or whirling storm. Finally, there is random movement—the occasional wandering of a nameless character across the trajectory of one of the book's more central figures, in chance encounters or isolated incidents that are nonetheless thematically related to some major idea or action. In a succession of crosscuts between shots tracking central and incidental characters as they traverse the city and struggle with its demands, Dos Passos creates a montage conveying the sensation of life in New York City from 1913 through the early 1920s. Manuscripts of the novel as it progressed show that he initially created each of the central narratives separately, then broke them apart and spliced the various pieces into the order he sought, a process remarkably like film editing. Fragmentation, then, was both the technique and the theme; but his montage created simultaneity among his narrative threads—although the narratives do not always progress at precisely identical speeds—and created meaning by juxtaposing narrative threads, images, and themes.

The theme of fragmentation, of the individual's struggle for identity and humanity against the inexorable mechanical nature of city life, extends into every facet of the novel. In fact, the city itself may be said to be the novel's primary subject: the structure of the work disallows "heroes" or protagonists in the usual sense, since characters abound and the relationships among them are not, as in the traditional novel, organic or familial but rather are arbitrarily determined by the city. But among the welter of lives viewed at an uninvolved focal distance, two characters, Ellen Thatcher and Jimmy Herf, are given backgrounds, families, and articulated emotional lives. These characters represent different responses to the city as an embodiment of the corrupted ideals of success in American culture. To achieve the characterization of Ellen and Jimmy and underscore the sense of simultaneity created by his montage, Dos Passos connects these characters to major themes and patterns of motion in the novel via repetitive imagery. Eventually, these two characters' lives intersect in one of the few significant relationships the novel depicts, and in the contrast between the ways each of them chooses to confront the pressures of American capitalism lies one of the novel's most overt comments on the myth of success.

Both Ellen's and Jimmy's characters and fates are naturalistically determined from their earliest appearances in the novel. As the novel begins, Ellen is born to an ineffectual father and an unstable mother whose subsequent withdrawal into hypochondria leaves Ellen emotionally detached but compelled to manipulate her father to win the approval she craves. Early, she learns to dance, to charm, and to capture her father's attentions—both emotional and material—for her grace and beauty. Thus she acquires a method of success that she will use throughout her career as a dancer, actress, and editor of a society and fashion periodical.

Likewise introduced early in the novel, Jimmy Herf first appears as a child returning to the United States on a liner after having long been abroad with his mother. Dos Passos underscores the identification of Herf with American dreams and myths as the boy catches his first glimpse of the Statue of Liberty and begs his mother to unpack his small American flag so that he may join in the Fourth of July celebration on deck. Through his mind wander phrases from "Yankee Doodle" as he disembarks within sight of immigrants segregated from the upper-class crowd at the dock. Left in the care of her socially prominent family when his mother suffers a stroke and subsequently dies, the lonely boy—whose absent father and peripatetic "hotel childhood" suggest an autobiographical basis for the character—is subjected to the values of the family, the Merivales. Jimmy is too young to reason through his resistance to their social and ethnic bigotry and their unthinking materialism; but when he reaches college age and his Uncle Jeff assumes that Jimmy will begin a career with the Merivales' banking firm, Jimmy finally rebels. His uncle declares that for Jimmy to apprentice himself to the firm will assure his future—" 'if a man's a success in New York he's a success!' " (119). Jimmy, however, has a vision of himself in futile circular motion, "fed in a tape in and out of the revolving doors . . . the revolving doors grinding out his years like sausage meat" (120). Perceiving the dehumanizing cost of his uncle's—America's—version of the success ethic, Jimmy declares to himself that "Uncle Jeff and his office can go plumb to hell" (120). The tension between the idea of "success" inculcated in him by the family and his own instinct for honesty and humanity shapes Jimmy's choices, career, and relationships throughout the novel.

Ellen's career and relationships as an adult demonstrate the degree to which she is dehumanized by her superficial idea of success. Her first marriage, to veteran actor John Oglethorpe, secures for her a mentor and connections in the theater. She progresses from chorine to the principal in various musicals by exploiting her looks and pursuing compro-

mising flirtations with producers. After she abandons the sexually ambiguous Oglethorpe, a series of involvements with progressively more
prosperous men eventually prompts one of them, the attorney George
Baldwin, to sneer that she is " 'no better than a common prostitute' "
(229). When she does fall in love, it is with Stan Emery, the self-destructive
ne'er-do-well son of a prominent New York family. His ambitions to be
an architect are thwarted by his family's insistence that he undertake a
more lucrative profession. His drunken death by self-immolation pro-
pels Ellen, pregnant with his child, into a marriage of convenience with
Jimmy Herf, who nevertheless loves her and devotes himself to her and
the child despite the boy's paternity. By this time, however, Ellen is
incapable of reciprocating: " 'I guess I don't love anybody for long
unless they're dead' " (346), she explains to Jimmy as they discuss
divorce.

Stan's death merely crystallizes in Ellen the hardness, the mechanical
distance, that she has developed to survive the pressures of the city
and achieve success on its terms. Communicating Ellen's loss of humanity with images of machines and inexorable cyclic motion, Dos Passos
makes her characterization a part of the dynamic mechanism of the
novel. She becomes "an intricate machine of sawtooth steel whitebright
bluebright copperbright," with a voice "like a tiny flexible sharp metal-
saw" (228) when she dances with Jimmy in an effort to banish her
feelings for Stan. After his death, she feels like "a stiff castiron figure in
her metalgreen evening dress" (261) as she continues her professional
ascent. After her divorce from Jimmy, finding editorial work tedious, she
returns to George Baldwin; but steeling herself to accept his proposal
and the security it will provide, she feels as if she has become a "dollself,"
"as if she had set the photograph of herself in her own place, forever
frozen into a single gesture" (374–75). Sealing the engagement with a
kiss in a taxi, she feels "like someone drowning," sees "out of a corner
of an eye whirling faces, streetlights, zooming nickleglinting wheels"
(376). With any trace of an authentic self eradicated by her compromises with success, she is pulled into the vortex of the city's amoral
energy.

Jimmy likewise must choose between becoming a success on the
city's terms and maintaining his integrity and values. As with Ellen's
career, Jimmy's job as a newspaper reporter exposes him to urban corruption. To characterize Jimmy's struggle with the commercial goals of
journalism and the cheapening of language and life those goals dictate,
Dos Passos intercalates bits of newspaper stories into the montage; he

illustrates the effects on readers of the press's distortions of reality; and he shows how journalistic formulas creep into Jimmy's thinking. Dutch Robinson, for instance, a minor character, picks up "a torn piece of pink evening newspaper" as he wanders hungry and jobless past Child's, a restaurant frequented by Herf. The headline reads "$50,000 HOLDUP": "In the busiest part of the noon hour two men help up Adolphus St. John, a bank messenger for the Guarantee Trust Company, and snatched from his hands a satchel containing a half million dollars in bills" (317). Dutch's heart begins to pound as he reads, and when he next appears, he has a gun; in the next sequence, he is suddenly well dressed and confides in his girlfriend Francie that he has held up a cigar store, and "it was a cinch" (363). Two narrative segments later, a reporter "writing up the crime wave" ingratiates himself with the cigar-store proprietor, Goldstein. Goldstein, however, refuses to give him the story: " 'Vat vill you do but print it so that other boys and goils will get the same ideas.' " The reporter argues that " 'Publicity . . . is as necessary as ventilation' " and that, in any case, he's taking " 'the human interest angle . . . pity and tears' " (366); he points out that the publicity will boost business. Goldstein then talks, and the reporter manipulates the information he receives to fit the title he's already got—"The Gilded Bandits." Two segments later appears a follow-up story: Dutch and the hapless, pregnant Francie, now being characterized in the press as the "Flapper Bandit," are in custody.

These segments of the montage punctuate the narrative of Jimmy's growing disillusionment with newspaper work and the press's abuses of power and language. When Jimmy witnesses a fight between bootlegging gangs over a shipment of liquor, he finds himself planning how to sell the story to the newspaper's Sunday supplement. Instead of honest reporting, what comes to his mind are clichés and formulas: "In a lonely abandoned dancehall on Sheepshead Bay . . . lovely blooming Italian girl . . . shrill whistle in the dark" (ellipses Dos Passos's; 319). Briefly, he chides himself for being, as he says reporters are, "a parasite on the drama of life" (320). But when he recounts the story to friends later that night, he plays up the sensational aspects of it—hydroplanes, drownings, spilled cases of champagne—rather than dealing seriously with the gravity of the incident and its human dimensions, such his injured friend Congo Jake.

However, he does begin to realize how dehumanized his work, the city, and his association with Ellen are making him. Any menial job, he swears, would be "better than spending all your life rooting into other

people's affairs until you're nothing but a goddam traveling dictograph.
. . . You get so you don't have any private life, you're just an automatic
writing machine" (344). Indeed, he realizes his private life with Ellen is
over; she has become incapable of the kind of love and humanity he
needs. But disengaging himself from the taint of the city and its compromised language is more difficult than he reckons. Even after he resigns
his job, he imagines a newspaper account of his failure to succeed in a
surreal parody of glib journalistic formulas: "Deported: James Herf
young newspaperman of 190 West 12th Street recently lost his twenties.
Appearing before Judge Merivale they were remanded to Ellis Island for
deportation as undesirable aliens" (353). He can tell the press and its
willful distortions to go to hell, as he did his Uncle Jeff Merivale early in
the novel, but the debased language he has learned in his trade cannot be
easily displaced in a culture that uses words only for profit. Finally, with
its collage of journalistic effects, the text demonstrates that the charges
John Oglethorpe levels against Herf earlier in the novel are true: " 'How
do you like being a paid prostitute of the public press? How d'you like
your yellow ticket? . . . I know that every sentence, every word, every
picayune punctuation that appears in the public press is perused and
revised and deleted in the interests of advertisers and bondholders. The
fountain of national life is poisoned at the source' " (195).

That Jimmy recognizes the truth of Oglethorpe's closing charge becomes clear in his jumbled thoughts once he has rejected the newspaper's dishonest use of language and, by implication, the false values of
the city and the culture for which the newspaper speaks. In the age of
the machine, as urbanization, technology, and the massive organizations
of business and government threaten to overpower and dehumanize the
individual, is there any meaning left in what Dos Passos called "the old
words" on which the nation was founded—"the old words of the immigrants . . . the old American speech of the haters of oppression" (*Big*,
469), "the great formulations of the generation of 1776" (*Occasions*, 64)?
From Herf's first appearance in the novel—on the Fourth of July, with
the Statue of Liberty in the background—the character has been identified with a fundamental questioning of the fate of American values in an
age of superficial materialism. Now, in a pivotal passage that inter-
weaves central images and patterns of motion and extends their significance to a symbolic level, Jimmy struggles to reclaim "the old words":

Pursuit of happiness, unalienable pursuit . . . right to life liberty and . . .
A black moonless night; Jimmy Herf is walking alone up South Street.

... All these April nights combing the streets alone a skyscraper has obsessed him, a grooved building jutting up with uncountable bright windows falling onto him out of a scudding sky. Typewriters rain continual nickelplated confetti in his ears. . . . And he walks round blocks and blocks looking for the door of the humming tinselwindowed skyscraper, round blocks and blocks and still no door. Every time he closes his eyes the dream has hold of him, every time he stops arguing audibly with himself in pompous reasonable phrases the dream has hold of him. [Y]oung man to save your sanity you've got to do one of two things . . . one of two unalienable alternatives: go away in a dirty soft shirt or stay in a clean Arrow collar. But what's the use of spending your whole life fleeing the City of Destruction? What about your unalienable right, Thirteen Provinces? His mind unreeling phrases, he walks on doggedly. There's nowhere in particular he wants to go. If only I still had faith in words. (365 – 66)

In his confusion, with his "mind unreeling phrases" from the original conception of America, he seems compelled to circle vainly the skyscraper that "has obsessed him": while in thrall to the monolithic city whose symbol is the skyscraper, the apex of the machine culture, he can never regain "the dream," never construct truth from the culture's compromised language.

If he is ever to regain "faith in words," then, he must reject the city, and so he does. He walks out of Manhattan without the money or the desire to travel at the city's pace or by means of its rapid transit, whose images and sensations zoom through the novel's pages. In fact, in the image of a horse wagon loaded with flowering plants that Jimmy passes, Dos Passos introduces a rare element of the natural, perhaps to suggest that Jimmy's escape from the machine will return him to a state of organic wholeness, of hope for the individual, and of belief in the possibilities of language. He is as uncertain of his destination as he is of how language can be reinvested with meaning or transformed to communicate the human experience as it has been remade in the machine age. But he has begun the process of discovery and reinvention—he is actively in search of his freedom—by making the gesture of "fleeing the City of Destruction" (366).

Like his protagonist, Dos Passos seeks an alternative to the language that has been debased by American culture; the creation of the form of *Manhattan Transfer* is that search. Even more than in *Three Soldiers,* in *Manhattan Transfer* he finds in other arts, particularly painting and film, elements of a new language more capable of achieving his goal: "to describe in colors that would not fade, our America that we loved and hated" ("What," 30), to convey the essence of life in America as it had become. Besides the precisionist and futurist aesthetics that shape its imagery, the novel reflects the beginning of Dos Passos's working with the techniques of cubism to achieve the multiplicity and simultaneity that characterize his fully developed modernist style. But more useful for Dos Passos in creating this moving portrait of the city, in evoking not just its parallel lives but its speed, clamor, and looming presence, were the techniques of film, since by the time he was writing *Manhattan Transfer* he was consciously aiming for a style that transcended the limitations of the page or the static picture plane, a style that would make life "stand up off the page" ("What," 9).

A schematic of one chapter of one of the book's three sections can demonstrate generally how crosscutting and the splicing of segments into montage create meaning through juxtaposition and simultaneity. "Steamroller," the fifth chapter of the first section, consists of five narrative segments. The segments are preceded by one of the prose poems that heads every chapter, and two of the segments are punctuated by fragments of songs.

The prose poem immediately reinforces the tone set by the title "Steamroller." By creating a sense of the oppressiveness of the city, the poem suggests inexorable forces at work crushing and fragmenting the individual: "Dark presses tight the steaming asphalt city, crushes the fretwork of windows and lettered signs and chimneys . . . and eyes and hands and neckties . . . into black enormous blocks. Under the rolling heavier heavier pressure windows blurt light. Night . . . squeezes the sullen blocks until they drip red, yellow, green into streets resounding with feet. . . ." (112).

The first narrative segment following the prose poem opens with the image of a steamroller compacting a road leading from a cemetery. Jimmy Herf walks rapidly down the road away from the site of his mother's burial; he is trying to escape the platitudes of the funeral service, the cloying scent of lilies, and the knowledge that his beloved mother is gone. With memories of her face swarming through his mind, he walks on. From previous glimpses of his life, the reader knows that Jimmy is now an orphan and that his fate will be determined by impersonal forces and an extended family that feels little connection with him and whose primary concerns are materialistic.

The chapter cuts to a second narrative that demonstrates how deterministic forces control characters' lives. In this brief scene, an illegal

French immigrant, Emile, bumps into May, a streetwalker, outside the delicatessen owned by Madame Rigaud. Early in the book, Emile jumped ship in New York, motivated by the American dream in its most reductive form: "In America a fellow can get ahead. Birth don't matter, education don't matter. It's all getting ahead" (21). Single-mindedly subscribing to that formulaic myth, Emile aspires to property ownership and prosperity—and to that end, he is wooing the widow Rigaud, with his eye on her business. Untroubled by integrity, he has schemed to manipulate Madame Rigaud into marrying him, and May chides him for having used her to make Madame Rigaud jealous by kissing May publicly within sight of the delicatessen. As Emile enters the shop, a fire engine "shatter[s] the street with a clattering roar" (114), directing the focus of the scene toward policemen dragging a black man away from the scene of a fire in an adjacent building. Onlookers speculate that the police have finally caught the "firebug" whose ugly crimes and sinister presence have already appeared in the novel twice. Emile's only concern, however, is to discover how much insurance Madame Rigaud carries on the delicatessen and to use the incident as an occasion to importune her once again about marriage.

Besides presenting a simultaneous picture of another kind of determinism at work and comparing Jimmy Herf's lack of genuine familial connection to Emile's false intimacy with Madame Rigaud, this segment complicates the significance of the arsonist, who has already crossed paths with both Herf and Ellen Thatcher's father, Ed. Both of these encounters occur in connection with incidents that permanently and catastrophically alter the characters' lives—Jimmy's mother's stroke and the birth of Ellen that unhinges her mother and fragments the family. Both Jimmy and Ed note the arsonist's appearance: he smells strongly of coal oil and has "tallowy sagging cheeks and bright popeyes" (14).

Given the description of the man as pale and shadowy, then, it seems unlikely that the police, by this time anxious to arrest someone for the series of fires, have found the culprit in the black man. The significance of this mistake is compounded by the police officers' brutal treatment of the suspect—"whose arms snap[   ] back and forth like broken cables" as three of them "crack[   ] the negro first on one side of the head, then on the other" with billy clubs (115). The kind of prejudice that would cause this kind of persecution, that would elicit the kinds of comments that come from the onlookers—" 'It's a shine 'at set the fire' " (115)—is as monolithic a force in American culture as is the dream of freedom it denies. Its eruption in this lower-class setting echoes its earlier appearance among the upper-class Merivales, who complain that the city has become " 'overrun with kikes and low Irish' " (101). The fire engine that announces the firebug's appearance, that clamors in and out of narrative segments, heralds the dangers of the forces at work in each segment and builds the novel's synaesthetic quality. The frequency of the intrusion of the fire engine suggests Dos Passos's awareness of it not only as a vehicle for moving with continuity from one shot to another but also as a sign of the nature of the city—a volatile, consuming power like fire. Dos Passos's identification of the fire engine with the city is also a painterly technique recalling the vibrant portrait the precisionist Charles Demuth painted of William Carlos Williams's poetic evocation of the machine, "I Saw the Figure Five in Gold."

The third narrative segment implies the destructive force of unbridled ambition, as did Emile's scene, but with greater subtlety, perhaps because this segment concerns Ellen Thatcher, whose characterization unfolds gradually throughout the novel. As the segment opens, Ellen and her new husband, John Oglethorpe, head for an Atlantic City honeymoon. They have just changed trains at Manhattan Transfer, a railway station in northern New Jersey where trains bound for New York City switch to electric power to accommodate the city's underground transit system. En route, Ellen feels resistance to Oglethorpe; his affectations and effeminacy presage the second section's revelation of his bisexuality, which is depicted in unsympathetic caricature unlike the more complex portrait of his fellow actor (and possible lover) Tony Hunter. In bed with Oglethorpe in Atlantic City, Ellen is sickened by the physical contact she has had with him. She composes herself rigidly on the opposite side of the bed and falls asleep. She has prostituted herself for an entrée into the theater—another actress says of Ellen that she'd " 'marry a trolley-car if she thought she could get anything by it' " (156)—and has had to detach herself from her feelings, from genuine human response to others, to countenance her rank opportunism. Her driving need for recognition, glamour, and luxury—her devotion to the success god—dehumanizes her, as Dos Passos illustrates with the machine imagery increasingly associated with her. Like the two previous scenes, this one dramatizes a paradigmatic instance of the action of the oppressive force that threatens each individual's humanity and connection to other humans.

The fourth narrative "cut" reveals another of these instances, but it relies for its meaning on juxtaposition with the previous scene concerning Ellen. This is the scene previously discussed in which Jimmy, now

16, listens to his Uncle Jeff platitudinously advise him to pursue success on the city's terms in Merivale's banking firm. But when offered the kind of professional advantage Ellen gained by marrying Oglethorpe, Jimmy sees in the career path dangled before him the potential for "grinding" (120) the life out of him. He steps from his uncle's posh club into a street teeming with the vital mixture of nationalities that animate the city; the catalog of immigrant workers reminds the reader that they were drawn to the city by the promises of equality and opportunity, of which Uncle Jeff's job offer and career are a perversion. Squaring his face into the gritty wind, Jimmy resolves to reject Merivale's path.

Cinematically, the scene functions in relation to the other segments in this section in significant ways. Subtly, it communicates a time shift in the novel that synchronizes Ellen's and Jimmy's stories, since the first segment in this section presented Jimmy as a boy. The reader is made aware by Dos Passos's "editing" techniques in the section—the time shift and the subsequent abrupt cuts in simultaneous time—of how pivotal the chosen scenes are, a consciousness reinforced by the growing perception of the continuity among the scenes. Secondly, the scene demonstrates the possibility of an alternate response to the "steamroller" of deterministic forces. Whereas Emile and Ellen are controlled by the cultural myths and dreams they have internalized, Jimmy resists. Granted, he has a propensity to evade painful realities: as a boy he constructs a fantasy world rather than face his mother's illness and he runs away from his mother's funeral. And he will attempt to avoid confronting his complicity in the devaluation of the individual implied by his newspaper's abuses of language. But the juxtaposition of the two sequences concerning Jimmy in the "Steamroller" section implies his potential to grow from mere avoidance of the oppressive forces in his life to an attempt, however ineffectual in the urban world, to assert his own values against those circumstances. The scene prepares the reader for Jimmy's ultimate rejection of the city and its corruption.

Yet if the fourth segment in this montage suggests, by juxtaposition with the earlier scenes, some hope for the individual, the fifth and final segment seems to create its meaning by parallel with the scenes concerning Emile and Ellen. This segment, the longest in the chapter, brings back Bud Korpenning, a wanderer who enters the book on its first page and reappears six times in the first four chapters. At 25, Bud fled his home on a farm in Cooperstown, New York; earlier segments hint that he has been party to a crime that left an old man—perhaps his father—dead. He arrived in the metropolis hoping to escape his past and reform his life in the city that he imagines is " 'the center of things' " (4). But after being swindled and exploited and finding that he is too much of a bumpkin to secure lucrative work, he is reduced to living in a flophouse. The sequence opens there, with Bud unable to sleep in the middle of the night, paranoically convinced that " 'bulls an detectives' " are watching him. He listens to the disheartening story told by another insomniac of his 10 years of futile efforts to establish a decent life in the city, only to wind up a Bowery bum. The bum advises Bud to go home to the farm and " 'the ole folks' " (122) while he still can.

Outraged at the concept of family as an alternative to the brutality of the city, Bud reveals to the bum and to the reader, finally, what he is hiding from and why he cannot go home. A "mass of white and red deep-gouged scars" (122) bears witness to Bud's account of years of beatings from the man who was supposedly his father. Finally retaliating, Bud killed the man and escaped. After his revelation, guilt makes him imagine that everyone he meets knows the truth, and he strikes out into the city that was to have provided refuge, convinced that his capture is inevitable. Having reached this heightened state of paranoia and fatalism, he is acutely aware of his surroundings as he walks the Brooklyn Bridge, imagines the life he dreamed of, and jumps from the rail of the bridge into the river. A tugboat crew hauls his lifeless body from the water.

This final scene of the chapter echoes the focal themes of the earlier segments. It shows once again an individual whose closest human connections, by blood or by marriage, are sterile or perverted. It depicts a figure overwhelmed by oppressive forces either caused or significantly augmented by the city. Unlike Emile's or Ellen's case, however, here the city kills not only the spirit or the self, but the body as well. In placing Bud's suicide at the end of the "Steamroller" section, Dos Passos creates a pessimistic closure in this montage. Shifting the point of view in the scene as he might choose different camera angles to achieve certain effects, he closes the "Steamroller" chapter by reemphasizing the city's existence as a machine. Detached from self and resolved to die, Bud in his last minutes perceives the bright power of the machine in images recalling the precisionists' crisp, impersonal cityscapes: from his vantage point on the bridge, streets appear to be "dotted lines of lights between square blackwindowed buildings." The bridge itself, in literature and painting long a symbol for the city, is "a spiderwork of cables" (124), a visualization from paintings such as those Joseph Stella created around the time Dos Passos was writing the novel. Once Bud drops from the bridge, the point of view shifts to the tugboat captain who sees Bud jump and, complaining of the inconvenience, pulls him from the river. The callousness of the captain reiterates that the city-machine is a dehumanizing force. The reader, too, experiences something of the captain's emotional distance when the shift to this detached point of view at the very culmination of the section forcefully distances the reader from the narrative. In this way, as with other revolutionary techniques—the speed of the narrative, its fragmentations, its uses of simultaneity and juxtaposition, and its patterns of motion created by structural effects and images—Dos Passos recreates an experience of the city.

The Bud Korpenning segment in the final montage of the first section of the book suggests something of how revolutionary Dos Passos's conception of the novel actually was. As Cecelia Tichi points out, "To read Manhattan Transfer . . . is to realize how radically Dos Passos rejected the established fictional tradition in which characters' relationships are based on lineage, ancestry, kinship patterns, or the common culture of a region" (200). In Bud, Dos Passos follows a character in some detail from the first page of his novel through five chapters. Devoting that much attention to a character, yet never creating any connection between him and another character, and then depicting his death barely a third of the way through the novel—this conception of character departs in disturbing ways from fictional conventions that implied order, relationship, and the intrinsic meaningfulness of existence to the culture of the generation before the modernists.

That culture, however, was swept away by the war, the rise of science, and the ascendency of technology—the advent of what Dos Passos called mechanical civilization. To assert meaning in the face of the massive organizations spawned by the mechanical civilization—the military, government in the service of industry and commerce, and monopoly capitalism among others—he searched for narrative structures that, by appropriating the mechanisms of the systems they opposed, would attain their power as well. Like Jimmy Herf, Dos Passos had lost faith in words; the systems that were a part of "superpower" had devalued language and the human in American culture; and, in any case, the transformed world had outgrown traditional narrative forms. In Manhattan Transfer, he constructs out of the very mechanisms of urban, industrial America the essence of its life. Especially with the visual aesthetics of cinema, the art form with which America became virtually synonymous, he recreates the fragmentation of modern culture and renders visible the machines that threaten the individual. In so doing, he wrote the novel that was his purest—if not his most innovative—modernist expression, since it strives as much as is possible to diminish evidence of the artist's subjective consciousness, a romantic characteristic, and to give a direct experience of its subject.

The year *Manhattan Transfer* was published, 1925, produced many of the most important books in the modernist canon: Theodore Dreiser's *An American Tragedy,* Ernest Hemingway's *In Our Time,* F. Scott Fitzgerald's *The Great Gatsby,* and Virginia Woolf's *Mrs. Dalloway,* among others. But even among this company, Dos Passos's novel was recognized as innovative. Sinclair Lewis declared that it was "the first novel to catch Manhattan, . . . a novel of the first importance. . . . The dawn of a whole new school of writing" (361). D. H. Lawrence, apprehending the structural basis of the novel, called it a "very complex film . . . [of] New York" (364). This was Dos Passos's fourth novel, and it bespoke a maturing command of materials and techniques. Characteristically, within a year after its publication, Dos Passos was deeply immersed in new directions—radical politics and experimental theater. And by 1927, he was making notes for what was to become his most ambitious work, the *U.S.A.* novels, whose style would originate from the structures of *Manhattan Transfer,* but whose scope—the entire nation—was evidence of Dos Passos's growing concern for "the America that we loved and hated" ("What," 30).

Chapter Nine

The Speech of the People: *U.S.A.*

With its vaultingly ambitious scope—"the broad field of the lives of these times . . . during the first three decades of the present century"[1]—*U.S.A.* sets out to bring to life nothing less than the transformation of a nation into a superpower in a new century. As it does so, the trilogy also charts the transformation of its author's politics from committed leftist activism to disillusioned anti-Communism that became increasingly conservative during the last three decades of Dos Passos's life. And, for this writer, whose very earliest publications demonstrated the inevitable and dynamic symbiosis between his politics and his aesthetics, reconceiving the one necessarily involved reconceiving the other. The resultant art of the trilogy likewise traces a transition. The first edition of the first novel reanimates and even complicates the high-modernist devices of *Manhattan Transfer*. But in the second two novels, written subsequently, and most evidently in the revision of the first novel, undertaken in preparation for uniting and publishing the works in one volume, Dos Passos retreats from the decentered structures of *Manhattan Transfer* that indict the mechanisms of urban technological culture even as they catalyze the novel.

Redefining his political views meant redefining his notion of the artist's position in politics and in history, as well as reconceptualizing the artistic subject's relationship to the novel itself as it embodies politics and history. Where in *Manhattan Transfer* Dos Passos consciously tried to eliminate the subjective consciousness of the artist, even as the artist's hand was implicitly experimenting with the novel's structure, in *U.S.A.* he acknowledges both his own consciousness and the purposes informing the structures he creates and, this time, explicitly defines. The voice of the "Camera Eye," it becomes clear, belongs to the same consciousness who owns the hands wielding the camera, choosing the "Newsreel" shots, focusing the angle of vision in the novel's biographies, and manipulating the characters in the fictional narratives. The modes of *U.S.A.* reintroduce the romantic subjective consciousness, and, even as the novels seek to "take in as much as possible of the broad field of the lives of these times" ("Introductory," vii), their scope reflects the gradual redirection of Dos Passos's political and aesthetic journey toward a carefully considered and constructed conservatism after the 1930s.

That shift had its origins, paradoxically, as did the novels themselves, in radical politics. With *Manhattan Transfer* behind him and an inconclusive engagement to Crystal Ross, a member of his literary circle, amicably broken, Dos Passos characteristically invested his considerable energies in new projects, all in some way related to the divisive political issues that galvanized the Left in the mid-1920s. At age 30, with a full sense of the potential of his literary powers, he sought ways to unite them with his belief in the importance of a "native American radicalism" (*Best*, 165) that, transcending political dogma, could infuse all individual expression. Out of this greater willingness to be publicly active in the specific programs and positions of the Left grew the reintroduction of the narrative subject into the text that distinguishes *U.S.A.* from the disengagement that characterizes *Manhattan Transfer*.

For instance, when Dos Passos was contacted in 1925 about the revival of the *Masses*, the radical journal well known before the war that had been suppressed by the Wilson administration in 1918, he volunteered to serve on its executive board and to be identified with it in any way that would benefit the publication. Yet even in this step forward he typically maintained his individuality. When in early 1926 he wrote the piece "The *New Masses* I'd Like,"[2] one of his first contributions to it, he was perhaps chafing at being called a mere "bourgeois intellectual" by the journal's new editor, Mike Gold, an avowed Communist who would soon impose a party agenda on the publication. In reaction, Dos Passos asserted his hope that the magazine would not confine itself to "always find[ing] [only] what they are looking for." Instead of predictable leftist dogma, he calls for a free expression of contending ideas that will articulate "what's in the air in the country." Echoing the American romantic Ralph Waldo Emerson, Dos Passos argues that "Ever since Columbus, imported systems [of thought] have been the curse of this continent. Why not develop our own brand?" (*"New Masses,"* 20). Gold's complaint that Dos Passos's politics were not sufficiently radical or well defined anticipated the attitudes of the radical Left toward Dos Passos throughout the 1920s and into the 1930s. During that period, as the movement urged him to identify himself explicitly with it, he consistently resisted, maintaining his individualism as events and the tactics of the Communist Party itself alienated him slowly from the Left.

In his work for the New Playwrights Theater, the experimental repertory group begun in 1926, Dos Passos again joined an artistic endeavor whose organizers specifically intended to combine revolutionary aesthetics and politics. His interest in the potential of drama to escape the limitations of conventional aesthetic techniques and bridge "the idiotic schism between Highbrow and Lowbrow"[3] in America had already led him to write the expressionistic play *The Moon Is a Gong*. Produced by the Harvard Dramatic Club in 1925 and later moved to New York, the play shared with the works of his friend John Howard Lawson, a radical playwright, unconventional approaches to every aspect of dramaturgy. Later published as *The Garbage Man*,[4] a title Dos Passos preferred, *The Moon Is a Gong* was less successful than Lawson's *Processional*, subtitled *A Jazz Symphony of American Life in Four Acts*. Dos Passos's play less effectively combined the diverse goals of "show" and "art" theater (Knox and Stahl, 98). But the commonality of their beliefs and methods inspired him to join forces with Lawson and three other artists to form the New Playwrights, for which the five wrote, directed, designed and created scenery, publicized, reviewed, and pursued backing until the group disbanded in disagreement in 1929.

Dos Passos defined the group's goals, defended its productions, and finally analyzed its demise in a trio of articles spanning the lifetime of the project. His 1925 *Vanity Fair* article, "Is the 'Realistic' Theatre Obsolete? Many Theatrical Conventions Have Been Shattered by Lawson's *Processional*," reviewed the play that seemed to him to epitomize the group's aims. The review describes this new form of theater as a healthy alternative to the superficiality of Broadway productions and a necessary direction in which drama needed to move to compete with movies and radio. His details about the company's revolutionary staging devices evoke an impression of self-conscious attempts to arrest attention: the illusion of reality is discarded, the "convention of the invisible fourth wall [is] . . . abandoned," raucous jazz music incongruously intrudes, vast, immovable, brightly colored backdrops resemble constructivist paintings, and actors charge into the audience from the orchestra pit. Such techniques, he explains, are attempts "to invade the audience's feelings by the most direct and simple means that come to hand" (" 'Realistic,' " 114).

"Toward a Revolutionary Theatre,"[5] which appeared in the *New Masses* in December 1927, focuses on the difficulties that confront the "revolutionary" theater. Here, unlike in his previous essay, Dos Passos explicitly states the group's political agenda: "[I]t must draw its life and ideas from the conscious sections of the industrial and white collar working classes which are out to get control of the great flabby mass of capitalist society and mold it to their own purpose." The group's productions would reject the escapist subjects of mainstream theater and dramatize instead the conflicts they believed their intended audience experienced: labor disputes, racial discrimination, ethnic prejudice, the stifling effects of oppressive institutions—the government, the military, banks, bosses—on the worker. Presciently, he observes that such a radical effort faces the obstacles of "internal organization and money" ("Revolutionary," 20). But he optimistically assumes that any group of like-minded people with a worthy goal will devise some way of preventing individual problems from interfering and that the audience of workers for whom the plays exist will make the theater self-supporting.

In fact, these two problems—money and internal organization— were what finally ended the New Playwrights Theater. During its three years, the group managed to produce plays by each member—Dos Passos, Lawson, Mike Gold, Em Jo Basshe, and Francis Faragoh—as well as by Paul Sifton, a playwright-director who often worked with them, and by a few other notable artists such as Upton Sinclair.[6] In recounting briefly the impact of each of those plays in his final *New Masses* essay dealing with the group, "Did the New Playwrights' Theatre Fail?",[7] Dos Passos finds that most of the plays themselves were worthwhile, despite often poor reviews. But patrons—like critics—were simply unprepared to accept the innovative techniques that characterized the productions: "It was fairly natural that the audience, being used to the conventions of the pictureframe and to the carefully pigeonholed distinctions of farce, musical comedy, drama, didn't like" many of the plays ("New Playwrights," 13). In their enthusiasm to depict working-class struggles, the radical artists had failed to take into account the realities of working-class lives. Many of the productions played to sparse audiences most nights, suggesting that most proletarians were not not inclined to spend their nights watching avant-garde interpretations of problems they wrestled with at work during the day. Even though the group conscientiously charged very low admission prices—prices the worker could afford—seats in the small theater in Greenwich Village went unsold most nights; and the lack of revenue contributed to the financial worries the group suffered during its three years of activity. Correspondence between individual members of the company and their primary backer, Otto Kahn, a financier and wealthy patron of the arts, documents the group's increasingly frequent requests for additional funds and Kahn's growing impatience with them, despite his munificence at the beginning of the venture.

Even if the plays had generated sufficient revenue to sustain the company, the other problem that Dos Passos cited—weak internal organization—would eventually have proved fatal to the effort. In his letter resigning as one of the company's directors, Dos Passos describes the members' differences as "a typically New York confusion of aims" (*Fourteenth*, 390) and alludes to conflicts between the company's interests and the self-promotion or political agendas of unnamed members. Lawson, for instance, may have regarded Dos Passos's *Airways, Inc.,* one of the plays the group staged, as "insufficiently social-revolutionary" (Wilson, 167). In fact, differences were already beginning to surface between Dos Passos and Lawson, an ardent Communist, that would end their friendship bitterly in 1937 when Dos Passos publicly expressed his disillusionment with the party's tactics in the United States and in the Spanish Civil War.

More immediately, however, Dos Passos was ready to resume his solitary work on his next fiction, *The 42nd Parallel*. Keeping the late hours and performing the multiple jobs necessary to stage the productions prevented him from writing steadily. The theater experiment had given him a chance to vary his mediums. Later in his life, in fact, he declared that he had been "more interested in scene designing than in the drama per se,"[8] and for the New Playwrights he designed and created a number of striking sets whose styles evoke the work of Diego Rivera or the contemporary urban-industrial art of the masses. And, in the plays he had written, he had dramatized not only the problems he would address in *U.S.A.* but also some of the techniques with which he would express them. *Airways, Inc.,* the company's final production, layers the speeches of strikers with those of corporate public relations officials in a counterpoint that lays bare the exploitation of the workers. The New York critics panned the play, but the *Daily Worker* loved it. Less predictable an assessment, however, came from Edmund Wilson, who alone of the major critics found the play, for all its faults, a vital representation of the motion and confusion of an urban nation—all of which Dos Passos would try to encompass in *U.S.A.* He acknowledged later that his "excitement over the 'expressionist' theatre" of the 1920s "had a great deal to do with shaping [the trilogy's] style" ("Looking Back").

As in his writing for the *New Masses* and his involvement with the New Playwrights Theater, Dos Passos sought in his travels during the late 1920s artistic means to achieve his political ends. Leaving temporarily behind the mixed motives of the repertory group, he traveled in 1928 to the Soviet Union to view firsthand the workings of a theater that he felt successfully used art, without sacrificing its integrity, in the service of revolutionary politics. His visits to the productions of Soviet dramatists such as V. E. Meyerhold reinforced his optimism about the potential of radical art, as did his discovery of informal theater productions staged by workers. These partly improvised short plays, which the workers called "Living Newspapers," dramatized the personal element in the flow of political events; its goal of uniting the human and the historical was one of his, too, in the work he had undertaken in the months before departing for Russia, a novel that eventually became the first edition of *The 42nd Parallel.*

But an even more crucial influence on this new work was his exposure to Russian film. In fact, as he wrote to E. E. Cummings, the "most interesting and lively people" he met during his stay in Moscow were "the movie directors" (*Fourteenth,* 386) of the many films that depicted the Russian Revolution and read history in terms of Marxist ideology. He noted Sergei Eisenstein particularly as having "one of the most brilliantly synthesizing minds" of any of the artists whose work he had ever seen (Ludington 1980, 270). Biographers such as Ludington, as well as critics analyzing the photographic and film dynamics of Dos Passos's trilogy, cite as a major influence the work of Eisenstein: like Dos Passos in his modernist works, he exploited montage and opposition, combined fiction and history, and theorized about how art could effect political action.[9]

But possibly more influential on the development of *U.S.A.*—and, unlike the influence of Eisenstein, a source never acknowledged by Dos Passos in his lifetime—were the films, writings, and theories of Dziga Vertov. As Carol Shloss persuasively argues in her chapter "John Dos Passos and the Soviet Cinema," Vertov's works would have been playing in the Moscow theaters during Dos Passos's visit, and the film "manifestos" that Vertov published in the mid-to-late-1920s would have been available to the writer, whose enthusiasm for Soviet film and film theory emerges powerfully in his letters home at this time: "Even the bum ones [films] have redeeming features," he enthuses to Cummings (*Fourteenth,* 386). The theories and terms Vertov originated in his film journal *Kino-pravda* and elaborated on throughout his career uncannily anticipate the dynamics by which Dos Passos structured *U.S.A.* and, by means of these devices, dealt with the role of the artist in the unfolding of history. In her discussion of why Dos Passos never mentioned Vertov as a source of inspiration, Schloss theorizes that Vertov's concept of the "kino-eye" (film-eye) and the implications it carries of the artist's involvement in creating the narrative—of a film, of a fiction, of history—was "too closely related" both to the name and the function of the trilogy's "Camera Eye" device "for Dos Passos's aesthetic comfort" (151). Certainly, as an exploration of the structures of the trilogy will show, the devices he originated for the novels move beyond Eisenstein's principle that montage creates and resolves oppositions. That principle more nearly informs the earlier *Manhattan Transfer,* although Griffith was the more likely influence on that work, as chapter 7 discusses. Vertov, on the other hand, acknowledges fragmentation and in part creates a center of consciousness in the work by revealing the hand—or, in Vertov's terms, the eye—of the maker and exploring its impact on the events it records. So, too, Dos Passos, in moving slowly toward a re-placement of the subjective consciousness into the narrative as the trilogy develops, questions the degree of the artist's power and grapples with the imperative for the artist's involvement as a precondition of change in the nation, the "power superpower," whose throes he charts.

The more immediate creative result of Dos Passos's Russian adventure was a series of impressionistic essays about how Communism affected the people, conditions, and the arts in the Soviet Union. Eventually published in his 1934 book of reportage *In All Countries,*[10] his perceptions did not move him toward any public declarations about whether Communism could effectively address the problems he felt so keenly in America's social, economic, technological, and governmental systems. As invigorating as his exposure to a revolutionized culture had been—a "bath of energy," he called it (Ludington 1980, 274)—it had also had dark undertones. By the time he finally published his account of the journey, he had grown sufficiently suspicious of the Communists to evoke in his writing the terror in the eyes of a bystander who had witnessed the brutality of Communist purges of dissidents or other factions. Even as he left Russia, as his friends there prevailed upon him to publicly declare himself their partisan, he demurred, feeling that his stance was too complex for him to articulate in the Russian language he had learned only imperfectly.

Although, when he returned to the United States at the end of 1928, he was unwilling to identify himself completely with an ideology, he had nevertheless the previous year committed himself openly and outspokenly to the most controversial cause espoused by the Left in the 1920s—the defense of Sacco and Vanzetti. The trial and subsequent execution of the Italian immigrants accused of robbery and murder moved Dos Passos to the most radical political position he was ever to occupy, but characteristically he maintained his independence of organized political movements such as the Communist Party. Even though he agreed with their social ideas, he would only identify himself wholeheartedly with a movement devoted to gaining justice for particular individuals. This is the deep concern from which the trilogy emanates—how can the common individual prevail against the massive systems of industrial capitalism that have turned the promises of the American dream into a lie? The major impetus for Dos Passos to write *U.S.A.* was the case of Sacco and Vanzetti.

Although historians today question their innocence, Dos Passos was one of a multitude of leftist writers, artists, and intelligentsia who were convinced that the 1920 arrest of the shoemaker Nicola Sacco and the fish peddler Bartolomeo Vanzetti was the result of rampant prejudice against immigrants exacerbated by the Red Scare of 1919 and 1920. The case became not only a cause célèbre but also the subject of diverse artistic outcries, from a play by Maxwell Anderson to poems by Edna St. Vincent Millay and paintings by Ben Shahn. Dos Passos himself identified closely with the accused men: they were political radicals who opposed war and whose very foreignness brought them under suspicion, just as Dos Passos's own Portuguese name and slightly European air and accent had rendered him an outsider as a child. Out of his sympathy for them and his conviction that they were being persecuted for their anarchist views, he responded to the case with a number of important pieces in 1926 and 1927: "The Pit and the Pendulum," his coverage of the case for the *New Masses;* "Sacco and Vanzetti," an impassioned *New Masses* review of a Eugene Lyons book about the sequence of events leading to the trial; "An Open Letter to President Lowell," published in the *Nation,* condemning the president of Harvard for his role in advising the governor of Massachusetts against clemency for the pair; and *Facing the Chair,* a 127-page pamphlet for the Sacco-Vanzetti Defense Committee.[11] In each of these forceful documents, Dos Passos argued that the case embodied both the struggle of the individual for justice in America and the plight of the working class endangered by "hatred of the new young vigorous unfamiliar forces" of ambitious immigrants, by an economic system that increasingly disenfranchised the worker, and by the "stealthy soulless mechanism of the law" ("Pit," 10–11).

Thus, as Dos Passos conceptualized and began to immerse himself in the novel that would become *The 42nd Parallel,* he knew his theme—the "basic tragedy" that, he observed later, all his work expresses, "man's struggle for life against the strangling institutions he himself creates"

("Looking Back"). He knew his scope, too, and his materials—"as much as possible of the broad field of the lives of these times" ("Introductory," vii), 1916 to 1919, the years of America's involvement in World War I and its immediate aftermath. He wanted to create "a contemporary commentary on history's changes, always as seen by some individual's eyes, heard by some individual's ears, felt through some individual's nerves and tissues" ("What," 31). And he knew that his aims in this new novel, more overtly political than those in *Manhattan Transfer,* would require methods that could articulate his conviction that the writer is the "architect of history" who has the responsibility to "write straight." Yet, to achieve both his artistic and his political goals without "preaching,"[12] he realized he needed to be both inside and outside of the narrative, both engagé and dégagé ("What," 31), as he expressed the goal of the artist even at the end of his career. Such an equipoise between passion and objectivity could only be gained through a dynamic structure that required the reader's involvement. The structure he evolved placed into tension fiction and history, the subjective and the objective, in interactive relationships that created meaning in the same way the planes and forms of a cubist painting interact dynamically.

The vehicles of these relationships are the four modes of *The 42nd Parallel* and the two subsequent novels, *1919* and *The Big Money,* which in 1937 were published together as *U.S.A.* Although he was conceptualizing only a single novel and not a trilogy when he first began writing *The 42nd Parallel* in 1927, as he gathered material for the four modes and considered the extent of the matter he wanted to treat, "it became obvious that the thing was going to be so long that it would be better to publish it in sections." Even as he gathered material for each mode, however, he already had "a plan about the end," although characters would change and grow while he wrote ("Interview," 15).

Dos Passos described the functions of the four modes in the introduction he wrote to the 1937 Modern Library edition of *The 42nd Parallel* that was part of *U.S.A.,* after all three novels had appeared individually. The "long narrative" of the trilogy, he explained, "deals with the more or less entangled lives of a number of Americans during the first three decades of the present century"—fictional narratives. Three other "sequences . . . [thread] in and out among the stories." Biographies of "real people are interlarded in the pauses of the narrative because their lives seem to embody so well the quality of the soil in which Americans of these generations grew." "Newsreel" sequences, which consist of fragments of newspaper headlines, phrases of stories from newspapers and tabloids, snippets of popular songs, and lines from speeches, "give an inkling of the common mind of the epoch." The "Camera Eye" "aims to indicate the position of the observer" ("Introductory," vii). These segments consist of impressionistic, autobiographical observations in a stream-of-consciousness style. They emanate from the point of view of a persona who is contemporaneous with the era of the novel; the persona's experiences and perceptions chart the growth of a writer's commitment to his vocation and articulate the genesis of his realization that "we have only words against POWER SUPERPOWER" (*Big,* 1210). Although the novel's modes function fully only in relation to one another, understanding the construction of each novel and each mode provides a basis that makes the dynamic of the whole more accessible.

The Fictional Narratives

Although these novels are densely populated with dozens of characters, they follow central portions of the lives of 12 principal figures who are buffeted, elevated, and borne along naturalistically by the rush of forces and events in the first third of the twentieth century. In each of the three novels, the experiences of one or two of these 12 establish an overarching theme that extends to the lives of all the other characters in the novel. Also, as exploration of the other modes reveals, the central concern in each novel governs the author's choices of actual figures who are subjects of the biographies, his choices of materials for the "Newsreel" segments, and, perhaps most important, his selection of autobiographical fragments from which to structure "Camera Eye" sequences. It is a mark of the "hidden" nature of Dos Passos's art, as Sartre phrased it (Sartre, 85), that the possibility of the "Camera Eye" persona's control of all the narrative choices never asserts itself until very late in the trilogy, at a point where form and theme are revealed to be synonymous.

The primary fictional character of *The 42nd Parallel,* the trilogy's first novel, is Fenian McCreary, who comes to be known as Mac. Mac is a rootless, working-class printer who becomes involved in radical politics through his association with the Industrial Workers of the World. Despite his participation in the major IWW-led miners' strikes in Nevada, over which "Big Bill" Haywood, the charismatic labor leader, presided, Mac deserts the movement and betrays his own ideals for the comforts of a middle-class life and marriage. But his relationship with Maisie, whom he marries because she is pregnant, sours because of her aggressive materialism. After leaving her he returns intermittently to radical causes, but the last narrative segment in *The 42nd Parallel* dealing exclusively with Mac makes clear that the labor movement and American radicalism are seriously threatened by America's entry into World War I. Tempted as he is by the ease of petit bourgeois involvement in the benefits of capitalism, Mac's ultimate lack of commitment to the radical movement and its dedication to improving workers' lives implies what Dos Passos sees as a defining direction in America from 1900 to the end of the war: the emergence of monopoly capitalism and all the enticements and enterprises it creates threatens to overpower not just the labor movement or radical politics but also the possibility for any authentic belief or expression of belief in the original promises of America. In a technique that Pizer calls "interlacing" (Pizer, *Dos Passos' U.S.A.*, 65), Mac's story intersects briefly with the narrative of the other central male figure in the novel, J. Ward Moorehouse. But their encounter in Mexico, where Mac has drifted after leaving Maisie, is so casual that rather than creating much traditional narrative unity it reinforces the sense that these characters are directed by naturalistic forces.

The stories of the other two central characters of *The 42nd Parallel*—Janey Williams and Eleanor Stoddard—intersect more traditionally and integrally with the Moorehouse narrative. In general, the interlacing of characters intensifies as the trilogy progresses. If Mac suggests the threats to radicalism from capitalistic systems, Moorehouse represents the emerging ethos and practices of the systems themselves. Although only three narrative chapters in *The 42nd Parallel* are devoted to his story—and none in the two subsequent novels—his presence and what it represents resonate throughout the trilogy.

Born on the Fourth of July, from childhood Moorehouse singlemindedly pursues the American version of success. As a boy he commands a marbles competition not only because of his skill but also because he has "maneuvered with the help of a little Jewish boy named Ira Goldberg" a "corner in agates"; "they managed to rent out agates to other boys for a cent a week for ten" (156). As he matures, he becomes more and more adept at seizing the main chance, until, through a mixture of advantageous but corrupt marriages, ambition, and a facility for manipulating language, he establishes his own successful public relations firm. Supremely confident in his skill at constructing images that will sell, he believes so implicitly in them—"American industry like a steamengine . . . charging through the night of old individualistic methods" (234)—that belief in anything substantial or genuine is unnecessary and even detrimental. Seeing in the European war "America's great opportunity"

(237), he represents the interests of capitalists trying to get the most lucrative deals possible with labor. The reader's last sight of Moorehouse in this novel finds him heading for Europe to exploit the war efforts of the Red Cross. Throughout the trilogy, he epitomizes the betrayal of the original promises of America and the distortion of the "old words" of the nation's founding by the massive forces of industry and government, which work in the interests of power and greed, not for the people they ostensibly serve.

Around Moorehouse's narrative revolve the stories of the other two main characters of *The 42nd Parallel,* Janey Williams and Eleanor Stoddard. Both women illustrate how business and the seductions of material success in America can transform people whose natures are initially open to genuine feelings and relationships into mechanical beings who repress and ultimately lose their natural impulses to love. Janey's is a lower-middle-class version of this story; Eleanor's, ambitiously middle-class. Janey rises from her position as secretary in a Washington, D.C., law firm to become the personal assistant of Moorehouse; in her position, she can serve him and adore him without risking actual involvement because of his unavailability and her deeply conventional values. Eleanor likewise parlays her talents—she is an interior designer—into a business that provides her escape from her average background into a world of taste, culture, and contacts with patrons such as Moorehouse. Her determination to maintain the image of respectability and refinement she has created for herself disallows any relationship—particularly sexual—that might disrupt her control and her facade. Thus, in their opportunism and sexual mistrust, Eleanor and Moorehouse are in fact perfectly suited for the sterile, mutually exploitive relationship they have throughout most of the first two novels: she wants the prestige he lends her as an escort, patron, and financial advisor; and he wants the impeccable taste and aura of class that accompany her. When Eleanor assures Moorehouse's wife that their "relations are pure as the driven snow" (311), her characterization is as true of their sexuality at that point as it is untrue of their social and business exploitation of one another.

In all his narratives focusing on women in the trilogy, Dos Passos depicts them as being as much under the control of cultural forces as are his male characters. But the predictability of the forces in the lives of the women—conventionality, the drive for respectability, shallow materialism—has led some analysts of the trilogy to criticize it as sexist or even misogynist.[13] Indeed, with the exception of Mary French, who in *The Big*

Money becomes a serious worker for the American Communist Party, the women in the trilogy are often controlled by stereotypically female concerns. Janey and Eleanor in particular seem cast in the same limited mold as were the only two primary women characters in Dos Passos's previous works. Like the woman central to *Streets of Night*, whom Dos Passos described in a letter as "that tiresome bitch Miss Nan Taylor" (Landsberg ed., 200), Janey is shackled emotionally by her fear of her sexuality and of men; and, like Ellen Thatcher of *Manhattan Transfer*, Eleanor creates a sterilely aesthetic world in which success takes precedence over love or ethics in a relationship. But as Robert Rosen points out, the naturalistic method, which is so evident in the novels of the trilogy, necessarily involves stereotypes; a naturalistic novel uninformed by feminism will "reflect not only its author's unexamined assumptions but the sexism of the society it depicts" (Rosen, 85). Yet half of the trilogy's main fictional characters are women, and Mary French's story certainly creates sympathy and, in fact, incorporates autobiographical elements of the author's experiences in the Sacco-Vanzetti defense. On the other hand, of the biographies in the trilogy drawn from a period in which women won the right to vote, in addition to other advances, only one concerns a woman, the dancer Isadora Duncan; there are no historical depictions of women outside traditionally female spheres. Both positively and negatively, *U.S.A.* reflects and reconstructs its era accurately.

Whereas *The 42nd Parallel* depicts the political and economic transitions of the years before and at the beginning of World War I, the next novel of the trilogy, *1919*, takes place during and immediately after America's involvement in the war. This second work, more sharply focused and more pointedly satirical, was written between 1929 and 1931, a time when it was becoming clear to Dos Passos that Woodrow Wilson's war had not, indeed, ended all wars and that the economy it created had been integral in precipitating the stock market crash of 1929. To Malcolm Cowley, Dos Passos suggested that "the later part of the book shows a certain crystalization (call it monopoly capitalism?) of society that didn't exist in the early part of 42nd Parallel (call it competitive capitalism?)." But in 1932, when he published *1919*, he could not be sure whether the third volume, yet to come, would ameliorate the bitterness of the second: "as for the note of hope—gosh who knows?" (*Fourteenth*, 404).

The four central characters in *1919* are balanced and interlaced in much the same way the characters of the previous novel are. Like Mac in *The 42nd Parallel* and Bud Korpenning before him in *Manhattan Transfer*,

Joe Williams is relatively isolated from the other three main narrative figures, but establishes a theme that will be powerfully and completely developed via their lives. Unlike his sister Janey Williams, Joe commits himself to experience, sexuality, and his version of fulfillment. But it is a mark of the growing pessimism of the works that his very openness to authentic feeling dooms him as it meets the hardships and disenfranchisements endemic to his lower-middle-class background and repressive family. The adventures Joe encounters as a seaman surely reflect Dos Passos's affection for the Spanish picaresque novel; but these scrapes intensify into genuine danger as Joe's lack of direction and his own nature make every facet of his itinerant life easy prey for brutal exploiters. In his diffuse search to realize the American dreams his working-class upbringing has engendered in him—freedom, "money and a good job and a girl of his own" (407)—he is victimized and overwhelmed by the conventions and economic restrictions of his class, realities that, in American life, create desire and thus control the dreamer.

The other central male character in *1919*, however, is actually the presiding presence of the novel. Richard Ellsworth Savage is as aware of how to use the class system to his advantage as Joe Williams is unaware of its crushing effect on him. Yet the narrative concerning Savage, woven as it is out of the fabric of Dos Passos's own life and those of his Harvard friends, is not the unambiguous indictment of betrayers of America's promises that Moorehouse's story is. Instead, Savage's story is a portrait of how privilege and self-interest can combine to produce a life of self-deception and moral irresponsibility. Even though he accepts a position in Moorehouse's postwar public relations office knowing the falsity of the business, he has been opposed to the war, has in fact been dismissed from his Red Cross ambulance unit for condemning America's tainted participation in the slaughter, just as Dos Passos himself did. As Harvard aesthete, combat ambulance driver, and army officer relishing the freedoms of France as he celebrates the Armistice, Savage represents the experiences of Dos Passos's own class and generation, many of whom the writer must have seen relinquish their radical and pacifist ideals after the war in their effort to benefit from the wealth to be made in the postwar economy.

Dos Passos communicates Savage's lack of moral rigor in part through the character's ambiguous sexuality. In this novel, in which sexual relationships are a trap for both men and women and sexuality renders one either predator or prey, Dos Passos extends this naturalistic depiction through Savage's homosexual tendencies, implicit in *1919* but

overt by the end of *The Big Money.* As with Dos Passos's ambivalent portrayal of Tony in *Manhattan Transfer,* this characterization suggests that
Savage's orientation is influenced by his parents' flaws and his own
almost feminine good looks. His moral weakness becomes explicit late
in the novel in a variety of ways: as noted, he joins Moorehouse's firm
even after seeing firsthand the grotesque difference between the reality
of the war, which he undergoes, and the manipulative rhetoric of war
disseminated by public relations experts such as Moorehouse; and Savage callously seduces, impregnates, then deserts his sweetheart, Anne
Elizabeth Trent. In his initial opposition to the war and his subsequent
willingness to profit from it and in his opportunistic dishonesty both
with himself and others, Savage suggests what Dos Passos saw as America's own self-serving, self-justifying participation in the war and the
manipulation of language and reality by which the nation's corporations
and government seduced the public into supporting it.

This novel's two primary female characters are, as in *The 42nd Parallel,* satellites to the commanding central male of the work. Anne Elizabeth Trent, or "Daughter" as she is called in the narrative titles, begins
as a wholesome all-American Texan with a vigor and freedom that nurture the openness of her character. Like Joe Williams, however, that
openness will make her vulnerable to exploitation by men such as Savage as she searches for a strong male around whom to center her life.
Again like Joe, whose wandering ends in a meaningless death in a bar
fight, Daughter wills herself to destruction and death through reckless
behavior once Savage, the force that shapes her life, advises her to marry
someone else to legitimize his child that she is carrying. Savage's dishonesty destroys her life, just as the falsity of the war rhetoric he helps to
create dooms those who must actually fight the war.

Eveline Hutchins, the other central female figure in *1919,* similarly
becomes prey to an unscrupulous seducer, Moorehouse. In this relationship, once again Dos Passos constructs a parallel between the personal
immorality and the public corruption of national values. Eveline, a
peripheral character in *The 42nd Parallel,* follows her friend Eleanor
Stoddard to assist her in the Red Cross public relations office soon
headed by Moorehouse. To allay Eveline's fear that he is involved with
Eleanor, Moorehouse uses the sentimentalized, platitudinous rhetoric of
the "spiritual" relationship free of the degradingly sensual—the same
obscurantist language with which Eleanor characterized her association
with him to his wife in the previous novel. The mutual opportunism of
that relationship has extended to the sexual once Eleanor and Moore-

house, working in Paris, are free of his wife's scrutiny and the possibility of damaging their public images. When Eveline discovers the couple in bed, she escapes into a conventional engagement with a sturdy American doughboy. When she reveals that she is pregnant, he gallantly insists on expediting their wedding. She acknowledges neither to him nor to herself that she is unsure of the child's paternity. Moorehouse's exploitation of Eveline by means of language that misrepresents his motives echoes his contribution to the rhetoric by which the nations negotiating peace at the end of the war disguised their self-interest.

Of all the ways in which Dos Passos denounces the war in this novel—through the characters' lives and speeches, through the "Newsreel" and "Camera Eye" segments and the biographies, as we shall see— no denunciation is clearer or more affecting than the final section of *1919*, "The Body of an American." Technically a biography, this segment recounts in Whitmanesque, expressionist terms the life, death, and interment of the Unknown Soldier buried at Arlington National Cemetery. It is a cubist portrait whose elements interact to create an image not just of a soldier but of the country that bred him and then sent him to France to die in confusion in a war fueled, Dos Passos makes clear, by cant and masked self-interest. The elements counterpose in a devastating tension: fragments from the congressional resolution designating a memorial to an unidentifiable casualty of the war; newspaper accounts of the burial ceremony; lines from President Harding's speech at the site; vulgar conversations among the morgue workers selecting the remains; composite details of the childhood and growth of the typical American boy; the voice of John Doe himself as he is groomed by the military, enters battle, and becomes separated from his unit; and the angry but factual voice of the narrator—whose identification with the "Camera Eye" persona will charge *The Big Money* with a metafictional dimension. In this terse but complex and ironic finale to *1919*, Dos Passos makes clear that the government, sacrificing the individual to its national economic and political interests, regards the soldier as a nonentity. Dos Passos, however, makes of the soldier at once an American individual and an everyman.

As startling and virtuoso a piece of writing as "The Body of an American" is as a conclusion to the second novel of the trilogy, in *The Big Money*, Dos Passos has raised the stakes: with the peace and the crash of 1929 behind him, and the Communist Party at home and abroad becoming as repressive as the systems he had once hoped the Left would transform, he broadened the scope of this volume as he wrote it between 1932 and 1936 and achieved the potential effects of the stylistic machinery he had created. His falling-out with John Howard Lawson over Lawson's insistence that Dos Passos echo the playwright's doctrinaire party line had forced Dos Passos yet again to declare his independence of creed. That assertion had found its way from his letters to Lawson in 1934 to the essay Dos Passos wrote for the Communist-influenced Writer's Congress in 1935. In that address, "The Writer as Technician," Dos Passos reaffirmed the writer's responsibility to "take crossbearings on . . . abstractions" as often as necessary to keep himself "honest." He articulated his belief that the writer who remains true to himself and his vision can "influence[ ] ways of thinking" and "rebuild[ ] the language, which is the mind of the group": "At this particular moment in history, when machinery and institutions have so outgrown the ability of the mind to dominate them, we need bold and original thought more than ever. It is the business of writers to supply that thought, and not to make themselves figureheads in political conflicts."[14]

The overpowering weight of social and industrial institutions in modern life, the centrality of the writer's vocation in "rebuilding the language," and the identification of a culture's valuation of language with the culture's commitment to individual freedoms—these concerns became Dos Passos's themes in *The Big Money*. Published in 1936, this novel spans the 1920s, picking up where *1919* concluded, with American troops returning from Europe after the demobilization. With the exception of the story of radical activist Mary French, the primary and secondary fictional narratives in this book depict characters grasping for success as it is coming to be defined in postwar boom America—grabbing for "the big money"—and allowing this hollow American dream to construct their identities. Unlike the previous two, this novel's sharply satiric aim is leveled more broadly at American culture and definitions of success. It introduces a different set of narrative figures although some earlier ones reappear; it bodies forth those characters more fully despite its still-naturalistic intent; and, most important for understanding the direction Dos Passos's career was about to take in the late 1930s, it extends its satiric vision to the working of the American Left, sharply criticizing it as yet another impersonal force controlling and often destroying its adherents. For these reasons, many critics regard this novel not just as the most independent and fully realized of the three but also as the most pessimistic.

In terms of the structure of its fictional elements, the novel achieves a unity its predecessors lack, a unity almost akin to that of a traditional novel, although the almost "hidden" working of its modes is chiefly responsible for that impression. No single linguistic manipulator dominates the book; instead, language, representation, and sign are false coin everywhere, and the perpetrators of false promises fall victim to the very systems they help to build. Instead of a prominent male figure around whom the women characters revolve, as in the first two novels, *The Big Money* cofeatures a man, Charley Anderson, and a woman, Margo Dowling, in an almost equal number of alternating segments. Although they struggle for success in different spheres and with different results, Dos Passos clearly intends a parallel between the two: although one lives and one dies, both kill a vital humanity in themselves to achieve success in the American capitalist system. Similarly, the third major character, Mary French, suffers a death of the self, but under the influence of her belief that communism, not capitalism, is the remedy for the soul sickness of the culture she sees around her.

The three major characters represent arenas of American life that defined the swirl of social and economic transition that was the 1920s. Charley Anderson, first introduced on his way to the war in France in the last section of *The 42nd Parallel,* returns to America. after the war as *The Big Money* opens. His observation as he docks in New York that he remembers the Statue of Liberty as "lookin' bigger" (773) presages his dissatisfaction at returning to his old life in Minnesota; he becomes determined to settle in the city, get a glamorous girl, and "make a lot of money right away quick" (821), as Eveline Hutchins expresses the goal of the era when he meets her and her husband in New York. He achieves each of these goals but at considerable cost: his wife Gladys, a banker's daughter, is an upper-class version of the grasping materialistic wives of Mac and Joe Williams; and to amass a fortune, he has to leave behind his production job, in which he delighted as a talented mechanic, and enter management, playing the market and ultimately betraying his partner and his own aviation firm by speculating in company stock. The allure of easy money and prestige transforms him from an ingenious technician who takes pride in his skill into an executive who spouts probusiness slogans—"We've got a responsibility towards our investors . . . the industry's the first line of national defense" (1030–31)—while he ostentatiously professes to be on the side of his laborers. After a crash in which his honest old friend, a fellow mechanic, is killed, some genuine self in Charley seems to have died as well. He heads for Florida to recuperate but, for the most part, only drinks and speculates in the Florida land boom, the emptiness of his pastimes signaling that his material success has effectively cost him the talents and human warmth that made him an individual. He dies of an infection resulting from an automobile crash in which, befuddled with drink, he tries to beat an oncoming train across the tracks.

In Florida before his death he meets Margo Dowling, whose story parallels and interlaces with his. If Charley's career represents the boom in the early airline industry, Margo's represents another of the pure products of America—the movies. Naturalistically impelled early in her life into a mistrust of men by her father's desertion of her and her stepfather's sexual abuse, Margo learns how to manipulate masculine sexuality to her advantage. This equips her perfectly to achieve her version of the American dream—to be a movie star, a career that depends on her ability to create desire, to be an advertisement for the unattainable, to be the same kind of product J. Ward Moorehouse creates. Yet unlike Moorehouse, Margo elicits some sympathy from the reader because her path is so clearly shaped by the exploitation she suffers as a girl and by her wit and resourcefulness.

Having married Tony, a young Cuban, to escape her stepfather, and having seduced an American official to escape from Tony and Cuba, she survives by exploiting her beauty and sexuality. Yet her amorality in the interests of self-preservation is mitigated by her sometimes fatal kindness of heart: she loses the chance to marry a wealthy Yale man when she takes pity on Tony, who has reappeared, penniless and now obviously homosexual. As in Richard Ellsworth Savage's story, homosexuality is once again an unambiguous sign of a corrupt character.

This same good-heartedness in Margo brings her together with Charley when both are in Florida and where she becomes his mistress. Although at one level their relationship is an economic transaction, at another level they discover in each other the human self each has repressed to attain success. For a brief section of the novel, they share the only genuinely affectionate relationship between major characters in the work. Yet as he lies dying, Margo tries to elicit one last check from him. The annihilation of genuine feeling she has managed will enable her to leave Florida, where swamps are passed off as prime real estate, to make her run on Hollywood, a city built on the business of creating illusion, where lower-class girls from Brooklyn can recreate themselves as foreign heiresses.

Such is Margo's disguise when she meets Margolies, a director whose autocratic control over her subsequent career resembles what Dos Passos saw of Josef von Sternberg's management of Marlene Dietrich's rise to stardom while the writer spent a brief stint in Hollywood working on scripts. Like Charley, Margo gains the big money; like him, she pays with her integrity; but unlike him, she survives to live out her fleeting success. That life, however, consists of an extravagant construction of lies: she passes Tony off as her chauffeur and he later dies in a sordid brawl; she marries the voyeuristic Margolies and, under his direction, simulates graphic passion on screen and off with her dim, alcoholic costar. At the end of the novel, the woman whom Margolies proclaims as "the nation's newest sweetheart" seems nothing more than a "porcelain doll" (1126, 1234), whose stardom is now doomed, ironically, by the coming of sound motion pictures. An already false language of signs will be augmented by an even more powerful and meretricious language as the film industry—the one American business that did not lose money during the depression but actually expanded—enlists words as well as pictures in the fabrication of destructively false dreams and desires.

Whereas Margo Dowling banishes feelings that would impede her in her drive to stardom, the third major character in *The Big Money*, Mary French, cannot construct a meaningful life for herself without them. Her sympathies for the downtrodden lead to her commitment to radical social causes, including the Sacco-Vanzetti case. Although Mary is not a Communist Party member, she works for the its causes because she believes its methods can most effectively remedy the economic and social injustices that affect her. Yet her sympathies make her vulnerable to the lovers she takes from among the party members, who disappoint and abandon her, justifying their callousness by saying that they must subordinate their own needs to the work of the party. The very commitment that creates meaning for her, however, ultimately conflicts with Communist ideology during the last days of the party's effort to secure a stay of execution for Sacco and Vanzetti. Exhausted by her frustrated hopes that she can save the men's lives, she finds strength in the commanding presence of Comrade Stevens, a party official she admires. Working for the futile campaign in the anarchists' behalf, Mary finds she is "least unhappy" doing errands and paperwork for Stevens. Thus, when she hears him declare of the accused men, "It doesn't matter whether they are saved or not any more, it's the power of the working-class that's got to be saved," and sees him organize a demonstration he acknowledges "will spoil the chance that the governor will commute at the last moment" (1153), she allows her commitment to individuals to be overridden by the rhetoric of the organization. Her capitulation to the impersonal forces of the party seems complete when, now Stevens's lover, she refuses to shelter her former lover, Ben Compton, destitute after having been expelled from the party as an oppositionist, for fear that she will jeopardize Stevens's standing in the party. And when Stevens deserts her to enter into a party-arranged marriage, Mary represses all feeling as she devotes herself entirely and impersonally to ideologically correct Communist activities.

When her story ends, she is perfunctorily helping to organize a protest meeting at Madison Square Garden. As if the party's exploitation of Mary French were not sufficient to suggest the critical stance Dos Passos had now assumed toward it, he concludes her story with an allusion to a meeting similar to a highly publicized 1934 meeting, which also took place in Madison Square Garden, in which factional rivalry led the Communist Party to disrupt a rally of the Socialist Party. The Communist Party, as it had become in America, would not tolerate individual dissent. That position was anathema to Dos Passos, ever the individualist thinker but now, moving counter to the tide of the American Left, militantly so. To Malcolm Cowley he wrote in 1935, while *The Big Money* was underway, "I don't believe the Communist movement is capable of doing anything but provoke oppression and I no longer believe that the end justifies the means" (*Fourteenth,* 477).

The intersection of fiction and history is evident not only in this narrative, which incorporates much of Dos Passos's own experience with the Sacco-Vanzetti defense, but also throughout the trilogy. In the work of a writer who defined a novelist as "a sort of second-class historian of the age he lives in,"[15] it is not surprising to find major characters whose stories are drawn from the lives of people Dos Passos knew and people he met in his extensive travels. J. Ward Moorehouse, for instance, grew partly out of Dos Passos's conversations in 1928 with Ivy Lee, cofounder of the American public relations industry (*Best,* 178). Moorehouse's belief that language is merely a tool to control public opinion echoes Lee's advocacy, articulated in his book *Human Nature and Railroads* (1915), of practices such as substituting the inoffensive phrase "readjustment of finances" for the more realistic "bankruptcy" (quoted in Pizer *Dos Passos' U.S.A.,* 126). For Moorehouse's protégé Richard Ellsworth Savage, who lends his glib skills to the Paris treaty negotiations, Dos Passos acknowledged that he "cribbed from [the] career and some peace conference stories" of Robert Hillyer, his friend since their Harvard days (*Fourteenth,* 543). The two friends had served in the Norton-Harjes ambulance corps and together had written "Seven Times round the

Walls of Jericho" during the war. Hillyer apparently saw enough resemblance between his experiences and those of the compromised, unscrupulous Savage to protest Dos Passos's use of his friends as novelistic material. But Dos Passos assured him that "Savage was a synthetic character as all the characters in my novels are" (*Fourteenth*, 544) and not an unflattering portrait of his friend. The postwar job Savage assumes and his avoidance of responsibility for his pregnant sweetheart, Anne Elizabeth Trent, do echo events in the life of John Howard Lawson, Dos Passos's wartime friend and cofounder of the New Playwrights. Lawson had been reluctant to marry his pregnant girlfriend, Kate Drain, an attractive woman whom Dos Passos befriended while she worked as a nurse's aide in wartime Paris (Ludington 1980, 162). In her vigor and her Texas background, Trent resembles also Dos Passos's onetime fiancée Crystal Ross. But unlike F. Scott Fitzgerald, who permanently damaged a friendship when he appropriated for *Tender Is the Night* the lives of Gerald and Sara Murphy, who were gracious hosts and benefactors of Fitzgerald, Dos Passos, Hemingway, and many other notable artists of the period, Dos Passos did not regard his friends' lives as his fictional territory. Rather, his interest was in building "a contemporary commentary on history's changes" ("What," 31), and he found his material for that part of the novel that would convey the texture and psychology of the times in the public lives of the era.

Biographies

In the introductory note to the 1930 edition of *The 42nd Parallel*, Dos Passos explained that the biographies of "real people . . . interlarded in the pauses of the narrative" were chosen "because their lives seem to embody so well the quality of the soil in which Americans of this generation grew" ("Introductory," vii). Actually, the 26 biographies, all of deceased public figures, work far more integrally toward the impact of each novel than this brief characterization suggests. Not only are the objects of the portrait representative of their times but also they adumbrate the themes of each novel and provide ironic parallel or counterpoint to the significances of the lives of fictional characters. Whereas the fictional narratives emanate from a naturalistically detached point of view in a relatively objective style, the biographies are impressionistic prose poems that use detail, repetition, and structure to create clearly subjective, sometimes devastatingly critical pictures. For instance, in *1919*, the biography of Woodrow Wilson—titled "Meester Veelson"—

immediately follows three other modal segments dealing with the Armistice: the narrative depicting Joe Williams's violent death during a peace celebration, "Newsreel XXIX" communicating the journalistic and popular giddiness about the Armistice, and "Camera Eye 36," in which the segment's persona empties slops over the side of a troopship on which he is returning to France to serve out his enlistment during demobilization. The subsequent biography traces Wilson from his religious upbringing to when "Wilson became the state (war is the health of the state)." In America, the biography notes,

> War brought the eighthour day, women's votes, prohibition, . . . high wages, high rates of interest, cost plus contracts, and the luxury of being a Gold Star Mother. . . .
>
> In Europe they knew what gas smelt like and the sweet sick stench of bodies buried too shallow and the gray look of the skin of starved children; they read in the papers that Meester Veelson was for peace and freedom and canned goods and butter and sugar.

The peace conference, Dos Passos writes, was "Three old men shuffling the pack, dealing out the cards" and "oil was trumps" (568–70). The contrast between Wilson's lofty rhetoric and the horrible reality of the war, and the detached wielding of power in the peace talks, where Wilson, George, and Clemenceau casually bargain countries and lives for power and profit, intensify the reader's outrage at the waste and hypocrisy of the war. Wilson's biography unifies and completes the effect built by the sequence of the four modal segments.

The power of the biographies and the anger that sometimes emerges from them were evident to those who stood in the path of the criticism. Harper's Publishing Company, for instance, refused *1919* because it contained a damning biography of the financier J. P. Morgan. Lambasting the Morgan firm because it exploits the war for financial gain while it maintains the appearance of a beneficent patron of the arts, Dos Passos writes,

> (Wars and panics on the stock exchange,
> . . . bankruptcies, warloans, starvation,
> starvation, lice, cholera and typhus:
> good growing weather for the House of Morgan.)
>
> (648)

But the "House of Morgan" had loaned money to Harper's during financial difficulties several years before, and the publishing company's executives had no wish to alienate their backer. Dos Passos published the book with Harcourt, Brace in 1932.

The biographies in each novel are chosen to echo the central themes and occupations of the narrative figures; thus, as *The 42nd Parallel* charts the fervor and decline of the labor movement, it offers the biography of "Big Bill" Haywood; *The Big Money* uses biographies of industrialists such as Henry Ford, efficiency experts such as Frederick W. Taylor, and entertainers such as Rudolph Valentino to create its picture of the boom of the 1920s.

Newsreels

The other major source of public history in the novels is the "Newsreel" segments. They contain, as the author said, "Everything. . . . Songs and slogans, political aspirations and prejudices, ideals, hopes, delusions, frauds, crack-pot notions out of the daily newspapers" ("What," 31). The "Newsreels," he explained, were "to give an inkling of the common mind of the epoch," ("Introductory," vii), "to give the clamor, the sound of daily life" ("Interview," 10), whereas the biographies were to provide the pictures. He suggests that the "Newsreels" bear the same kind of relationship to the biographies, which are more substantial and graphically more unified, that the score of a film bears to the images. The viewer of a film is not usually conscious of how the music enhances the visual impressions or how the score, more or less in the background, guides and even manipulates responses. Likewise the "Newsreels" work sometimes almost subliminally but at other times quite directively to echo themes, prepare for events, provide ironic contrast to events in the biographies or narratives, effect transitions from one mode to the next, or simply create the "clamor," as Dos Passos puts it, of the era. The analogy to film works in another way as well: characteristic of their name, the elements in these segments, when they work in conjunction, function in the same kind of interactive relationship, although one that is much less complex, that the modes enact together.

The reader searching for signs of the modernist sensibility in *U.S.A.* can locate them in the workings of the more directive "Newsreels." "Newsreel LI," immediately preceding the introduction of Mary French in *The Big Money,* presents fragments of classified advertisements and headlines concerning the possibilities for good jobs and favorable working conditions in the city for young girls. Mary goes to the city not only to seek a direction through work but also to minister to young women who have been lured there by the promises these ads hold out to them only to find the jobs menial, grinding, and paying poverty-level wages. Interspersed in this "Newsreel" are lines from the song "St. James Infirmary," which tells the story of a young girl who, having left her home, ends up as a corpse being claimed by her lover in the infirmary. Although the forces at work on Mary will not actually take her life, she will sacrifice her unborn child to the demands of party dedication and will eventually sacrifice her ability to care—"I haven't any feelings at all any more, I've seen how it works in the field," she will finally declare (1233)—to the numbing commitment to the party's work. The fragments form a kind of cubist poster portrait of the character and her fate.

But it is not always possible to find ways in which the fragments shore against the ruins of the culture they represent; and, especially as Dos Passos originally intended the "Newsreels," and given the evidence of the first edition of The 42nd Parallel, this mode seems to involve a more sliding, decentered use of language than the other narrative methods. In their almost dadaistic absurdity, many of the original "Newsreels" and others as they were eventually published in the trilogy implicitly reinforce Dos Passos's suggestion, via characters and events in the rest of the novels, that language can be manipulated into meaninglessness and that the cacophony of our culture, the welter of words and sounds emanating from print and other media, can easily mask that emptiness. The Library of America edition of U.S.A. lists in its notes the elements that were later edited out of the original "Newsreels" of The 42nd Parallel, the first edition of which is now relatively difficult to find. Studying the direction of these changes makes one more aware of the undertone of instability that pervades these novels ominously. Sometimes the form as well as the meaning states that things do fall apart and that the center will not always hold, either in American language or in its cultural life.

Camera Eye

Even if both the fragmented structure and the chaotic events of these novels frequently offer only dislocation and instability, the trilogy is nonetheless a work that at least implies a center, unlike Manhattan Transfer, in which the characters cannot find "the center of things." True, U.S.A. is built around fictional and real characters who are master manipulators of language, whose business and belief is the distortion of language for profit and illusion. In both its form and its content, the trilogy offers countless examples of how words can be rendered meaningless. If Dos Passos is suggesting in his form and content that language in American culture is hopelessly dislocated, then he also intimates by the same methods that meaning—not universal meaning, but personal—originates only in the imaginative act of the individual that creates a center for the self and, possibly, for the culture. Dos Passos then takes a subtle but radical turn away from the high modernism of *Manhattan Transfer* and the first edition of *The 42nd Parallel*, and initiates a return to an essentially romantic idealism: he validates the individual perceiving consciousness.

This individual consciousness, the origination of the imaginative act that creates meaning, is enacted in the fourth mode of the trilogy, the "Camera Eye." This element of the narrative, Dos Passos said, was "to indicate the position of the observer" ("Introductory," vii), but later in his life in interviews he explicitly identified the point of view in the "Camera Eye" with his "own subjective feelings," as he told interviewer David Sanders.[16] Using this mode as a "safety valve" for them, he explained, had enabled him to approach a greater objectivity in the rest of the book. Although Dos Passos neglected to acknowledge that the biographies are clearly not objective, his acknowledgment of his involvement with the content of the "Camera Eye" segments clarifies their function both in the architectonics of the novels and in the totality of their meaning. Although contemporary readers of *U.S.A.* might not have recognized the autobiographical basis of the "Camera Eye," modern readers have the benefit of two lengthy biographies of the writer published in the 1980s to illustrate how directly the segments correspond to Dos Passos's life. But a knowledge of the narrator's identity is not necessary to perceive the effect of the mode and how it interacts with the other modes to generate meaning.

These stream of consciousness segments—John Wrenn calls them "stream-of-memory" (155)—ranging in length from a couple of paragraphs to a couple of pages, chart the development of different kinds of consciousnesses in an unnamed narrator from childhood to adulthood. Although through much of *The 42nd Parallel* the experiences of the narrator seem to have little relevance to the lives of the fictional characters, by its end, as Moorehouse, Eleanor Stoddard, and Charley Anderson head to France in war-related activities, the "Camera Eye" narrator is also aboard ship headed for service in an ambulance corps. In *1919* his

experiences fall even more specifically within the events the novel depicts, as he sees duty in France and emerges from it hopeful of the peace
and caught up in the anarchist, revolutionary spirit of the Paris of 1919.
In this novel, the various levels of significance of the "Camera Eye" segments emerge more clearly; Savage's superficial willingness to turn
wartime service into a prestigious job contrasts with the narrator's
immersion in the chaos and destruction of warfare. The narrator's sensory delight and youthful optimism at the peace as he "step[s] out
wideawake into the first morning of the first day of the first year" (651)
are undercut by the cold machinations of the peace conference and Savage's shabby opportunism, depicted in segments that quickly follow the
"Camera Eye." Finally, in *The Big Money* the correspondences become
even more explicit, as the "Camera Eye" narrator returns to America
and becomes involved in radical politics, just as Mary French and Ben
Compton do. The events the "Camera Eye" narrator witnesses—the
Sacco-Vanzetti trial, the Harlan County, Kentucky, miners' strike—are
those the characters live as well.

In the arrangement and frequency of the "Camera Eye" segments and
in the intensification of the narrator's identity with the events that occur
in the fictional and biographical modes, Dos Passos gradually asserts the
validity of the individual consciousness in the narrative and in history;
and, after intending to remove the evidence of the artist's hand and presence in the narrative in *Manhattan Transfer*, he acknowledges the artist's
agency even as he demonstrates it in the structure of the trilogy as a
whole. In creating the "Camera Eye" and clarifying its functions in *The
Big Money*, where it asserts control over form and theme and imposes
unity on them, Dos Passos creates a metafiction that the "Camera Eye"
segments themselves enact—"the opportunity to chart the genesis of the
speaking voice of the text within the text itself" (Shloss, 27).

Early in the trilogy, for instance, the "Camera Eye" segments are frequent and diffuse; the narrator has little sense of himself as an agent in
history and seems caught in his own isolated imagination. But by *The
Big Money*, he has transcended his isolation. Although the last novel contains only 9 of the segments, whereas the first contained 27, in *The Big
Money* the narrator has begun to define himself within the struggles of
his times. He bears the "hated years in the latrine-stench at Brocourt
under the starshells" (790); when he returns from the war he feels the
press of "Coca Cola signs Lucky Strike ads pricetags in storewindows . . .
money in New York" (892–94), and he searches for a redeeming value
in the deaths of "the brave men our friends" Sacco and Vanzetti, exe-

cuted by "strangers who have turned our language inside out," the "betrayers" of truth (1156–57). Recognizing the complicity of "the prosecutingattorney the judge . . . the political boss the minesuperintendent the board of directors the president of the utility the manipulator of the holdingcompany" in the plight of the impoverished in the "dark strike-silent hills" where the coal miners live (1208–9), the narrator struggles for some weapon to bring to bear against the institutions that rob individuals of identity and substance. In identifying himself with the struggle against oppression in all its forms, he has become part of the "we"[17]—the defense of Sacco and Vanzetti, the strikers in Harlan County and their defendants, the common people who militate against "Power Superpower" as it has come to be represented by the forces of monopoly capitalism and its attendant institutions and vices.

Moreover, in defining himself as an individual, the narrator has also defined himself as an artist. In the penultimate "Camera Eye," he believes that "our nation has been beaten," despite "the scribbled phrases the nights typing . . . stringing words into wires the search for stinging words to make you feel who are your oppressors America." But even in the face of the defeat of individual freedoms symbolized by the execution of Sacco and Vanzetti, he asserts that "the old words of the immigrants are being renewed in blood and agony . . . the old American speech of the haters of oppression" (1157) is being renewed in the continuing efforts of common people such as he to combat the corruption of the "old words" of America—the principles of individual liberty and equal opportunity on which the nation was founded. And although the narrator recognizes the seemingly invincible complicity of law and government, industry and finance, against the common workers he encounters in Kentucky, he ends the final "Camera Eye" by asserting that "we have only words against" that "Power Superpower" (1210). In identifying language and its practitioners with the only possible defense against the multiple forms of oppression in America at the beginning of the twentieth century, he has assumed and acknowledged his vocation as an artist. Undertaking and acknowledging the redemptive quality of the imaginative act, the narrator-author has enacted his own theme.

This replacement of the individual consciousness within the text not only makes possible a kind of synthesis of structure and meaning Dos Passos had not fully achieved before. It also signals a subtle but significant shift away from the definitive modernism *Manhattan Transfer* represents. By affirming the primacy of the individual, *U.S.A.* hints at the return of a kind of romantic sensibility that characterized Dos Passos's earlier work. By the time he finished *The Big Money,* whose narrative modes work in a more traditional parallelism than those in the earlier novels, he had just begun, as he said of himself later in his life, "to come back to center" ("John Dos Passos," 69).

The way Dos Passos used film techniques, probably the most obvious artistic source for the trilogy, underscores the subtle shift that had occurred in his inseparable aesthetics and politics by the time the trilogy was finished in 1936. Ludington, Evans, and Shloss among others have explored the degree of the artist's borrowing from the Soviet filmmakers he met in the late 1920s. Dos Passos acknowledged his debt to the methods of Eisenstein and the American D. W. Griffith, but he never discussed what he may have learned from the work of Dziga Vertov, whose films, Shloss argues persuasively, Dos Passos almost certainly would have seen in Moscow in 1928. Examining Vertov's theories and practices, however, suggests that the American author might have been indebted. Vertov, for instance, developed a series of short, realistic films he called newsreels or, alternatively, *Kinopravda,* "film-truth," which he envisioned as a film periodical. He wrote also in one of his manifestos on film of his conception of the "kino-eye," the camera eye: "I am kino-eye, I am a mechanical eye. I, a machine, show you the world as only I can see it. . . . I, a camera, fling myself along . . . , maneuvering in the chaos of movement, recording movement."[18] Comparison to Dos Passos's impressionistic notes as he developed his conception of the "Camera Eye" is suggestive:

> The upside down image on the retina, piece by piece . . .
> Camera Eye— . . . how could you warp the paper figures to simulate growth— . . . shove him through the various terrible velocities of time. Imagine paper boats that will indicate the swirls and eddies of the stream. (quoted in Ludington 1980, 259–60)

The identification of the machine and the human eye, the goal of capturing the flux of time—the two artists share these ideas. They differ slightly in that Vertov explicitly acknowledged that it is he whose eye is the camera; that acknowledgment would come later for Dos Passos, or would at least be revealed to the reader of his trilogy only in the third novel.

Vertov and Dos Passos also had similar visions of how to structure a work. Dos Passos claimed that montage was the central ordering device of his modernist works, and *Manhattan Transfer* certainly bears out his

claim. The fragmentation of its structure points to the fragmentations of
the lives in the novel and the culture they inhabit. The segments of
U.S.A. instead point the reader back to a center, where is located an
individual and an artist in the fullness of history. The novel's structure
resembles more nearly Vertov's use of the interval, "the thought that
the space between fragments could invite participation, that the film-
maker/writer/technician's job was to edit, to provide the juxtaposition of
information that, when assembled in the viewing/reading, would lead to
a recognition of the importance of each unit within the whole" (Shloss,
158–59). With this structure, Vertov intended to show "life, to note its
turns and turning points, to catch the crunch of the old bones of everyday existence beneath the press of the Revolution, to follow the growth
of the young soviet organism" (47)—to depict, in other words, the lives
of the times of the artist as they changed under the influence of an economic and social system in transition, essentially the same goal that Dos
Passos articulated in his introductory note to *The 42nd Parallel.*

If, in fact, the concepts of structure that Dos Passos was developing
for his trilogy were sparked by his exposure to Vertov's films and writings in the late 1920s, he may have been reluctant to define that influence because of the radical difference between the two artists' political
contexts that had become clear by the time Dos Passos finished his
work. Vertov filmed laborers of all sorts and all the activities of daily life
in postrevolutionary Russia to show the dynamism and productivity of a
burgeoning new system. He inserted himself as the artist explicitly into
his films to demonstrate that the artist is yet another worker in the system, not an idiosyncratic, individualistic throwback to the decadence of
the old system. Dos Passos, on the other hand, created his trilogy to
reflect the dangers of totalizing systems and made central to the growth
of the work an enactment of the individual consciousness and its imaginative potential. Dos Passos's *U.S.A.* emanates from the conviction that
the political impetus that produced Vertov's art was invalid in American
society. Neither the socialist program nor any program that denied individuality, repressed free expression, or devalued and distorted the
"straight" use of language would work for the America that had been
founded on the "old words."

In fact, as early as 1934, in one of his lively exchanges with Edmund
Wilson, Dos Passos was complaining that "the whole Marxian radical
movement is in a moment of intense disintegration." "The only alternative," he continued, "is passionate unmarxian revival of AngloSaxon
democracy or an industrial crisis helped by a collapse in the director's

offices." Such a movement, he explained, would be "a reaction towards old time Fourth of July democracy" (*Fourteenth*, 435–36). The "old words" and principles he evokes in these letters—"Fourth of July democracy"—are among those that the "Camera Eye" persona implies have been corrupted by the complexes of power created in America by big money, big business, and big government, forces that "have taken the clean words our fathers spoke and made them slimy and foul." Even if the nation is imperiled by these forces, the language of its founding, the language of its people, "is not forgotten" (*Big,* 1157–58). In the final segment of the last novel of the trilogy, Dos Passos demonstrated in the "Camera Eye" persona's commitment to redeeming the language what he articulated in the opening segment written to introduce the three novels when published as a trilogy in 1937: America is the narratives of personal and private history; the stories of schoolchildren and workers and vagabonds and businessmen; the jokes, yarns, tall tales, speeches, facts and illusions—"the speech that [clings] to the ears, the link that [tingles] in the blood. . . . But mostly U.S.A. is the speech of the people" (2–3).

Chapter Ten

"A Dark and Garish Picture":
The Later Chronicles

The Spanish Civil War and Its Aftermath

Within a year after the publication of *The Big Money* in 1936, the reconsideration of the politics of the far Left that had begun during the writing of that novel attained sharper definition for Dos Passos after the Spanish Civil War. By the time the United States entered World War II five years later, the crystallization of his stance was evident not only in the direction of his content but also in the narrative forms he chose. Turning to reportage in essays such as those published in *The Villages Are the Heart of Spain* (1938), to directly editorial journalism in pieces such as "Farewell to Europe!" published in *Common Sense* (1937), and focusing on history in works such as *The Ground We Stand On* (1941),[1] the man who had been heralded as a groundbreaking radical writer and formal innovator signaled his growing fear that individual liberty was now under attack by Communism and began his search for solutions in the "heritage" ("Farewell," 11) of the governing principles of America. His disillusionment with radicalism that in part generates the despair of *The Big Money* gathered momentum with the events of the late 1930s as Dos Passos searched for a political ground to stand on. Having found it and announced it in "Farewell to Europe!" he stood by it and expressed it for the rest of his prolific career, characteristically undeterred by criticism from the Left. When it came from friends, such as John Howard Lawson and Ernest Hemingway, it hurt him; but he responded patiently in letters and in print even to those who held his political stance responsible for what they saw as a narrowness, a limiting didacticism, in the works he published between *U.S.A.* and his death in 1970.

Undeniably, his politics had always been inextricably related to his aesthetics, as his previous work had demonstrated; and certainly his writing had always been regarded in terms of its social and political impact. Thus perhaps it was inevitable that his writing too would fall into critical disfavor when his views came into conflict with what he disparagingly called "this middleclass communism of the literati" in a 1935 letter to Edmund Wilson (*Fourteenth*, 468). Yet, after the events in Spain and at home that produced the vehemence of "Farewell to Europe!" and out of which his next novel, *Adventures of a Young Man*,[2] grew, Dos Passos had indeed lost some vital kind of energy, perhaps that which had been sparked by the hopes and idealism shared by his generation between the wars. The changes in his writing, politics, and thinking about the course of his nation are discussed at length and from differing critical angles in the major biographies of Dos Passos as well as in more specialized works, such as Rosen's.[3] They chart the causes and effects of Dos Passos's reconsideration of radicalism that left the American Communists feeling so betrayed by one whom they had supposed to be of their camp.

But as the major explorations of his career suggest and as study of his works demonstrates, the theoretical position Dos Passos assumed after the Spanish Civil War was in fact consistent with the political commitments he had thoughtfully evolved early in his career. In a 1959 article for the *New York Times*, "Looking Back on *U.S.A.*," he himself asserted that "on the whole the attitude of mind exhibited by the '*U.S.A.*' books doesn't seem to me too different from my attitude today. What has occurred is a complete transformation of the social background. . . . [T]he basic tragedy my work tried to express seems to remain monotonously the same: man's struggle for life against the strangling institutions he himself creates" ("Looking Back"). It was the source of the threat to individuality and freedom that had changed, he argues; whereas in the 1920s and early 1930s, the systems of industrialism, government, and monopoly capitalism that developed in the nation seemed the most urgent dangers, by the late 1930s, he perceived a more pernicious enemy in other monolithic organizations that had the power to exploit and deny individuality—the Communists, primarily, or any other group vulnerable to Communist manipulation, such as the labor unions. In the statement of his goal for the major series of historical essays he undertook in 1939, he said his primary concern had always been "individual liberty, where it comes from and what it amounts to," which was the "American tradition" (quoted in Ludington 1980, 398). Because of its "heritage" of revolution and "the Bill of Rights and the fact that democracy in the past has been able, under Jefferson, Jackson, and Lincoln . . . to curb powerful ruling groups," he believed, America was in "a better position" than any European country or system "to work out the problem: individual liberty vs. bureaucratic industrial organization," as he wrote in "Farewell to Europe!" (11).

Whether it was he who changed or the "social background" of his beliefs, the new direction of his writing had many possible sources both private and public. In 1929, he had married Katharine Smith, a childhood friend of Ernest Hemingway, whom Dos Passos had met the year before while visiting the other writer in Key West. His life with Katy, as he called her, was no less peripatetic than it had been before, but it now acquired a permanent home base, their house in Truro, near Provincetown, Massachusetts. Hoping to add greater financial security to the pleasures of their life together, Dos Passos seriously investigated for the first time since his father's death obtaining clear title to his share of John R.'s considerable land holdings in Westmoreland County, Virginia. Finding fiscal deception of the part of the relatives to whom he had given legal authority to collect income on the land since his father's death, he brought a lawsuit and obtained not only the estate, where he settled permanently in 1949, but also a cash settlement that enabled him to work and travel in greater comfort after a time. At middle age, with his domestic life established as he gravitated back toward the Virginia home of his youth and of his conservative father, the transitions his life and career were undergoing in the late 1930s may have seemed a part of the natural course of maturity.

Seeking greater personal satisfactions and reinvesting in his own "chosen country," as he came to call America, may also have been an inevitable response to the political sorrow he felt when his hopes for a social revolution in Spain were crushed by the factionalism of the country's Civil War and the violent repressiveness of its central government. It was more than a political cause to him, however. He had felt early in his life a kinship with the individualistic spirit of Spain, with its arts and its long and varied traditions; and his love of the country and the people had been nurtured by long stays there throughout his life. Moreover, fluent in Spanish and mindful of his own Iberian heritage, he had many Spanish friends. One of them, José Robles, a professor of Spanish literature at Johns Hopkins University, was in Spain when the fighting began and elected to stay and help with the cause. Dos Passos himself conceived of a project to elicit relief funds from Americans to help the people's fight. To write, film, and produce a documentary about the plight of the Spanish people, he helped organize a group calling itself Contemporary Historians, consisting of writers that included Archibald MacLeish, Lillian Hellman, and Ernest Hemingway. Dos Passos traveled to Spain in 1936 to prepare for the filming; there he was to meet Hemingway, who would narrate the film, and Joris Ivens, the director, who was a Communist himself.

To familiarize himself with the situation, Dos Passos headed first for Valencia, which was then the capital of the republic. When he found that Robles had disappeared, he questioned every official and connection he knew, eliciting conflicting and evasive rumors about Robles's fate but no answers. Worried but proceeding to Madrid where Hemingway and Ivens awaited, he continued his questioning there until Hemingway and Ivens warned him that to pursue the matter further would be to jeopardize the film project and its possible benefits. Outraged that they could place their cause, however righteous, above the life of an individual, and in fact believing that both men were using the project to their own advantage in different ways, Dos Passos finally learned that Robles had been executed by one of the Republican "special sections," probably Communist, for reasons that were murky. He also discovered that the Republicans had purposely misled him earlier about his friend's fate because they did not want to lose Dos Passos's sympathy for their cause.

Whatever the reasons behind Robles's death, Dos Passos could see that the Communists were gaining control of the Republican cause and undercutting it. Furious and disgusted by the time he joined Katy in Paris to make their way back to the United States, Dos Passos characteristically resolved to tell the truth he had learned about Communist interference and perfidy once he had completed his study of the situation. But Hemingway, suddenly turning up at the train depot in Paris to confront Dos Passos as he and Katy were departing, warned him that taking such a position publicly would undermine his stature with the New York reviewers. Dos Passos refused to rise to the bait, and Katy, Hemingway's old friend, dismissed his threat as "despicably opportunistic" (quoted in Ludington 1980, 374). Dos Passos cooperated with the completion of the film, *The Spanish Earth,* despite his political and aesthetic differences with Hemingway and Ivens, and it succeeded in raising thousands of dollars for the Spanish struggle. But Hemingway's bravado in Madrid, his confrontation with Dos Passos in Paris, a subsequent insulting letter to Dos Passos, and several published articles purporting to know the truth about the Robles affair and insinuating Dos Passos's cowardice and political naivete—these made the break permanent between the two writers who had long been friends. The Spanish war had cost Dos Passos not only the life of his friend Robles and his association with Hemingway but also the last shreds of his belief that any force could militate against "the infectious formulas for slavery that [were] preparing in Europe on every side," he wrote in bidding farewell to European political movements in favor of American solutions ("Farewell," 9).

The Robles tragedy confirmed in Dos Passos a mistrust of the Communist Party that had been brewing for years. He felt, for instance, that the Communists had manipulated the striking miners in Harlan County, Kentucky, for the party's purposes and then had abandoned the jailed workers; he later wrote that he as well as the other writers who came to the strikers' defense in 1931 had merely been "pawns in the game" (*Best,* 208). And he had withdrawn his name and his support from the *New Masses* after it had become "a sort of literary supplement to the Daily Worker" (quoted in Ludington 1980, 310), he wrote in his last contribution to the magazine that had become a Communist Party instrument. He had simultaneously begun to publish regularly in *Common Sense,* a journal whose platform announced that it was "an independent publication devoted to the interests of the American people." Although it was "not connected with any political party," it nevertheless advocated the view that "a system based on competition for private profit can no longer serve the general welfare" and that, to achieve "the American ideals of liberty, democracy, and equality of opportunity," the nation must "adapt the principles of the American Revolution of 1776 to modern needs" (quoted in Ludington 1980, 311). While he had begun to fear the oppressive tactics of the Communist Party, he nonetheless still questioned capitalism and, as of the mid-1930s, referred to his beliefs as "libertarian" (*Fourteenth,* 515).

But the fatal evidence of Communist brutality in the Spanish Civil War and the knowledge that the brutality would be added to the fascism and other afflictions about to descend upon Europe catalyzed Dos Passos's uneasiness about the party into pessimism and an overriding opposition to Communism that fueled everything he was to write after the late 1930s. His "farewell to Europe," Rosen writes, echoing the opinions of many other critics writing about Dos Passos's career after *U.S.A.,* "turned out to be a farewell to any real hope for radical change in America, and the blow to his idealism proved to be a setback to his art" (96).

Chronicles of Change

The changes that did transform the United States in the following years were not the utopian ones Dos Passos had championed earlier in the 1920s and 1930s; and despite the strengths of some of the work of the last three decades of his life, in which he chronicled with growing despair the transitions in both his own and the world's politics, more often than not his work was poorly received by the critics and the public alike. At times stung by dismissive or condescending reviews from fellow writers whom he respected, Dos Passos nonetheless persisted in working out his ideas on American history and culture that seemed increasingly vital to articulate in the face of what he saw as national crises that vindicated his suspicion of Communism—World War II, the Cold War, the resurgence of the American Left in the 1960s, and the military action in Vietnam. In each of the genres he chose—reportage, history, and fiction—he blended his politics, the events of his life as they bore out his views, and the heritage of his chosen country to create the works that now often leaned toward "telling" rather than "showing," as Hemingway characterized them in the late 1930s (Ludington 1980, 304).

Of the three types of works, his journalism generally received the most positive reception in the 1940s, possibly because the articles he wrote for major magazines such as *Life* and *Harper's Magazine* frequently do, in fact, show rather than tell, given his interest in the voices and the experiences of the people involved in the events he reports. After a series of articles about the Spanish Civil War he published in 1937 and 1938 in *Esquire* and in *The Villages Are the Heart of Spain,* his subsequent related short book of essays, the next reportorial projects Dos Passos undertook were coverage of World War II, its effects both at home and in the theater of war, and its aftermath. In these wartime projects, having bidden farewell to Europe, he embraced his own country in a search for hope and a characteristic determination to document its physical and social breadth and to understand its thinking. "[C]ontinually tortured by curiosity" about the "big untidy soulstirring country we live in," as he wrote to Robert Hillyer in 1943 (*Fourteenth,* 536), he promised a series of articles to *Harper's Magazine* in order to fund a year traveling across the country to see the burgeoning productivity of a nation galvanized by the war effort. Whereas in the 1930s he had flatly denounced war and capitalism as coconspirators in the obliteration of individual freedoms, now, in the face of a worldwide threat to democracy, he praised the energy generated by the war and the economic system it had invigorated. Still, however, he hoped for the preservation of the small family farm, with its resonance of "popular selfgovernment,"[4] under federal regulations that seemed to favor major corporations. Although a departure from his positions of less than a decade earlier, his slant on the business of the nation in the 1940s retained its advocacy of individualism and its caution about big government. The series he produced, "People at War," became part of *State of the Nation,* published in 1944.

The second group of articles, originally written for *Life* and subsequently published as *Tour of Duty*[5] in 1946, was less optimistic about the beneficial effects of the war, since his travels for this series took him to the Pacific and to Europe. Once again he was encouraged by the efficient vigor of America's war effort and in individual responses to it, this time among the troops stationed in the Pacific; but he realized, too, the horror and desolation of the European cities that he had loved. Dismayed by the political maneuvering among the three major Allied countries and particularly discouraged by America's ineffectuality at heading off what he saw as a growing Communist threat from Russia, Dos Passos felt that this war, like the last one, would prove to be a costly, futile undertaking.

He continued to express his pessimism about the peace in late 1947 and early 1948 in two more articles for *Life*, "Britain's Dim Dictatorship" and "The Failure of Marxism," and in another volume of essays in 1950, *The Prospect before Us*,[6] which collected and revised many of the revealing *Life* articles from that period, including "Britain's Dim Dictatorship."[7] These pieces all echo Dos Passos's career-long belief that massive systems threaten individual liberties. But whereas the Dos Passos of the 1920s and 1930s located that threat frequently in capitalism or the military, now he saw the danger in all the "corporate organizations" that had become the "dominant social pattern of the life of a large part of the human race"—and the pattern, he wrote in *The Prospect before Us*, is "uniform" all over the industrial world: "In the United States we call it Capitalism. If you go over to England you'll find people behaving in much the same way but calling it Socialism. In the Soviet Union and its satellite states you'll find a remarkably similar social structure going under the name of Dictatorship of the Proletariat, or by the oddest reversal of the meaning of terms, People's Democracy" (5–6). Yet even if Soviet socialism resembles the "monopoly Capitalism" of the United States, he continues, the Soviet system lacks "the palliatives which come to us from surviving competition and from the essential division between economic and political power which has so far made it possible for the humane traditions of the Western world to continue" (6–7). His distinctions between the two systems are vague, but Dos Passos seems to be striving for a balanced comparison between what he sees as two evils in the essays in this volume.

But in "The Failure of Marxism," he had already spelled out unsubtly his conviction that any system with a taint of socialism—even Britain's postwar Labor government, which is the focus of the two *Life* essays and much of *The Prospect before Us*—inevitably threatened individual liberty and ultimately opened the door for the kind of tyranny the Soviet version of socialism imposed. *The Prospect before Us* attempts to examine objectively the status of individual freedoms in three industrial cultures—postwar Great Britain, South America, and the United States. Incorporating the previously published *Life* essays and new material, Dos Passos structures the book as a series of lectures delivered by a professorial "Mr. Lecturer" to an American audience, which responds with questions. Dos Passos is clearly the lecturer, and he adopts a mild, self-deprecating tone that wryly insinuates his belief that he had become a political back number. Mr. Lecturer is witty, but once he launches into a lecture, he drones—a style that he acknowledges, but persists in nonetheless. Despite the appearance of objectivity that might have been created by the persona and the book's format, the "lectures" recapitulate Dos Passos's charge in "The Failure of Marxism" that Britain's Labor government was oppressively and dangerously socialistic. As the lecturer relates his experiences in postwar Britain, based on the time Dos Passos and Katy had spent there in 1947, he directs the auditors' sympathies. The plucky workers he describes are thwarted by the government in their efforts at individual initiative. Apathy and mediocrity in services are rife under government regulation of enterprise. Government ministers, their minions, and socialist sympathizers are slick, manipulative, and affected, extolling England's recovery from the war while government inefficiency allows much-needed food to rot in the fields.

The problem with the British system as well as the American, Dos Passos declares, is that the organizations of society have become so complex that an individual who tries to live an independent life out of the mainstream fails to learn how to "test the self-serving propaganda" of the "political climbers who use corporations, labor unions, stratified organizations of any kind, as ladders to positions from which they may ride to glory on the backs of their fellows" (8). The "antithesis between Capitalism and Socialism is beside the point," he claims, in the face of the "centralization of power and the isolation of the individual" that are inherent in the modern world's "great stratified industrial enterprises" (7). Radically indicting the very structure of all of industrial society, the solutions he seeks are for his own country. Its "survival . . . as a nation with hopes and purposes essential to mankind" depends upon acknowledging and addressing with "reason" the "social and political problems of a corporate industrial society" (12–13). Stressing the urgency of recognizing the problems, he nevertheless enumerates them only generally:

U.S. society must control "the power over men's lives of these stratified corporations which . . . are so admirably adapted . . . to the uses of despotism" (8); and "we must get out of our heads the paralyzing Marxist doctrine . . . that teaches that these problems will solve themselves if we wait long enough." Solutions lie in individual "patient daily efforts of people like the reader of these lines, the printer who sets them up, the bookseller who sells the books" (13)—telling examples from a writer who in his greatest fiction had created as his villains the abusers of language and posited as his nation's hope the recuperation of its "old words."

On the basis of "Britain's Dim Dictatorship," "The Failure of Marxism," and *The Prospect before Us,* Dos Passos was publicly regarded as having severed himself irrevocably from liberalism. Prominent reviewers savaged him for what they felt was an extreme bias that kept him from examining postwar Britain fairly.[8] By seeking solutions to the problems he outlined in the individual initiatives of citizens who recognize the value of the old words, he did take a traditional stance that revealed itself to be a conservative one in the conclusion to *The Prospect before Us.* The penultimate section, "The Country We Came Home To," dwells on the energy and productivity of corn farmers and wheat producers in the Midwest. Here, by contrast to the stagnancy of the Labor-dominated economy of Great Britain, Dos Passos suggests that solutions for the United States lie in the old ways as well as the old words. Having early in the book defined monopoly capitalism as a lesser evil than socialism because capitalism nurtures individual effort, in the final section on farming he nevertheless unabashedly praises the system of "free enterprise" that can "keep our social structure evolving and improving" (326). He had already written in the 1946 *Tour of Duty* that the "untrammeled power of the ruling class in the Soviet Union makes you wonder whether the profit motive is as bad as it has been painted" (327). In the success and efficiency of large farming operations such as the one he describes in detail, he sees a paradigm of what good can happen when enterprising individuals have free rein to realize their potential. He does not acknowledge the contradiction between his indictment of large, stratified organizations and his praise of modern agrarian enterprises in which one owner uses massive machinery, a few laborers, and some tenant farmers to cultivate increasingly large spreads. The description of Bob Garst's Iowa corn operation—clean, mechanized, using up-to-date methods and technology—is Dos Passos's implicit answer when a "round pale" economist asks him how food production in the United

States will keep up with the "increase in mouths to feed in this country and in the entire world." Garst himself calls farming "the most exciting occupation in the world" (276–77). Even in downtrodden England, one of the lecturer's respondents conveniently notes, the farmers are happier and more prosperous than any other group. Illustrating the sound values and restorative virtues of agrarian life, Dos Passos retreats toward cultural and governmental structures of the past in his disillusionment with the present.[9]

Likewise, in his historical narratives, Dos Passos turned to the past to search for the wellspring of American democracy. In works such as *The Ground We Stand On,* published in 1941, he chose as his subjects revolutionary figures such as Tom Paine, with whom Dos Passos clearly identified as someone who had persisted in his convictions even when they became unpopular in an era of transitions. The volume examines the lives of other early Americans who had also exemplified individualism— Roger Williams, Samuel Adams, and Thomas Jefferson, among others.

Jefferson is the subject of Dos Passos's most significant volume of historical comment, *The Head and Heart of Thomas Jefferson,*[10] published in 1954. To Dos Passos, Jefferson represented a kind of moral virtue and political and intellectual balance lacking in the world at midcentury. In this biography and in later volumes of history or historical narrative, such as *The Men Who Made the Nation* (1957), the writer sought among the founders of American democracy the model of self-government and an active, responsible individual freedom without which the nation would not be able to "counter the deathdealing illusions of Europe," as he had written earlier in *The Ground We Stand On* (2). He creates a Jefferson who embodies the writer's own principles and the attributes out of which he believed the nation had been built: dedication to country even at personal sacrifice; an Enlightenment investment in reason as a tool to improve society for all; and optimistic belief in the potential of the nation to provide a prosperous egalitarian life for all. Central to Jefferson's democratic vision was the agrarian model of independent landowners with substantial power and eminent ability to govern themselves. The historical studies Dos Passos wrote during this period and later, like his reportage, reveal his conviction that the nation must reclaim its old ways along with its old words in order to restore its commitment to democracy. This biography, he stated shortly before its publication, was an expression of his persuasion that "decentralization of power, i.e., the opposite of the Soviet system, is highly important" in "the American system" (quoted in Ludington 1980, 462). "The great formulations of the generation of 1776," he wrote a few years after the book appeared, are "as valid as ever" (*Occasions,* 64).

But could social and governmental models from two centuries past realistically be expected to deal effectively with the complex metastasizing political and economic organizations of industrial society he had described in *The Prospect before Us?* The vision he presented in his histories of a nation structured by Jeffersonian principles is as idealized as his representation of the man himself in the biography—"a triumph of imagination over inquiry," as John Diggins observes in his analysis of Dos Passos's historical writing. The book drew considerable criticism for the romanticized representation of Jefferson and his times. It substituted detail, "the jangling bric-a-brac of Americana," for intellectual substance, Irving Howe charged; another reviewer agreed that, although "[n]o earlier biographer [had] the heart as expertly" as Dos Passos, Jefferson's "head was considerably harder" than Dos Passos was willing to admit. Other reviewers, however, saw his use of detail to build the texture of Jefferson's life and evoke his attitudes as one of the book's strengths. Granville Hicks called the biography "solid" and "conscientious" but "dull."[11]

Conscientious though it is in many respects, and despite the democratic aims for which Dos Passos intended it, *The Head and Heart of Thomas Jefferson* fails to confront some distinctly undemocratic aspects of the system of governance Jefferson advocated: it represents the experience of the landowning class as definitive, and it glosses over the racial attitudes that allowed Jefferson and his fellow gentry to justify perpetuating slavery. It suggests, for example, that Jefferson developed "that seasoned sense of responsibility for the conduct of his world" that would fit him for national leadership in the course of learning to manage a "Virginia plantation manned by irresponsible slaves kept at work by low grade white overseers, whose cast of mind was hardly more responsible than that of the blacks" (*Jefferson,* 69).[12] In these respects, however, the biography is in keeping with much postwar American historiography. Exhausted by the protracted research and anticipating yet another hostile reception from reviewers, he wearily reported in a 1951 letter to Edmund Wilson that the "Jefferson operation" was "a hell of a lot of work, with only the prospect of another goddam book to shove down the goddam rathole" (*Fourteenth,* 596).

At least the extraordinary effort Dos Passos had put into researching the work did not escape the attention of Hicks and the other reviewers. The biography had taken him over a decade to produce, years filled with upheavals in his personal life as well as steady work on novels and articles. Amid the problems, dismal sales, and mixed reviews that beleaguered him in the early 1950s, the *New York Times* reviewer who called *The Head and Heart of Thomas Jefferson* the writer's "best work since *U.S.A.*" seemed to validate the investment Dos Passos had made in the biography and in the principles from the nation's founding that informed it.[13] As he grew older, he increasingly longed for these traditional values, for a vision of human perfectibility to replace the utopian dreams of the 1920s and 1930s. The end of the war brought no satisfaction to him politically, as his reportage showed, and no relief from critical disapproval from the Left.

Superseding his professional worries, however, was the personal tragedy he sustained when his beloved companion Katy was killed in September 1947 in an automobile crash that left Dos Passos, who had been driving, blind in one eye. Within a year after his loss, he relocated his life from Provincetown, where the memories of his rich life with Katy overwhelmed him, to the land in Westmoreland County he had inherited from his father. There he made plans to finish refurbishing the pre–Revolutionary War brick house standing on the property overlooking the banks of the Potomac. Renewing his personal ties with Virginia, settling at Spence's Point in 1949, and working toward making the farm a self-sustaining, independent agrarian venture constituted a gesture toward living the Jeffersonian ideals he had been writing about. In establishing a new home far away from the literary world of the northeast and marrying again in August 1949, he insulated himself against his detractors and disappointments and established a foundation for continuing the work that was always central to his life, no matter how unpopular it might prove. His life with his second wife, Elizabeth Hamlin Holdridge, provided a steady framework within which he continued his constant traveling and restless exploration of the issues that were pressing to him. And the birth of a daughter, Lucy Hamlin Dos Passos, in 1950 added to the equilibrium he had gained after the years of confronting his declining literary reputation, diminishing book sales, and sorrows over lost hopes, lost friendships, and the loss of his first wife.

Like the reportage and historical writing Dos Passos published after *U.S.A.,* the fiction he published after the apex of his critical reputation charts the growth of a disillusionment with radicalism that reached a crescendo between the Spanish Civil War and World War II. The consciousness informing all these works reaches into the past for answers to the crisis of the nation, hope for a solution, and, finally, escape from insoluble problems. The fiction, however, provides an increasingly auto-biographical perspective on the transitions and events that the other genres depict. Perhaps because of his personal investment in these nov-els, he felt angry, misunderstood, and betrayed when he read the nega-tive reviews of his fiction that began with *Adventures of a Young Man* (1939), the first novel he published after *U.S.A.*[14] Not until the final novel he completed, *Midcentury* (1961), in which he returned to an approximation of the innovative form of *U.S.A.*, did reviewers respond again to his work with anything like the praise that had greeted his books of the early 1930s.

But it was perhaps precisely that personal involvement with these later novels that cost him the objectivity necessary to create work that was more than polemic rendered into traditional narrative form, as the critics characterized these novels. The urgency of his politics after the Spanish Civil War found expression in autobiographical narratives so transparent that the critics inevitably identified the works completely with the writer; when the novels were reviewed, it was Dos Passos's controversial politics that were actually under scrutiny. And, given the prevalence of the "com-munism of the middleclass literati," as Dos Passos had complained of the New York literary community, the work was bound to draw fire. Although the New York reviewers did not bury him, as Hemingway had warned, and although some of the novels received moderately positive notices from some critics, Dos Passos's work was never again to gain the superlative reputation *Manhattan Transfer* and *U.S.A.* had earned.

The immediacy of Dos Passos's disillusionment with the tactics of the Communists in the Spanish Civil War informed the first fiction he pub-lished after *U.S.A. Adventures of a Young Man* ultimately became part of Dos Passos's second trilogy, *District of Columbia,* published as a unit in 1952. What loosely links the three novels of the trilogy—*Adventures, Number One,* and *The Grand Design*—is not form or a developing concept integrated with technique, as in *U.S.A.*, but merely a diffuse focus on three members of the Spotswood family and a general commonality of purpose, elements that demonstrate the evils of Communism, the dan-gers of demagoguery, and the potential of each of these forces to exploit idealism. The idealist in *Adventures* is Glenn Spotswood, whose experi-ences as a youthful radical in the 1930s somewhat resemble Dos Pas-sos's. Spotswood, however, ultimately joins the Communist Party only to run afoul of its doctrinaire members when he opposes their callous sacrifice of the welfare of jailed striking miners to the greater goal of educating the working class about Marxism. As clearly as this episode reflects Dos Passos's objection to the party's treatment of the Harlan County strikers, even more obviously autobiographical is Spotswood's manipulation by the Communists during the Spanish Civil War. The protagonist's experience merges Dos Passos's own perceptions of the Communists' covert action with what he had learned of Robles's fate at the hands of the party. Still the idealist despite his expulsion by the party, Spotswood goes to Spain to help the Republicans. But there, the Communists, knowing he is a dissenter, accuse him of conspiring with "counterrevolutionary wreckers and spies" (316) and send him on a mission that they know will lead to his death.

Technically uninspired and blatantly grinding a political axe—Communists in the novel frequently "hiss" instead of speaking, for instance—the novel was attacked by reviewers on the Left such as Malcolm Cowley and especially Samuel Sillen, reviewer for the *New Masses:* "a crude piece of Trotskyist agit-prop," he called it. But less ideologically committed reviewers saw something instructive, if ominous, both in the novel and in its reception. John Chamberlain, covering the novel for the *Saturday Review of Literature,* pointed out that, even though the work was not on the level of *U.S.A.,* it was clearly a satire of American radicalism that would inevitably incur displeasure from leftist reviewers. Writing in the *American Mercury,* James T. Farrell warned that such reviewers' vehement damnation of the novel "reads like a warning to writers not to stray off the reservations of the Stalinist controlled League of American Writers to which more than one of the critics belong" (494).[15]

In the second novel of the trilogy, *Number One,*[16] published in 1943, Dos Passos is concerned with the dangerous rise to power of a single individual, a political demagogue, rather than with the machinations of a political group. Unlike *Adventures, Number One* not only was favorably reviewed but also sold as many copies as had any single volume of *U.S.A.* Perhaps in finding a subject from which he had some distance and perhaps, too, in turning momentarily away from his crusade against Communism, Dos Passos created a novel that addressed issues vital and immediate to the nation yet about which he had no personal vendetta. He had taken as his subject a politician, a thinly disguised portrait of Louisiana governor Huey Long, whose career the writer had followed since the 1932 Democratic Convention. The protagonist of the novel, however, is Tyler Spotswood, elder brother of Glenn and campaign manager for the Long character, Senator Chuck Crawford. Tyler Spotswood's idealism is tested and ultimately triumphs as Crawford's corrupt nature is revealed and as it eventually entangles Spotswood himself. The novel focuses on the conflict of an individual with his own ethics and on the conflict between a form of fascism and individual freedom of choice. Spotswood extricates himself from Crawford's machine by concluding that "If we want to straighten the people out we've got to start with number one, not that big wind. . . . I got to straighten myself out first" (297). In choosing a demagogue similar to Long as his subject and in depicting the moral dilemma of one of his supporters, Dos Passos was the first to use the characters and conflicts out of which Robert Penn Warren would structure his 1946 *All the King's Men*. Dos Passos's novel is distinguished also by its slight echo of the forms out of which his great modernist works were structured. Brief interchapters that recall the prose poems of *Manhattan Transfer* and the "Camera Eye" segments of *U.S.A.* preface each chapter of narrative and offer sketches of average anonymous lives in America.[17] The sketches are connected only thematically by their emphasis on the use and transmission of language in the construction of the nation's powerful organizations. But their inclusion differentiates this novel from its predecessor in the trilogy and marks the beginning of Dos Passos's gradual return to something of the modal structure and complexity of the early novels. This return becomes more evident in *The Grand Design*, the considerably more ambitious novel that followed *Number One*, and culminates in the relative achievements of *Midcentury*, his final completed novel.

Like *Number One*, *The Grand Design* (1949),[18] the trilogy's third novel, uses actual political figures as the basis for a critique of a contemporary political situation. This time, Dos Passos takes on the New Deal as it entered wartime and illustrates how the unnamed president in the novel, clearly a sharply critical treatment of Franklin Roosevelt, allows the once-promising programs he has initiated to come to serve the interests of a powerful few rather than the needy common people. Unlike the previous two novels of the trilogy, however, *The Grand Design* tracks the experiences of several central characters who have moved to Washington to take jobs in Roosevelt's ambitious organization for restoring the nation to economic health. The fictional technique is reminiscent of the multiple narratives of *U.S.A.*, and the 20 impressionistic prose poems that precede the chapters likewise recall the "Newsreels" and biographies of the first trilogy. Although the prose poems offer some of the most affecting writing in *The Grand Design* and although the lives of the busy characters evoke the tone of New Deal Washington, the novel's patent bias against Roosevelt and its grotesque stereotypes of Communists rob it of the observational, objective quality that contributes to the vitality of the great modernist works. Whereas in *U.S.A.,* Dos Passos constructed multiple points of view and placed them in a dynamic tension that demanded the reader's involvement, now that he believed he knew absolutely and specifically who the enemies of individual freedom were, he focused his narrative lens directly at them, allowing the reader no peripheral vision, no context or alternative view out of which ambiguity could arise.

Thus the central characters of *The Grand Design* move through a narrative pattern common to the three novels of *District,* from optimistic activism in a cause to disillusioned withdrawal from it. The novel once again includes the Spotswood family, although they are not as central as in the previous two novels. The father of Tyler and Glenn Spotswood, Herbert Spotswood, is an influential radio commentator who fails to understand the manipulative power of the language that is his tool. Self-absorbed in his position of power, Herbert becomes a Communist dupe: invited by the party to speak at one of their meetings about Glenn's death in the Spanish Civil War, he yields to the crowd's pressure to turn his eulogy into pro-Stalin propaganda.

Two other central characters in the novel resist manipulation more effectively but succumb to disillusionment with New Deal policies and presidential scheming. Millard Carroll, a businessman from the lower Midwest, and Paul Graves, a scientist from North Carolina, take leaves from their professions to serve their country by accepting positions in the Department of Agriculture. Despite some improvements that result from New Deal programs, Millard and Paul find themselves stymied in their idealistic efforts by the accumulation of power in the hands of centralized sources: the "Farm Bureau lobby" that serves the interests of "the big boys" rather than the "other seventyfive percent of the farming people" (75); the "operator," (369) financier Jerry Evans, whom the president appoints to head the newly formed War Procurement Board; and opportunistic union officials such as the Communist Joe Yerkes. Finally, both Millard and Paul resign from their New Deal posts, telling each other, as they evaluate their time in Washington, "Some day we may know whether it was worth it. . . . Maybe we'll never know" (437).

Georgia Washburn, the novel's only major female character, does not fare even as well as the male characters. Like women in Dos Passos's earlier novels such as Mary French and Daughter, Georgia is victimized by the men with whom she becomes involved and by their causes. Her lover, Joe Yerkes, decides to leave their life together in Detroit to work in Washington with the New Deal, which he dismisses as "only a social-fascist whiting of the sepulchre of depression but . . . a great opportunity to build a labor movement" (56). To facilitate his goals, he marries a Communist Party comrade and arranges for Georgia to abort the child she has conceived; then, when Georgia finally vents her anger at him, he retorts that she has no right to "upset him in the middle of an organizing campaign when he needed all his strength to give to the movement and that sex was only a flower picked by the wayside and that he was sorry she hadn't been able to restrain her bourgeois possessive feelings" (58). To forget her pain, she moves to Washington herself where, working as a researcher and secretary for Paul Graves, she is soon enmeshed in an affair with him before he has been able to relocate his wife and children from North Carolina. But despite his affection for Georgia, his dedication to his work and devotion to his family take precedence. Heartbroken, Georgia drifts into a superficial relationship with a party member who tries to induce her to steal information from Paul. Soon afterward, Paul appeals to her patriotism to provide information on her Communist acquaintances. Devastated that his political concerns outweigh their personal connection, Georgia kills herself by taking an overdose of pain pills.

In this narrative, the Dos Passos of *U.S.A.* seems visible for a moment: Georgia is prey to forces more powerful than she, whether embodied by the Communists' goals or by Paul's noble commitment to country. Were the tone of these episodes more objective, Georgia's suicide would seem as universally despairing as Mary French's numb immersion in curing social ills at the end of *The Big Money.* But in *The Grand Design,* Dos Passos's sympathies lie entirely with Paul's ethical struggle with Communist conspiracy and the centralization of power in the New Deal administration. Even while Paul attempts to use her to foil the Communists just after Jed Farrington tries to get her to spy on Paul, Dos Passos uses adjectives such as "kind and sorrowful" and "concerned" (405–6) to describe Paul as he tries to sway Georgia. Perhaps Dos Passos is suggesting that Paul is as much a victim of New Deal machinations and Communist manipulation as Georgia is of her own needs, since the episode seems to imply little criticism of Paul for his role in Georgia's destruction. Rather, his fear that his involvement with Georgia will be revealed publicly becomes the catalyst for his ethical rebirth. Realizing how his "career in government" has warped his values, he vows to redeem himself by joining a wartime navy project testing "intensive cultivation on some of our new Pacific bases to take a little of the strain off supply" (425). With relief, he pictures himself "turning over new soil for crops he didn't even know the name of, different plants, odd birds and insects" (440). Millard Carroll, too, finds salvation in a return to the land. When his son is killed in the military, he takes refuge from his grief working in his victory garden and ultimately escapes the duplicities of the wartime New Deal by returning to his home in "Texarkola."

Thus, the resolution of *The Grand Design* articulates in fictional form the same message that the writer sent in his reportage and his historical writing during the 1940s and into the 1950s: that hope for the nation lay in Jeffersonian, agrarian values. This is not a surprising conclusion, since Dos Passos was writing this novel in the years after Katy's death when he gathered material for the *Life* essays by visiting the Garst family farm in Iowa, arranging to relocate permanently to Virginia, and finding solace for his losses and disappointments by making plans to renovate and cultivate his own farm. Some of the most vividly realized scenes in this novel are those with rural settings. As Paul and Georgia travel to the Midwest to develop a field report based on actual cases for the Appropriations Committee, for instance, what Georgia sees from her train window resembles one of the idealized, symmetrical farm scenes the regionalist Thomas Hart Benton was painting during the same depression years the novel covers:

> wide undulations of wheat beginning to go blond for the harvest, green ranks of corn that caught a little of the blue of the sky in the shimmer where the leaves curled, immense oblongs of clover, frizzy alfalfa in parallelograms that stretched to the horizon. . . . Under a sky piebald with small cotton clouds palegreen trees huddled in wavy bands. . . . Here and there a rattletrap farmhouse spun slowly into view dwarfed by great silver barns or silos . . . or for an instant Georgia could study the figure of a woman in a gray smock who had just come out on her back steps to throw feed from a bucket into a scuttling of white fowls. (242)

The similarity between the work of the Kansas painter and some of Dos Passos's written landscapes—and his vibrant gouache landscapes from around this time as well, although with his seriously impaired vision, his painting became somewhat less experimental than in the 1920s and 1930s—is not surprising given both artists' turn toward nostalgia for a romanticized agrarian tradition in the face of national adversity.[19]

But in the same way that Benton's representations of rural characters sometimes edged into caricature, Dos Passos's characters in *The Grand*

Design verge on stereotype, just one of many flaws reviewers found in the book. To make his point about the Communist threat inescapably clear, the writer creates cardboard-cutout party members: Dr. Jane Sparling wears trousers, clenches a cigarette holder between her teeth when she talks, and makes leering, suggestive comments to the "buxom" (68) Georgia Washburn; effeminate Winthrop Strang speaks in a falsetto voice, adores modern English poetry, and blames his domineering mother for "starting his Oedipus complex" (321). The association of a lack of ethics or scruples with homosexuality and promiscuity that begins with Richard Ellsworth Savage in *The Big Money* now becomes absolute and overt.

Granville Hicks took Dos Passos to task for the narrow-mindedness of *The Grand Design* in his 1950 review: "It is strange that Dos Passos, who shied away from Marxist dogmatism when he was close to the Communist Party, who remained far more flexible and open-minded than most of the fellow-travelers, has now stumbled into a kind of absolutism."[20] His primary objection to the book was that Dos Passos's reading of history in it provided little "guidance for realistic action in the immediate situation" (98), a problem that had begun to characterize the writer's reportage and his historical writings as well.

Other critics, aghast at the skewering of Roosevelt, a liberal icon, flogged the novel for its bitterness and polemic against the New Deal.[21] Although the president in the novel is never named—characters call him "the boss"—it is clearly Roosevelt, jaunty despite his leg braces, who fully understands the manipulative power of language in a way that Herbert Spotswood never does. The president's voice in public addresses is "Carefully tuned to the microphones, the patroon voice, the headmaster's admonishing voice, the bedside doctor's voice . . . the pervasive confident voice . . . the insinuating voice"; "We danced to his tune" (4, 5, 60, 417), Dos Passos concludes ominously. Indeed, the president's wartime actions seem ominous: "[W]ithout asking anybody's leave [he] got to meddling with history; without consulting [his] constituents, revamped geography . . . divided up the bloody globe and left the four freedoms out" in the Yalta agreements (417–18). The novel criticizes still other characters who are easily recognizable syntheses of actual New Deal administrators with whom Dos Passos met in Washington while working on his wartime essays. Walker Watson, for instance, is a composite of Harry Hopkins and Henry Wallace. Dos Passos mistrusted Hopkins because of the increasingly exclusive power he gained as Roosevelt's closest advisor; and the writer was disgusted when Wallace, who

had served as vice president during Roosevelt's third term, ran for
the presidency in 1948 on a Progressive ticket that advocated more
power for labor unions and increasing U.S. cooperation with the Soviet
Union.[22]

But critics who objected to what they saw as the crudity of the book's
stereotypes, the superficiality of its characterizations, and the pessimism
of its politics were missing what Ludington explains was Dos Passos's
real intention in the book—to satirize the liberal vision of the New Deal
(Ludington 1980, 444). Certainly the *U.S.A.* trilogy often uses broad
brushstrokes to sketch characters and refuses to ameliorate the darkness
of its portrait of America in the boom years. *The Grand Design,* however,
takes aim at specific and unambiguously defined villains—Roosevelt
and other New Deal architects who hoarded bureaucratic power, and
insidious Communist infiltrators—rather than demonstrating the power
of the forces of the culture. *The Grand Design* demands assent to its overt
political agenda; the modernist novels had been critiques of American
culture at large.

For all the flaws critics perceived in it, however, no one could dispute
the urgency of the belief out of which Dos Passos wrote the novel—and
both that belief and its expression in the prose poems echo the theme
already articulated so innovatively in the trilogy of the previous decade.
In the final prose poem, Dos Passos returns to his conviction that "we
have only words against POWER SUPERPOWER," as his final "Camera Eye"
in *The Big Money* asserted, and he again voices the distinction between
words made corrupt, made into empty signifiers, and words that attain
the power of gesture, as he had written years before in *Rosinante to the
Road Again,* when his picaros searched for the gesture that would imply
the Spanish character. The only way to protect individual freedoms
against a man like "the boss," who by "the modulations of his voice into
the microphone . . . played on the American people" (443), is to rejoin
signifier to signified and language to gesture, to put into action the
"grand design" of the United States, to restore it to its old democratic
ways by seeking a Jeffersonian freedom.

The power of this tenet so central to Dos Passos's writing both early
and late is diffused, however, in the three novels of the third series Dos
Passos envisioned. With the exception of the first of the series, *Chosen
Country,* these novels transform autobiography into convincing narrative
even less successfully than those in the *District of Columbia* trilogy.
Although never published as a unit and never named as a trilogy, the
novels of this third series are linked by the scope of the autobiographical

territory they cover—from Dos Passos's childhood through the years around Katy's death—and by their delineation, through their political themes, of a journey from hope for a social revolution to betrayal of those hopes by the Communists and despair for the future of the country. But especially in the last two novels, the autobiography is so thinly disguised and the author's biases about the events he depicts so evident that the reader seldom gains a sense of fully realized characters or a crafting of the narrative. His difficulty in crafting effective fiction out of personal experience in these novels, however, perhaps shows the writer grappling with the personal, professional, and political transitions of his later life.

The first and most successful of the three novels, *Chosen Country* (1951),[23] creates the young Jay Pignatelli from the details of the writer's own childhood and young adulthood, details he had used more obliquely in *Manhattan Transfer* to characterize Jimmy Herf. Dos Passos's imagining of Jay's parents' illicit relationship and ultimate marriage brings to life his own parents and their difficulties. As had Dos Passos, Pignatelli experiences World War I, the Middle East, and the legal defense of two Italian workingmen accused of an anarchist crime. A young lawyer, Pignatelli loses his idealism about representing the Sabatinis, a father and son, when he realizes that the Communist Party members who he thinks are his allies in the case actually support it only to make working-class martyrs of the men. His somewhat stereotypically colorful immigrant cousin Nicolas Pignatelli acquaints Jay with proletarian revolutionary politics but tells him about the Communists: "They don't mind about one Italian man. You and me we want to save a life." Moreover, Nick warns, the case has become "a valuable property" to other groups besides the Communists: "The bourgeois liberals, . . . even Mafia interested." When Nick is subsequently murdered, Jay assumes that it is because of his cousin's outspokenness about the perfidy of the "communisti" (420). The radical lawyer's political disillusionment is complete.

In this narrative of Jay's professional dedication and disenchantment over the course of a few months, Dos Passos draws on the pivotal events of many years that robbed him of his own liberal idealism: his involvement in 1926 and 1927 with the Sacco-Vanzetti case; his disillusionment with the Communists' actions in the 1931 Harlan County miners' strike and in the Spanish Civil War; and his friendship with the Italian anarchist publisher Carlo Tresca, who was murdered in 1943, Dos Passos assumed, for his anti-Communist opinions.[24] Likewise, figures in

Dos Passos's life whose behavior furthered his political disillusionment appear in the novel in fictionalized versions. The minor character Jed Morris, based on John Howard Lawson, is a decadent Communist playwright who becomes the unattractive protagonist of the trilogy's second work, *Most Likely to Succeed.* A prominent character in the depiction of Lulie Harrington, who ultimately becomes Jay's wife, is George Elbert Warner, loosely patterned after Ernest Hemingway. Hemingway had spent the summers of his youth in Michigan near the family of Dos Passos's first wife, Katy, on whom Lulie is based. Katy and her two brothers had hunted and fished with the young Hemingway and had socialized with him again later when all were living in Chicago after World War I. In *Chosen Country,* Warner is an able woodsman and a likable, brash boy; but as a young man he affects a "bristling, conceited . . . mustache" (303) and, as a cub reporter, exploits the Harringtons to get a story that advances him from sports reporter to feature journalist. Lulie declares that Warner is "selling his own past history" (310), and the incident does recall an episode that alienated Katy's brothers from Hemingway. But Dos Passos's novelistic treatment of the falling-out is indeed fictionalized and clearly not mean-spirited: Lulie and her brothers are ultimately amused by Warner's sensationalized story about a scandal in their family.

Hemingway, however, was not amused by the echoes of his past in the Warner character. Hypersensitive about his public image, he lashed out at Dos Passos in letters to mutual friends, despite the fact that the story of Warner and his reportorial betrayal resembled actual events only in their broadest outlines. When Hemingway used thinly disguised autobiographical detail to write about his friendship with Dos Passos and Katy in *A Moveable Feast,* the portrait was explicit and vituperative.[25] The friendship that both writers had once valued, already broken over the Robles incident in the Spanish Civil War, had very tentatively been renewed in exchanges of sympathetic letters between 1949 and 1951 regarding Dos Passos's marriage to Elizabeth and the death of Hemingway's second wife, Pauline. But even though published posthumously, Hemingway's unflattering account confirmed the final enmity between two friends who had struggled with change and hardship in their lives and careers.

Besides creating autobiographical characters in *Chosen Country,* Dos Passos also used autobiography in part to structure the novel. Interspersed early in the narrative are three chapters, "Prolegomena," that profile central figures in the lives of Jay and Lulie. Portraits of Jay's mother and father are based on John R. and Lucy Madison Dos Passos, for instance. Three later interchapters, "Footnotes," use fictionalized portraits of actual historical characters to adumbrate themes in the novel. The "Footnote on Social Consciousness: Anne Comfort Welsh 1892–1929," for example, draws on the life and work of Mary Heaton Vorse, an early-twentieth-century social activist. But the primary use that Dos Passos makes of autobiography to structure the novel, and what is both the novel's greatest interest and its weakest aspect, is in employing the details of his courtship of Katy and their marriage to resolve neatly and speedily the protagonist's search for something to believe in once his idealism is undermined. After the Communists are revealed to have taken control of the Sabatini case and after Nick's death, Jay escapes to the East, to "a vague future with a firm of Jewish attorneys in New York who want a gentile name on their letterhead even if it is a wop" (475). Traveling to New York with Lulie and her brothers, Jay suddenly finds himself "inordinately happy" to be driving "through the raw magnificent country. . . . [A] newfound land, . . . still new and fresh as the day my grandfather. . . stumbled down the gangplank off a bilgy sailing ship. New means raw, unformed, disorganized. That's why we have to try and try again every time we fail" (465). He also discovers, in the space of a few pages, that he is in love with Lulie, and they marry in a small New England town in a scene that touchingly recalls Dos Passos's own happy but disorganized wedding in Wiscasset, Maine, in 1929. Ultimately, he embraces his "chosen country" as he and his wife stand together on the threshold of happiness. It is a romantic and unconvincing ending but represents Dos Passos's own need, after Katy's death and his remarriage, to affirm his personal and political choices.

The second novel, *Most Likely to Succeed* (1954), blending Dos Passos's experience with the New Playwrights and John Howard Lawson's career in Hollywood, is an unconvincing and judgmental narrative about playwright and screenwriter Jed Morris, who is manipulated and ultimately betrayed by his fellow Communists. The Communists are once again depicted as hissing villains, who this time control both the theater and the movies, and Morris is so unsympathetic a character that the novel works only if one takes it as satire, which was Dos Passos's intention; but it is too heavy-handed and angry to succeed consistently. Like Hemingway after the publication of *Chosen Country*, Lawson was offended by what seemed a personal attack in the novel's characterization of Morris. Nor were critics kindly disposed toward the novel. Many of them had personal involvement with political situations of the sort the book depicts, and the presence of Communists in the entertainment industry was a charged topic for artists and writers in the 1950s. Granville Hicks, now no longer seeking reasons for Dos Passos's political transitions as he had in earlier reviews, declared the novel "a literary debacle"; and Harold Clurman, who knew the New York theater and the work of the New Playwrights, called the book "a wretched piece of work" and "libelous."[26]

The very title of the third novel, *The Great Days* (1958), conveys its frankly nostalgic tone, and for readers familiar with the author's life, it is a poignant account of the reverses Dos Passos suffered in the late 1940s. To narrate the experiences of its protagonist, journalist Roland Lancaster, Dos Passos depicts episodes from his own life after Katy's death and, in so doing, evokes his loneliness during that time and communicates his sense that his work had come to be almost universally unappreciated in the past decade. Lancaster invites a younger woman to accompany him on a reporting trip to Cuba after the war, and the failure of their emotional and sexual relationship parallels Lancaster's realization that the United States has failed to maintain its postwar leadership in Latin America and the rest of the world. Accounts of Lancaster's experiences in the war are, embarrassingly, lifted verbatim from *Tour of Duty*. Emotionally and stylistically, the novel's tired quality suggests Dos Passos's sense of defeat after decades of defending his political beliefs against the barbs of critics who, contemptuous of his unfashionable political views, dismissed him as a literary figure. Discouraged by the poor reception of *Most Likely to Succeed* while he was putting together *The Great Days*, Dos Passos himself was aware that the story of Lancaster was not his best work, even though he reminded Edmund Wilson that it had been well received in England (Ludington 1980, 475). Although some critics such as James T. Farrell praised it, they largely agreed with Malcolm Cowley that "it [did] not belong on the same shelf as *Manhattan Transfer, U.S.A.,* or even *The Men Who Made the Nation.*"[27] But, characteristically, Dos Passos was already engaged in another work, a history, and more reportage by the time *The Great Days* appeared.

As the 1950s ended and the 1960s began, Dos Passos entered what was to be his final decade working on at least two manuscripts simultaneously. His energy for traveling did not abate—he published travel books on Brazil, Portugal, and Easter Island before his death—and he lectured, managed the production of crops and cattle at Spence's Point, delighted in his family, and kept up a prodigious correspondence with friends throughout the 1960s. Yet, for all the satisfactions he had secured through his commitment to writing and to his principles, the final novel he was to complete, *Midcentury*, is perhaps his darkest, even though it revives some of the best aspects of his modernist trilogy.

At the same time he was researching and writing a history, *Mr. Wilson's War*, he was working on several projects that influenced the themes and form of *Midcentury*,[28] which was also underway and would be published in 1961. For an article to appear in *Reader's Digest* in 1958, he was granted permission to explore the files of the Senate Select Committee on Improper Activities in Labor and Management Fields, chaired by Senator John McClellan of Arkansas.[29] The files contained thousands of letters from union members protesting the corruption of union leaders and the power they wielded over workers, and he was able to interview many of these correspondents. Also during 1958 and 1959, he cooperated in adapting parts of *U.S.A.* for the stage and, in the process, began to reflect upon how the structure of the trilogy served its political purposes. This project became a separate piece of writing, "Looking Back on 'U.S.A.' " for the *New York Times*.[30]

With the these projects and the material of *U.S.A.* fresh in his mind, he constructed in his new novel a chronicle of American culture in the middle of the twentieth century. *Midcentury* depicts a nation in which individual freedoms, initiative, and ethics are undermined by big labor unions, monolithic business structures, and pervasively insidious consumerism. This is familiar Dos Passos territory from both early in his career and later, but *Midcentury* succeeds in part where other Dos Passos novels of the late 1940s and 1950s failed because it returns to the structures of his greatest work. Reintroducing the modal techniques of *U.S.A.* allowed him to broaden the focus and point of view in *Midcentury* and encouraged the reader to explore the interaction of the segments. Using the forms he himself had created as a modernist also elicited from him writing that often attains the innovative quality of the earlier works.

The structure of *Midcentury*, which Dos Passos described in his correspondence with his Houghton Mifflin editor as "delicately cantilevered" (*Fourteenth*, 622), resurrects the modal concepts of the first trilogy but with some variations that reflect the differences between *U.S.A.* and the new book's aims. Impressionistic prose poems that resemble "Camera Eye" segments open each of the three major sections and close the book. These monologues are from the point of view of the narrator: "musing midnight in midcentury" (3), he walks with his dog through the quiet rural landscape. These segments, which allow Dos Passos to "bleed off" some of the subjective, as he noted of the function of the earlier "Camera Eye" narratives, contribute to the relative balance between political and artistic goals he achieves in this book. Twenty-five "Documentary" segments take the place of the earlier "Newsreels." The new name of these segments signals the writer's consciousness of the potential of that film genre. Like many of the nuclear-age film documentaries but unlike the earlier film newsreels, which create the sound and texture of a particular time, these segments convey a thesis: using segments of advertisements, press releases about technology, and portions of union testimony, they uncover, often humorously, the preposterous and seductive nature of media ads, the dismayingly frivolous applications of modern science, and the graft and abuses of power rife in the labor unions. The 14 biographies in *Midcentury* underscore these central themes, as in *U.S.A.,* and recreate the satirical impact of the biographies in that work. "The Promised Land (old style)," for example, captures in its portrait of Sam Goldwyn the particular combination of immigrant idealism, New World self-invention, media savvy, and capitalist acquisitiveness that characterized the early Hollywood film moguls. Other biographies, such as the segment on United Automobile Workers organizer Walter Reuther, represent the growing problems of the labor movement. A new mode, "Investigator's Notes," allows Dos Passos to present material he had gathered from his research into the McClellan committee's work. Along with the investigator, who in these seven sections interviews workers offering information on labor practices, the reader is shown how the labor movement, which the writer had depicted with hope in *The 42nd Parallel,* had become just another massive organization threatening workers' freedom. In the fifth mode, five major fictional characters are drawn from both labor and management in different businesses and trades. With one exception, their stories interlace, as in *U.S.A.* Jasper Milliron, an executive in a large grain-milling corporation, devises methods to decentralize the corporation and make its operations more efficient, but corporate bureaucracy and administrative greed stymie his efforts. Milliron's son-in-law, Will Jenks, starts a taxi business that challenges the rival cab monopoly, a company in the grasp of profit-hungry businessmen and union bosses cooperating with organized crime. As in the first trilogy, but more generally, the interaction of these narratives with the other modes helps create meaning. The first "Investigator's Note," for instance, ends with a newspaper notice of the murder of a witness just after he talked to the investigator about how powerful union officials use police and underworld connections to stifle workers who publicize the corruption. The following segment, a biography of John L. Lewis, powerful head of the United Mine Workers, begins to fill in the background of the unions' rise to power; and the subsequent fictional narrative undertakes the story of Frank Worthington, who idealistically organizes the rubber workers' union only to see it fall under the control of ruthless and crooked fellow union officials. The only fictional narrative that has no interaction with other characters' stories is the long monologue of Blackie Bowman, an old man in a hospital recounting his career as an idealistic labor organizer beginning in the first two decades of the century. Bowman vividly unravels his experiences with the old IWW, his life in Greenwich Village among other organizers, his account of the riotous 1913 Paterson strikers' meeting in Madison Square Garden. In this old-fashioned radical whose activism resembles that of the his own youth, Dos Passos creates one of the most plausible, human characters in all his later fiction, despite Bowman's function in the novel's structure as a disillusioning contrast to the self-interested compromises of contemporary union bosses.

What Dos Passos finally conveys through the structure and substance of this work is indeed bleak. In the pivotal biography of McClellan, Dos Passos catalogs the abuses McClellan uncovered in his investigations: "Denial of the working man's most elementary rights, the underworld's encroachment on the world of daily bread, sluggings, shootings, embezzlement, thievery, gangups between employers and business agents, the shakedown, the syndicate, oppression, sabotage, terror." Then follows the question that expresses McClellan's outrage, which is clearly Dos Passos's outrage as well, the question that is implicit in all of his later work: "Could this be America?" (272). Nor is there hope elsewhere in the culture. The shallow and seductive consumer culture he depicts is more sinister than the monopoly capitalism that threatened the individual in *The Big Money*, because it has at its disposal the advanced technologies of the age and—for the modern reader—because we now live in its midst. The youth of the nation, who might be a source of optimism for their potential to remedy the ills Dos Passos depicts, are instead most susceptible to consumerism; under its spell, they become self-absorbed, amoral materialists. Finally, deploring the proliferation of "tinpot pharaohs" dealing hate and lies, the narrator muses on "the century's decline" and concludes that "Man drowns in his own scum. These nights are dark" (495–96).

The darkness of this final novel—a clear expression of the writer's bitterness—ultimately undermines the narrative and structural benefits of returning in *Midcentury* to the methods he had originated as a modernist. The novel fails to achieve the stature of *U.S.A.* for some of the same reasons his other novels after 1939 faltered, although many critics praised the force of the work and the *New York Times Book Review* in a cover story asserted that it "[retrieved] his reputation at a single stroke."[31] But other critics found that *Midcentury*, like his other recent novels, in the end sacrificed its artistic goals to its political agenda. The biography of the actor James Dean as a representative of "The Sinister Adolescents" and the subsequent monologue of the fictional teenager Stan Goodspeed, who goes on a spending spree with the stolen credit cards of his uncle, Jasper Milliron, have a petulant tone and approach the heavy-handed caricature that Dos Passos had formerly reserved for Communists. Dishonest union bosses and their mob connections—who have Italian names and wear loud sport jackets—kill whistle-blowers and monopoly breakers without conscience. The narrative modes, promising in their conception, never interact as dynamically as they need to. Moreover, the contradictions among some of his central ideas suggest that Dos Passos was not seeking objectivity despite his use of a novelistic structure that introduces a wider perspective than in his other late novels. For instance, clearly it is consumer capitalism that creates the kind of advertising in the "Documentaries" that show how it preys upon greed, desire for status, and gullibility; but Jasper Milliron and Will Jenks, both depicted as waging noble struggles against racketeers, are both capitalist entrepreneurs. The invariably corrupt labor unions in *Midcentury* rob the worker of choices and initiative, but Blackie Bowman's story demonstrates the need for unions. Once again, Dos Passos sidesteps the complexity of the problems; once again, salvation may lie in an agrarian life—Milliron longs to retire to a farm; and the narrator muses pessimistically as he walks through night woods richly described— but in the decline of the century, urban and suburban life prevail. "Man is a creature that builds institutions" (119), Dos Passos writes, but he offers no antidote to the power these institutions have to efface their builders. In the contemporary decline, language is fully corrupted in the service of the powerful economic forces that overmaster the individual: "A word is a package. Packaging is the national obsession. No need to look inside if you say the right word" (189).

Dos Passos himself saw the grimness of his last completed novel, published when he was 65, as the natural stance of a satirist faced with the transitions in American culture in the last half of a turbulent century. In a 1960 speech at Carleton College, he declared, "It was in the cards that the writing of a would-be chronicler like myself should become more and more satirical as the years went by" (quoted in Ludington 1980, 484). With the upheavals of those recent years and the growing disorder of the century, he had seen every source of his earlier idealism demolished. These crucial disappointments, the historian John Diggins explains in his analysis of Dos Passos's political journey, were "the failure of the labor movement to achieve genuine trade union democracy; the failure of capitalism to free itself of external controls on the one hand and inner cupidity on the other; and the failure of science and technology to fulfill Veblen's dream of liberating modern culture from all that was irrational, wasteful, stupid, and oppressive" (248). The frustration of these hopes and his unswerving conviction that Communist infiltrators and sympathizers were actively dismantling American democracy motivated Dos Passos to contribute his support and a number of articles to the *National Review* beginning in 1956. Just as he had once contributed to the *New Masses* while ultimately maintaining his political autonomy, in his association with a group of conservative intellectuals spearheaded by William F. Buckley Jr., Dos Passos retained his individualistic, libertarian stance. His central political principles, he believed, had not shifted much since the 1920s. His work, as always, tried to express "man's struggle against the strangling institutions he himself creates" ("Looking Back"). Rather, he complained in the 1950s, "All the concepts have been stood on their heads. 'Liberalism,' for example, used to be equated with enthusiasm for individual rights; now it tends to mean identification with central governing power" ("Looking Back"). In *National Review* essays that appeared until his death in 1970, he often brought an acerbic satirist's tone to treatments of the issues that engaged him. "Please Mr. Rip Van Winkle, Wake Up Some More," later reprinted in *Occasions and Protests,* took the occasion of reviewing Edmund Wilson's *The Cold War and the Income Tax* to admonish Wilson for sounding like "another robot of the ventriloquists of Communist propaganda" (*Occasions,* 296). In "The New Left: A Spook Out of the Past," Dos Passos suggested that student protests of the mid-1960s were part of a Communist conspiracy.[32]

In fact, as the 1960s waned, Dos Passos frequently criticized student protests against both the conflict in Vietnam and the establishment that they believed had produced it. The violence and what he saw as the petulance of the protests appalled him, and he once again took an absolutist stance about the movement. It was spoiled "rich kids"—the kind he had berated in his portrait of the sniveling narcissistic Stan Goodspeed in *Midcentury*—who were joining the New Left, he told a journalist from the *Washington Post Potomac Magazine* in 1968 (quoted in Ludington 1980, 500). Working-class youth, he declared, with his familiar idealism about the proletariat, tended toward conservatism. In private, he was characteristically gentler on the matter, as evidenced in one of the letters he wrote to his daughter Lucy, by then a college student herself. He conceded that the "new college generation" had the advantages of good education, but, after seeing the documentary about the 1969 Woodstock festival in upstate New York, he blamed the generation's drug use and ineffectual complaining on its being "weaned and raised on TV." Instead of railing against the system, he wrote, young people should "try to develop themselves, physically and morally and mentally into decent human beings." Besides, he wondered, why all the rejoicing at the festival over the fact that over 200,000 people had attended it? "At any time in my life if I'd taken a young lady out to the Catskills, I'd have wanted a little privacy," he wrote dryly. Still, for all the issues he raised in his reply to Lucy's long letter, he had read "every word . . . with pleasure and agree with more of it than you think" (*Fourteenth*, 631–32, 638–40).

When he wrote about his own rebellious youth, he made clear distinctions between the activism of the New Left and that of his own World War I generation, which had been, he believed, more constructive. And he cast his memories of his own days of protest in an engaging light in *The Best Times* (1966), the memoir he was writing at about the same time he was taking aim at the Woodstock generation. His account of the education and experiences of the generation that came of age during and after the First World War recreated the excitement of his first encounters with modernist art, his shock at the carnage at the French front, the personal and political passions of bohemian Greenwich Village in the 1920s, and the fascination of life among the American literary expatriates in France. His respectful, interesting portraits of the artists he knew, Hemingway among them, and his benevolent tone in the reminiscence contrast with the gossipy, vindictive manner in which Hemingway in *A Moveable Feast* recounted his own life among the artists in France during the early 1920s. Writing about *The Best Times* in *Saturday Review*, Granville Hicks faulted it for downplaying politics but compared it favorably to *A Moveable Feast*. Unlike that book, Hicks noted, Dos Passos's memoir left one respecting the character of the author. Other critics likewise praised the book for its dignity and energy.[33] It was as widely and positively reviewed as any of his books had been since

U.S.A. Some critics echoed the question asked by Dos Passos's old friend and frequent political antagonist Edmund Wilson after reading the accounts of some of their mutual adventures: Why did the memoir stop in 1933, short of the pivotal experiences of the Spanish Civil War and after?

The answer lay partly in the fact that the first third of the century had been, in truth, the best times for Dos Passos. These were the years that produced most of the books against which all his later work was inevitably judged, the years during which his aesthetics became a dynamic vehicle for his political vision but were never subordinated to a message. Until the late 1930s, his activism embraced the transitions in American society and maintained hope that it could live up to its original promise to preserve the liberty and power of the individual. But in 1939, the betrayal of the cause of the Spanish Civil War and the sacrifice of an individual to an idea seemed emblematic to him of the treacherous direction the Left was taking. Thereafter, although he continued to invest himself and his principles in his work, his optimism—for the individual, for his nation, for the world—steadily diminished. Perhaps as a reaction to the betrayal of his early ideals, his political perspective ceased to change dynamically and neglected to factor in the new complexities and ambiguities of what the United States had become as the century waned.

What was becoming of America was his concern in *Century's Ebb* (1975), the novel he left incomplete at his death. Amid other projects, he worked on this novel sporadically during the latter part of the 1960s despite increasing cardiac problems that would cause his death of congestive heart failure on September 28, 1970. His final portrait of the century is, not surprisingly, grim—a "last forlorn Chronicle of Despair," he called it (quoted in Ludington 1980, 506). Its unfinished quality contributes to its forlornness: although the writer returned a final time to the basic structural ideas of his modernist trilogy, the segments are clearly unpolished and fall short of dynamic interaction, perhaps because his final intentions about their order were unclear.[34]

But its form and content, though unfinished, communicate Dos Passos's proposed aim in the book. He sought to chronicle the second half of a tumultuous century, to chart the manifestations of its decline as he saw it from the vantage point of someone who had lived its entire span. His slant is evident in the opening juxtaposition of an exuberant biography of Walt Whitman, one of his early heroes, with a segment entitled "Turnpike," a cross between a prose poem and a "Newsreel" that recreates a journey on the New Jersey Turnpike into 1960s New York City.[35] Commerce and new modes of transportation have transformed the "Vanished . . . croplands" and "salt meadows" of Whitman's day into a deadly, sulfurous vortex for traffic heading to the city to be "sucked underground" into the Lincoln Tunnel" (18). Other biographies sound another familiar theme. A biography of Joseph McCarthy, for instance, depicts the senator as misunderstood in his campaign to ferret out Communists, maligned and hounded by liberal enemies who eventually ruin him. Of McCarthy, Dos Passos makes the observation that "it is a brave man indeed who dares think straight about the dangers his country faces in a communist-dominated world" (165). Additional biographies profile figures such as George Orwell, John Foster Dulles, and, in a segment ominously entitled "The Coming of the Assassins," Lee Harvey Oswald.

Besides biographies and impressionistic sketches from across the country are fictional narratives interspersed with portraits of pivotal years in the characters' lives. A first-person narrative being spoken into a tape recorder—Dos Passos once again cannily adapts current media technology to narrative purposes—creates the character of Danny DeLong as he records notes for a ghostwritten autobiography. Dos Passos intended him as a "cross between Eddy Gilbert," a notorious embezzler of the 1960s whom Dos Passos met in Brazil where Gilbert was eluding prosecution, "and Bobby Baker," Lyndon Johnson's cohort who was convicted of defrauding the government (*Fourteenth,* 629). DeLong's childhood incorporates material about Dos Passos's boyhood already used in very early stories and in *Manhattan Transfer* to develop the character of Jimmy Herf, but the material is now cast in the language and given the slant of a 1960s hustler. The fulcrum of the novel's structure, however, is "The Later Life and Deplorable Opinions of Jay Pignatelli," seven lengthy segments that bring the protagonist of *Chosen Country* into the 1960s as they interweave with other narratives. Jay's story briefly reintroduces Jed Morris, tying this novel to *Most Likely to Succeed,* and Jay agrees to represent Danny DeLong in a lawsuit, although that subplot seems incomplete. But the central focus of the Pignatelli segments is the account of his experiences during the Spanish Civil War and what subsequently happens to his beliefs and career, an account based directly on Dos Passos's own sobering episode with the Republicans in Spain.

This narrative is Dos Passos's most revelatory attempt to deal in fiction with the murder of Robles and its repercussions on the writer's professional and political direction. The first and second Pignatelli segments in the book, "The Documentary" (35–56) and "The Trouble with

Causes" (67–99), and, to some degree, the third, "Thought Crime" (167–84), are essentially fictional continuations of *The Best Times,* which leaves off in 1933. As such, the Pignatelli narratives provide the reader with an important adjunct to the memoir. In Jay's experiences are all the details of Dos Passos's attempt to aid the Republican cause and rescue his Spanish friend: the Dutch documentary filmmaker who is a Communist; the execution of the Spaniard by a Communist "special section"; the bullying efforts of the swaggering writer and friend; and the huddling group of writers at the Hotel Florida. Jay's subsequent career is marked by his reaction to this episode, as was Dos Passos's. After he publishes an article revealing what he knows about the case, Jay's law partners turn on him and implicitly ask him to resign from the firm.[36]

As the book comes to a close, the segments create an increasingly bleak and violent image of a nation in decline. The biography of Lee Harvey Oswald is followed by one recounting the life and murder of Malcolm X. But amid these expressions of despair at what American is becoming, Dos Passos, for the last time and in the face of what he seemed to feel were insuperable forces, asserts that what Whitman called the "fervid and tremendous *Idea*" of the nation is not entirely "lost" (13). In the success of the Apollo 8 mission to orbit the moon in December 1968 and in the subsequent accomplishments of the Apollo program, Dos Passos saw a manifestation of the redemptive human quest for knowledge:

In this Century we have seen everything that is hideous in man come to the fore: obsessed leaders butchering helpless populations, the cowardice of the led, the shoddy selfinterest, the easy hatreds that any buffoon can arouse who bellows out the slogans, public derision of everything mankind has learned through the centuries to consider decent and true; but now, all at once, like the blue and white stippled bright earth the astronauts saw rise above the rim of the moon's grisly skeleton there emerges a fresh assertion of man's spirit. (472)

Century's Ebb is an uneven, diffuse, unfinished novel. The very incompatibility of its elements and moods demonstrates that even at the end of his life, despite political agendas that at times overshadowed his art, Dos Passos saw in America the ignoble failings and heady triumphs that cannot be reconciled easily. What he says at the end of *Century's Ebb* about humankind characterizes the writer at his best: "by his very nature, man has to know" (472).

In the course of a prolific career that spanned over half a century, Dos Passos grew increasingly frustrated with the "strangling institutions man himself creates" ("Looking Back") and sunk into bitter despair about the future of the "America that [he] loved and hated" ("What," 30). But that exacting vision of his country evolved precisely because he had early known and passionately felt its potential; and to "prod people into thinking"[37] about the gap between America's original promises and its betrayal of them, a gap that widened with every decade in the twentieth century, he became a satirist of his land and times. In the late 1950s, at a time when he was producing some of his most caustic and disillusioned work, he took the opportunity of accepting a prestigious Gold Medal for Fiction from the National Institute for Arts and Letters to make a statement about the satiric intentions of his work and his weary consciousness of its adverse reception:

> I wonder if any of you have ever noticed that it is sometimes those who find most pleasure and amusement in their fellow man, and have most hope in his goodness, who get the reputation of being his most carping critics. Maybe it is that the satirist is so full of the possibilities of human kind in general, that he tends to draw a dark and garish picture when he tries to depict people as they are at any particular moment. The satirist is usually a pretty unpopular fellow. The only time he attains even fleeting popularity is when his works can be used by some political faction as a stick to beat out the brains of their opponents. Satirical writing is by definition unpopular writing. Its aim is to prod people into thinking. Thinking hurts. ("Acceptance")

The pictures of American life he drew late in his life were indeed darker and more garish than the painterly, vibrant images with which he created his great modernist works, and it is for those—*Manhattan Transfer* and *U.S.A.*—and for his passionate antiwar novels *One Man's Initiation* and *Three Soldiers* that most readers know him. But until the end of his life, through a career in which he chronicled the motion and struggle of two-thirds of a century, he wrote to reclaim "the clean words our fathers spoke," to make sure that "the language of the beaten nation is not forgotten"—to make "the old words new" in his own time (*Big*, 1157–58).

Notes and References

Preface

1. John H. Wrenn, *John Dos Passos* (New York: Twayne Publishers, 1961), 8 (hereafter cited in text).
2. Jean-Paul Sartre, "John Dos Passos and 1919," in *Literary and Philosophical Essays*, trans. Annette Michelson (London: Rider, 1955), 96 (hereafter cited in text).

Chapter One

1. John Dos Passos, "A Humble Protest," *Harvard Monthly* 62 (May 1916): 116 (hereafter cited in text as "Humble"); reprinted in *John Dos Passos: The Major Nonfictional Prose,* ed. Donald Pizer (Detroit: Wayne State University Press, 1988), 30–34 (hereafter cited in text as Pizer 1988).
2. John Dos Passos, "Against American Literature," *New Republic* 8 (October 1916): 269 (hereafter cited in text as "Against"); reprinted in Pizer 1988, 36–38.
3. John Dos Passos, "Farewell to Europe!" *Common Sense* 6 (July 1937): 11 (hereafter cited in text as "Farewell"); reprinted in Pizer 1988, 183–86.
4. "A Second Talent," exhibition catalog (Chicago: The Arts Club of Chicago, 1971).
5. John Dos Passos, "Translator's Foreword," in *Le Panama et mes sept oncles* (Panama or the Adventures of My Seven Uncles), by Blaise Cendrars (New York: Harper and Brothers, 1931), vii–viii (hereafter cited in text as "Foreword").
6. See Kathleen G. Hjerter, ed., *Doubly Gifted: The Author As Visual Artist* (New York: Harry N. Abrams, 1986), 116-17. Because Dos Passos rarely dated individual paintings, I have relied for dating on several sources of information: the date of the notebook or sketchbook in which a work appears; conversations with Elizabeth Dos Passos and Lucy Dos Passos Coggin; correspondences between the types of paper on which dated and undated paintings appear; correspondences between style or subject and the influences or setting of a particular period of time; and the advice of Dos Passos's biographer, Townsend Ludington.
7. William Rose Benet, *The Reader's Encyclopedia,* 2d ed. (New York: Thomas Y. Crowell, 1965), 282.
8. John Dos Passos, *The Best Times* (New York: The New American Library, 1966), 130 (hereafter cited in text as *Best*).
9. Frank Gado, "An Interview with John Dos Passos," *Idol* 45 (Fall 1969): 17; reprinted in Pizer 1988, 276–92 (hereafter cited in text as "Interview").

10. John Dos Passos, "What Makes a Novelist," *National Review,* January 16, 1968, 30 (hereafter cited in text as "What"); reprinted in Pizer 1988, 29–32.

11. John Dos Passos, *The Fourteenth Chronicle: Letters and Diaries of John Dos Passos,* ed. Townsend Ludington (New York: Gambit, 1973), 95 (hereafter cited in text as *Fourteenth*).

12. John Dos Passos, *Manhattan Transfer* (New York: Harper and Brothers, 1925), 366 (hereafter cited in text as *Manhattan*).

13. Stephen Spender, "The Modern as a Vision of the Whole," in *The Idea of the Modern in Literature and the Arts,* ed. Irving Howe (New York: Horizon Press, 1968), 50 (hereafter cited in text).

14. John Dos Passos, *Occasions and Protests* (Chicago: Henry Regnery, 1964), 64 (hereafter cited in text as *Occasions*).

15. Wylie Sypher, *Rococo to Cubism in Art and Literature* (New York: Vintage, 1960), 98 (hereafter cited in text).

16. Herschel B. Chipp, comp., *Theories of Modern Art: A Source Book by Artists and Critics* (Berkeley and Los Angeles: University of California Press, 1968), 260.

17. William A. Johnson, "Toward a Redefinition of Modernism," *Boundary* 2 (Spring 1974): 542.

18. The three bibliographies are: Jack Potter, *A Bibliography of John Dos Passos* (Chicago: Normandie House, 1950); John Rohrkemper, *John Dos Passos: A Reference Guide* (Boston: G. K. Hall, 1980); and David Sanders, *John Dos Passos: A Comprehensive Bibliography* (New York: Garland, 1987).

19. Malcolm Bradbury, *The Social Context of Modern English Literature* (New York: Schocken Books, 1971), 42. For cogent and extensive attempts to define modernism, see Maurice Beebe et al., *Journal of Modern Literature* 3 (July 1974).

20. Wendy Steiner, *The Colors of Rhetoric: Problems in the Relation between Modern Literature and Painting* (Chicago: University of Chicago Press, 1982), 3 (hereafter cited in text).

21. Rene Wellek, "The Parallelism between Literature and the Arts," in *English Institute Annual* (New York: Columbia University Press, 1941), 33.

22. Jean Laude, "On the Analysis of Poems and Paintings," *New Literary History* 3 (Spring 1972): 471.

23. M. H. Abrams, *The Mirror and the Lamp* (New York: Oxford University Press, 1953), vi.

24. Jane Rye, *Futurism* (London: Studio Vista, 1972), 9.

Chapter Two

1. John R. Dos Passos Sr., *Commercial Trusts: The Growth and Rights of Aggregated Capital* (New York: n.p., 1901), 89.

2. John Dos Passos, *U.S.A.: The 42nd Parallel, 1919, The Big Money* (New York: Library of America, 1996), 77 (hereafter cited in text as *42nd, 1919, Big*).

3. John Dos Passos, *Chosen Country* (Boston: Houghton Mifflin, 1951), 32 (hereafter cited in the text as *Chosen*).

4. Virginia Spencer Carr, *Dos Passos: A Life* (New York: Doubleday, 1984), 40.

5. John Dos Passos, "July," *transatlantic review* 2 (September 1924): 170.

6. John Dos Passos, "Art and Aspiration," n.d., John Dos Passos Papers, University of Virginia Alderman Library, 2.

7. Jacques Barzun, *Classic, Romantic, and Modern* (Boston: Little, Brown, 1943), 49.

8. John Dos Passos, "Travel Diary of J. Madison (Dos Passos)," 1911–1912, John Dos Passos Papers, University of Virginia Alderman Library, 72 (hereafter cited in text as "Diary").

9. Hugh Honour, *Romanticism* (New Haven: Yale University Press, 1979), 212.

10. John Wilmerding, introduction to *American Light: The Luminist Movement, 1850–1875* (Washington: National Gallery of Art, 1983), 17 (hereafter cited in text).

11. John Dos Passos, "Les Lauriers Sont Coupés," *Harvard Monthly* 62 (April 1916): 48.

12. George Knox, "Dos Passos and Painting," *Texas Studies in Literature and Language* 5 (Spring 1964): 23 (hereafter cited in text).

13. John Dos Passos, "Journal of John R. Dos Passos Jr.," 1916–1917, John Dos Passos Papers, University of Virginia Alderman Library, 33 (hereafter cited in text as "Journal").

14. Townsend Ludington, *John Dos Passos: A Twentieth Century Odyssey* (New York: E. P. Dutton, 1980), 44 (hereafter cited in text as Ludington 1980).

15. John Dos Passos, "Diary of Italy," 1918, John Dos Passos Papers, University of Virginia Alderman Library, 49 (hereafter cited in text as "Diary of Italy").

16. Fernando Rossi, *Mosaics* (New York: Praeger, 1970), 27.

17. Bruce Cole, *Italian Art, 1250–1550* (New York: Harper and Row, 1987), 273 (hereafter cited in the text).

18. David Thompson, *Raphael: The Life and the Legacy* (London: British Broadcasting Corporation, 1983), 85.

Chapter Three

1. Malcom Cowley, "Dos Passos: The Learned Poggius," *Southern Review* 9 (January 1977): 6.

2. John Dos Passos, *John Dos Passos: Afterglow and Other Undergraduate Writings,* ed. Richard Layman (Detroit: Omnigraphics Inc., A Manly Book, 1990), vii.

3. Charles W. Bernardin, "John Dos Passos' Harvard Years," *The New England Quarterly* (March 1954): 14.

4. John Dos Passos, "The Shepherd," *Harvard Monthly* 61 (January 1916): 115–21 (hereafter cited in text as "Shepherd").

5. John Dos Passos, "An Aesthete's Nightmare," *Harvard Monthly* 60 (May 1915): 78–79 (hereafter cited in text as "Aesthete's").

6. John Dos Passos, "First Love," *Harvard Monthly* 61 (October 1915): 23.

7. John Dos Passos, "The Past," n.d., John Dos Passos Papers, University of Virginia Alderman Library, l. 41 (hereafter cited in text by line number).

8. John Dos Passos, "Bubbles and the Sea Wind," n.d., John Dos Passos Papers, University of Virginia Library, ll. 1–3 (hereafter cited in text by line number).

9. John Dos Passos, "From Simonides," *Harvard Monthly* 61 (January 1916): l. 3 (hereafter cited in text by line number).

10. E. Estlin Cummings et al., *Eight Harvard Poets* (New York: Laurence J. Gomme, 1917), 37–38 (hereafter cited in text).

11. John Dos Passos, "Book of Verses," 1914–1917, John Dos Passos Papers, University of Virginia Alderman Library, 47 (hereafter cited in text as "Book").

12. John Dos Passos, "Malbrouck: A Sketch," *Harvard Monthly* 59 (March 1915): 194 (hereafter cited in text by page number).

13. John Dos Passos, "An Interrupted Romance," *Harvard Monthly* 60 (June 1915): 119 (hereafter cited in text as "Interrupted").

14. Michael Wilson, *The Impressionists* (Oxford: Phaidon Press, 1983), 36.

15. Barbara Novak, *American Painting of the Nineteenth Century* (New York: Praeger Publishers, 1969), 246 (hereafter cited in text).

16. John Dos Passos, "Prairies," *Harvard Monthly* 61 (November 1915): l. 1 (hereafter cited in text by line number).

17. John Dos Passos, "The Bridge," in Cummings et al., 29 (hereafter cited in text by line number).

18. Barbara Novak, "On Defining Luminism," in Wilmerding, 27.

19. John Dos Passos, "Night Piece," in Cummings et al., 40–41 (hereafter cited in text by line number).

20. E. P. Richardson and Otto Wittmann Jr., *Travelers in Arcadia: American Artists in Italy, 1830–1875* (Detroit: Detroit Institute of Arts and Toledo Museum of Art, 1951), 171.

21. Malcolm Cowley, *Exile's Return: A Literary Odyssey of the 1920s* (New York: Penguin Books, 1934), 35 (hereafter cited in text).

22. Malcolm Cowley, *After the Genteel Tradition: American Writers since 1910* (New York: W. W. Norton, 1936), 169–70 (hereafter cited in text).

23. John Dos Passos, "The Almeh," *Harvard Monthly* 56 (July 1913): 174 (hereafter cited in text by page number).

24. John Dos Passos, "The Cardinal's Grapes," *Harvard Monthly* 61 (February 1916): 152–53 (hereafter cited in text by page number).

25. John Dos Passos, "A Pot of Tulips," *Harvard Monthly* 61 (December 1915): 78–79 (hereafter cited in text by page number).

26. John Dos Passos, "Orientale," *Harvard Monthly* 61 (November 1915): 43 (hereafter cited in text by page number).

27. John Dos Passos, "Romantic Education," *Harvard Monthly* 61 (October 1915): 3 (hereafter cited in text by page number).

28. John Dos Passos, "Incarnation," in Cummings et al., 32–33 (hereafter cited in text by line number).

29. Ernest Benshimol, "To a Mad Poetess," *Harvard Monthly* 61 (February 1916): 155, ll. 2–3, 13–14.

30. Horst de la Croix and Richard G. Tansey, eds., *Gardner's Art through the Ages,* 6th ed. (New York: Harcourt Brace Jovanovich, 1975), 468 (hereafter cited in text).

31. John Dos Passos, "Memory," in Cummings et al., 34–36, ll. 5, 9. 27–32 (hereafter cited in text by line number).

32. George Knox and Herbert M. Stahl, *Dos Passos and the Revolting Playwrights* (Upsala: A.-B Lundequistka Bokhandeln, 1964), 98 (hereafter cited in text).

33. Barbara Rose, *American Art since 1900* (New York: Holt, Rinehart and Winston, 1975), 9 (hereafter cited in text).

34. John Dos Passos, "Literary Diary of John Dos Passos," 1914–1916, John Dos Passos Papers, University of Virginia Alderman Library, n.p. (hereafter cited in text as "Literary Diary").

35. John Dos Passos, "English 5 Weekly Theme," John Dos Passos Papers, University of Virginia Alderman Library, 18 (hereafter cited in text by line number).

36. John Dos Passos, "Salvation Army," in Cummings et al., 30–31 (hereafter cited in text by line number).

37. John Dos Passos, "Genre," n.d., John Dos Passos Papers, University of Virginia Alderman Library (hereafter cited in text by line number).

38. John Dos Passos, "Satire as a Way of Seeing," in *Interregnum,* George Grosz (New York: Black Sun Press, 1937), 9 (hereafter cited in text as "Satire"); reprinted in Pizer 1988 as "Grosz Comes to America," 173–78.

39. Abraham Davidson, *Early American Modernist Painting, 1910–1935* (New York: Harper and Row, 1981), 166 (hereafter cited in text).

40. John Rewald, *Post-Impressionism from van Gogh to Gauguin,* 3d ed. (New York: The Museum of Modern Art, 1978), 147–48 (hereafter cited in text).

41. Edward Lucie-Smith, *Symbolist Art* (London: Thames and Hudson, 1972), 18 (hereafter cited in text).

42. For a comprehensive discussion of artistic and literary treatments of the temptation of St. Anthony, obviously a resonant symbol for Dos Passos as for many artists before and during his time, see Jean Seznec, "The Temptation of St. Anthony in Art," *Art Magazine* 40 (March 1947): 87–93 (hereafter cited in text).

Chapter Four

1. John Dos Passos, "The Evangelist and the Volcano," *Harvard Monthly* 61 (November 1915): 61 (hereafter cited in text by page number); reprinted in Pizer 1988, 25–26.

2. John Dos Passos, "A Conference on Foreign Relations," *Harvard Monthly* 62 (June 1916): 126; reprinted in Pizer 1988, 35.

3. Bernardino de Pantorba, *A Guide-Book to the Prado Museum* (Madrid: Compañia Bibliografica Española, S.A., 1970), 142 (hereafter cited in text).

4. See, for instance, the "Journal" entry for November 13, 1916, in *Fourteenth*, 54–56.

5. Ronald Paulson, *Representations of Revolution* (New Haven: Yale University Press, 1983), 294.

6. John Dos Passos, *A Pushcart at the Curb* (New York: George H. Doran, 1922), 23–24 (hereafter cited in text as *Pushcart*).

7. John Dos Passos, *Rosinante to the Road Again* (New York: George H. Doran, 1922), 94–96 (hereafter cited in text as *Rosinante*).

8. For a comprehensive exploration from the Spanish point of view of the effects of Spanish culture on Dos Passos's style, see Catalina Montes, *La Visión de España en la obra de John Dos Passos* (Salamanca: Ediciones Almar, S.A., 1980).

9. Kaja Silverman, *The Subject of Semiotics* (New York: Oxford University Press, 1983), 17 (hereafter cited in text).

Chapter Five

1. John Dos Passos, *One Man's Initiation: 1917* (Ithaca, N.Y.: Cornell University Press, 1969) (hereafter cited in text as *Initiation*).

2. Elena Wilson, ed., *Edmund Wilson: Letters on Literature and Politics, 1912–1972* (New York: Farrar, Strauss and Giroux, 1977), 85 (hereafter cited in text).

3. Melvin Landsberg, ed., *John Dos Passos' Correspondence with Arthur K. McComb or "Learn to sing the Carmagnole"* (Niwot: University Press of Colorado, 1991), 190 (hereafter cited in text).

4. As an editor of the *Harvard Monthly*, Dos Passos would have been aware of the imagist movement. For a discussion of Dos Passos and imagism, see Linda W. Wagner, *Dos Passos: Artist As American* (Austin: University of Texas Press, 1979), 4–11 (hereafter cited in text).

5. Michael Clark, *Dos Passos' Early Fiction, 1912–1938* (London: Associated University Presses, 1987) (hereafter cited in text).

6. John Dos Passos, *Streets of Night* (New York: George H. Doran, 1923), 102 (hereafter cited in text as *Streets*).

7. John Addington Symonds, *Renaissance in Italy* (New York: Random House, 1935), 1:125.

8. Richard Shiff, *Cézanne and the End of Impressionism* (Chicago: University of Chicago Press, 1984), 122 (hereafter cited in text).

Chapter Six

1. John Dos Passos, "Art and Baseball," n.d., John Dos Passos Papers, University of Virginia Alderman Library, n.p. (hereafter cited in text).

2. David L. Vanderwerken, "*Manhattan Transfer:* Dos Passos' Babel Story," *American Literature* 40 (May 1977): 264 (hereafter cited in text).

3. John Dos Passos, "An Edition of John Dos Passos' 'Seven Times round the Walls of Jericho,' " ed. Ruth Liggette Strickland (Ph.D. diss., University of South Carolina, 1981) (hereafter cited in text as "Seven Times").

Chapter Seven

1. Cecelia Tichi, *Shifting Gears: Technology, Literature, Culture in Modernist America* (Chapel Hill: University of North Carolina Press, 1987), xi (hereafter cited in text).

2. Stephen Kern, *The Culture of Time and Space, 1880–1918* (Cambridge: Harvard University Press, 1983), 2 (hereafter cited in text).

3. Kern reprints some of the appallingly self-congratulatory editorials from major newspapers of April 14 to April 21, 1912, on pages 65–67. The ironies of the tragedy, caused by a hubristic faith in technology, seem to foreshadow the way in which developments in contemporary technology more often than not precede the development of ethical or humanistic guidelines for using the technology.

4. J. Hillis Miller, *The Disappearance of God: Five Nineteenth-Century Writers* (Cambridge: Harvard University Press, 1963), 2 (hereafter cited in text).

5. Paul Fussell, *The Great War and Modern Memory* (New York: Oxford University Press, 1975), 80 (hereafter cited in text).

6. Citing literary and sociological accounts of soldiers' perceptions of the war zone, Kern discusses the "phenomenology" of the war landscape, 361.

7. Gertrude Stein, *Picasso* (New York: Charles Scribner's Sons, 1946), 11 (hereafter cited in text).

8. John Dos Passos, "Contemporary Chronicles," *The Carleton Miscellany* 2 (Spring 1961): 26 (hereafter cited in text as "Contemporary").

9. John Dos Passos, *Three Soldiers* (New York: George H. Doran, 1921), 148 (hereafter cited in text as *Three*).

10. Carolina Tisdall and Angelo Bozzolla, *Futurism* (London: Thames and Hudson, 1977), 54 (hereafter cited in text).

11. Marjorie Perloff, *The Futurist Moment: Avant-Garde, Avant Guerre, and the Language of Rupture* (Chicago: University of Chicago Press, 1986) (hereafter cited in text).

12. Gail Levin, *Synchromism and American Color Abstraction, 1910–1925* (New York: Whitney Museum of American Art, 1978), 19.

13. The frequency with which recent critics feature this poem as a modernist artifact suggests its significance. Perloff discusses the poem in detail, quotes from it at length, and prints a color illustration of the entire manuscript. Kern also provides an illuminating overview of the interaction of the various elements of the text, 72–74.

14. Roland Barthes, *S/Z,* trans. Richard Miller (New York: Farrar, Straus and Giroux, 1974), 174 (hereafter cited in text).

15. David A. Cook, *A History of Narrative Film* (New York: W. W. Norton, 1981), 14 (hereafter cited in text).

16. Perhaps the first critic to note the cinematic qualities of Dos Passos's mature work was D. H. Lawrence in a review of *Manhattan Transfer*, which appears in *Phoenix: The Posthumous Papers of D. H. Lawrence*, ed. Edward D. McDonald (London: Heinemann, 1936), 363–65. Subsequently, Claude-Edmonde Magny defined the film aesthetic in the American novel and discussed *U.S.A.* as the most important example of her theory; see *The Age of the American Novel: The Film Aesthetic of Fiction between the Two Wars*, trans. Eleanor Hochman (New York: Frederick Ungar, 1972), 105–43 (hereafter cited in text). Originally published in 1948, her discussion is the most extensive. Following Magny, a number of articles and studies on Dos Passos have acknowledged the film aesthetic as an influence. See critics such as E. D. Lowry, "The Lively Art of Manhattan Transfer," *PMLA* 84 (1969): 1628–38; Eric Mottram, "The Hostile Environment and the Survival Artist: A Note on the Twenties," in *The American Novel in the Nineteen-Twenties*, eds. Malcolm Bradbury and David Palmer, Stratford-Upon-Avon Studies 13 (London: Arnold, 1971), 40–51; Robert Rosen, *John Dos Passos: Politics and the Writer* (Lincoln: University of Nebraska Press, 1981); Michael Spindler, "John Dos Passos and the Visual Arts," *Journal of American Studies* 15 (December 1981): 391–405 (Rosen and Spindler hereafter cited in text); and Wagner.

17. Quoted in Iain Colley, *Dos Passos and the Fiction of Despair* (London: Macmillan, 1978), 62.

18. Thomas G. Evans, "Dos Passos and the Evolution of Montage," unpublished essay (1981) (hereafter cited in text).

19. For a lengthy discussion of the literary and philosophical implications of and relationships among the three characters, see Clark, 76–96.

20. During that period Dos Passos often attended concerts in the company of a young woman, Germaine Lucas-Championnière, whom he had met in Paris and who shared his musical tastes. As Ludington (1980, 180-81) describes the background of Mlle Lucas-Championnière and the nature of Dos Passos's close friendship with her, she seems to have been the model for the positive aspects of Andrews's friend Geneviève Rod.

21. Dos Passos's choice of the famous Russian filmmaker's name for this character must be accidental, since, as Spindler and Evans show, Dos Passos almost certainly would not have known of the film work of Eisenstein until 1925. The name choice is ironically prophetic in that this character sees more clearly than anyone in the novel except Andrews how the "system . . . turn[s] men into beasts" (46) to ensure their cooperation. Eisenstein claims to have gained this insight in part from reading Tolstoi, whose novels were the basis of some of the film epics of the Russian Revolution made by Eisenstein and Pudovkin (Cook, 398 n). In a further coincidence, the soldier Eisenstein is pointedly accused by a friend of Fuselli of being a "Goddam kike" (14), calling attention to the fact that he is a Jew, like most of the men who "invented Hol-

lywood," in the words of the title of the work by Neal Gabler, *An Empire of Their Own: How the Jews Invented Hollywood* (New York: Crown, 1988).
    22. Blanche H. Gelfant, *The American City Novel* (Norman: University of Oklahoma Press, 1954), 140.
    23. R. P. Blackmur, *Language of Gesture* (New York: Harcourt, Brace, 1935), 6.
    24. Alfred Kazin, introduction to *U.S.A.: The 42nd Parallel* (New York: New American Library, 1969), x (hereafter cited in text).

Chapter Eight

    1. Sinclair Lewis, "Manhattan at Last!" *Saturday Review of Literature* 2 (December 1925): 361.
    2. For references to the schools of painting detected in *Manhattan Transfer*, see Knox, 23–27, and Spindler, 394; and to film aesthetics, see Spindler, 401, Magny, 105, and Allen Tate, "Good Prose," *Nation*, February 10, 1926, 160–62. William Brevda, "How Do I Get to Broadway? Reading Dos Passos's *Manhattan Transfer* Sign," *Texas Studies in Literature and Language* 38 (Spring 1996): 79–114, explores the visual manifestations of 1920s popular culture in the novel—billboards, advertisements, Times Square—as signs of the illusory, evasive "center" in the novel.
    3. Lionel Trilling, "The America of John Dos Passos," in *The Merrill Studies in* U.S.A., ed. David Sanders (Columbus, Ohio: Charles E. Merrill, 1972), 21.
    4. Donald Pizer, *Dos Passos' U.S.A.: A Critical Study* (Charlottesville: University of Virginia Press, 1988), 17 (hereafter cited in text as "Pizer *Dos Passos' U.S.A*").

Chapter Nine

    1. John Dos Passos, introductory notes to *The 42nd Parallel* (New York: Modern Library, 1937), vii–ix (hereafter cited in text as "Introductory"); reprinted in Pizer 1988, 179–80.
    2. John Dos Passos, "The *New Masses* I'd Like," *New Masses*, June 1926, 20 (hereafter cited in text as "New Masses"); reprinted in Pizer 1988, 81–82.
    3. John Dos Passos, "Is the 'Realistic' Theatre Obsolete? Many Theatrical Conventions Have Been Shattered by Lawson's *Processional*," *Vanity Fair*, May 1925, 64 (hereafter cited in text as " 'Realistic' "); reprinted in Pizer 1988, 75–78.
    4. John Dos Passos, *Three Plays: The Garbage Man, Airways, Inc., Fortune Heights* (New York: Harcourt, Brace, 1934).
    5. John Dos Passos, "Toward a Revolutionary Theatre," *New Masses*, December 1927, 20 (hereafter cited in text as "Revolutionary"); reprinted in Pizer 1988, 101–3.

6. For the most complete account of the New Playwrights' productions and documentation of the writers with whom the group was associated, see chapter 3 in Knox and Stahl, 96–147.

7. John Dos Passos, "Did the New Playwrights Fail?" *New Masses,* August 1927, 13 (hereafter cited in text as "New Playwrights"); reprinted in Pizer 1988, 118–20.

8. John Dos Passos, "Looking Back on *U.S.A.,*" *New York Times,* October 25, 1959, sec. 2 (hereafter cited in text as "Looking Back"); reprinted in Pizer 1988, 235.

9. Carol Shloss, *In Visible Light: Photography and the American Writer, 1840–1940* (New York: Oxford University Press, 1987) (hereafter cited in text). In chapter 4, "John Dos Passos and the Soviet Cinema: Separate Frames of Truth," 143–75, Shloss analyzes the history of Dos Passos's exposure to the work of Eisenstein and Vertov, explores their exploitation of montage and the notion of the filming observer in the service of Socialist politics, and relates the Soviets' film techniques and theories to Dos Passos's own implementation of narrative montage and his involvement in the making of *The Spanish Earth.*

10. John Dos Passos, *In All Countries* (New York: Harcourt, Brace, 1934).

11. John Dos Passos, "The Pit and the Pendulum," *New Masses,* August 1926, 10–11 (hereafter cited in text as "Pit"); reprinted in Pizer 1988, 85–91; "Sacco and Vanzetti," *New Masses,* November 1927, 25; reprinted in Pizer 1988, 99–100; "An Open Letter to President Lowell," *Nation,* August 24, 1927, 176; reprinted in Pizer 1988, 97–98; *Facing the Chair* (Boston: Sacco Vanzetti Defense Committee, 1927).

12. John Dos Passos, introduction to *Three Soldiers* (New York: Modern Library, 1932), vii; reprinted in Pizer 1988, 146–48.

13. See, for instance, Eleanor Widmer, "The Lost Girls of *U.S.A.*: Dos Passos' Thirties Movie," in *The Thirties: Fiction, Poetry, Drama,* ed. Warren French (Deland, Fla.: Everett Edwards, 1967), 11–19.

14. John Dos Passos, "The Writer As Technician," in *American Writers' Congress,* ed. Henry Hart (New York: International Publishers, 1935), 80; reprinted in Pizer 1988, 169–72.

15. John Dos Passos, "Statement of Belief," *Bookman,* September 1928, 26; reprinted in Pizer 1988, 115.

16. David Sanders, "John Dos Passos," in *Writers at Work: The "Paris Review" Interviews,* ed. George Plimpton, 4th ser. (New York: Viking, 1976), 79 (hereafter cited in text as "John Dos Passos"); reprinted in Pizer 1988, 241–52.

17. Townsend Ludington, "The Ordering of the Camera Eye in *U.S.A.*." *American Literature* 49 (November 1977): 445.

18. Dziga Vertov, *Kino-Eye: The Writings of Dziga Vertov,* ed. Kevin O'Brian, trans. Annette Michelson (Berkeley and Los Angeles: University of California Press, 1984), 17 (hereafter cited in text).

Chapter Ten

1. John Dos Passos, *The Ground We Stand On* (New York: Harcourt, Brace, 1941) (hereafter cited in text as *Ground*).

2. John Dos Passos, *Adventures of a Young Man* (New York: Harcourt, Brace, 1939) (hereafter cited in text as *Adventures*); reprinted in *District of Columbia* (Boston: Houghton Mifflin, 1952) (hereafter cited in text as *District*).

3. See, for instance, Ludington 1980, 362–409, and Rosen, 93–98.

4. John Dos Passos, *State of the Nation* (Boston: Houghton Mifflin, 1944), 81 (hereafter cited in text as *State*).

5. John Dos Passos, *Tour of Duty* (Boston: Houghton Mifflin, 1946) (hereafter cited in text as *Tour*).

6. John Dos Passos, *The Prospect before Us* (Boston: Houghton Mifflin, 1950) (hereafter cited in text as *Prospect*).

7. *The Prospect before Us* contains, with some revisions, five important essays from *Life* in the following order: "Britain's Dim Dictatorship," retitled "Great Britain: Ordeal by Government"; reportage of Dos Passos's visit to South America, "Pioneers in Brazil," *Life*, December 20, 1948, 5–6, and "Visit of Evita," *Life*, April 11, 1949, 27–28; "Where Do We Go from Here?" *Life*, January 27, 1947, 95–96; and Dos Passos's account of his observations of the corn operation of Bob Garst, a farmer whom Dos Passos visited in Coon Rapids, Iowa, "Revolution on the Farm," *Life*, August 23, 1948, 95–98. Additionally, the collection includes two articles about Great Britain from *Harper's*. "The Failure of Marxism" is collected in a revised form under the name "Socialism Is Not Enough" in *The Theme Is Freedom* (New York: Dodd, Mead, 1956), 236–45.

8. See Rosen, 109 n. 22.

9. Reviewing and analyzing Dos Passos's definition of the problems of postwar life in *The Prospect before Us,* Granville Hicks assented to the writer's fundamental assertions but faulted them for not including solutions: "The program is all right as far as it goes, but I hope that Dos Passos doesn't think it offers a plain road to salvation." See Granville Hicks, "Dos Passos As a Lecturer," *The New Leader,* December 11, 1950, 27.

10. John Dos Passos, *The Head and Heart of Thomas Jefferson* (Garden City, N.Y.: Doubleday, 1954) (hereafter cited in text as *Jefferson*).

11. John P. Diggins, *Up from Communism: Conservative Odysseys in American Intellectual History* (New York: Harper and Row, 1975), 265 (hereafter cited in text); Irving Howe, "The Perils of Americana," *New Republic,* January 25, 1954, 16; Gerald W. Johnson, "A New Jefferson Seen through Men and Forces," *New York Herald Tribune Book Review,* January 24, 1954, 5; Granville Hicks, "A Dull Book, but It Also Ends Too Soon," *New Post,* January 1954.

12. As he labored over the extensive research for *Jefferson,* Dos Passos complained in a letter to Edmund Wilson that his work was slowed by having to sort through what he assumed were falsified documents insinuating Jeffer-

son's liaison with one of his slaves, and he concluded that Jefferson had fathered no mulatto children. In the letter he expresses his exasperation that historians waste time pursuing such insignificant matters that only obscure what in his judgment are important issues concerning historical figures. See *Fourteenth*, 593–94.

13. Charles Poore, "Books of the Times," *New York Times*, January 21, 1954, 29.

14. For a summary of the hail of negative reviews that greeted *Adventures* and a defense of the book, see James T. Farrell, "Dos Passos and the Critics," *American Mercury*, August 1939, 489–94.

15. Malcolm Cowley, "Disillusionment," *New Republic*, June 14, 1939, 163; Samuel Sillen, "The Misadventures of John Dos Passos," *New Masses*, July 4, 1939, 21–22; John Chamberlain, *Saturday Review of Literature*, June 3, 1939, 3–4, 14–15.

16. John Dos Passos, *Number One* (Boston: Houghton Mifflin, 1943) (hereafter cited in text); reprinted in *District*.

17. For a thorough analysis of how the interchapters in *Number One* contribute to its meaning, see Axel Knönagel, "The Interchapters in John Dos Passos's *Number One*," *Journal of Modern Literature* 19 (Fall 1995): 317–22.

18. John Dos Passos, *The Grand Design* (Boston: Houghton Mifflin, 1949) (hereafter cited in text as *Grand*); reprinted in *District*.

19. See, for instance, works by Benton such as *Planting* or the precise order in works such as Grant Wood's *Spring Turning, Fall Plowing*, or *Arbor Day*, and his depression-era portraits of rural Americans such as *American Gothic* and *Daughters of Revolution*. For a discussion of the regionalists and their responses to the depression, see Rose, 97–103.

20. Granville Hicks, "The Politics of John Dos Passos," *Antioch Review* 10 (Spring 1950): 98 (hereafter cited in text). Hicks is accurate about Dos Passos's consistently independent thinking during the time of his most extreme radicalism but inaccurate in intimating that he was ever a "fellow-traveler."

21. See, for instance, Maxwell Geismar, "Dos Passos' New Novel of the New Deal Years," *New York Times Book Review*, January 2, 1949, 4, 13; Diana Trilling, "Fiction in Review," *Nation*, January 22, 1949, 107–8.

22. For complete information about the biographical bases of the characters in *The Grand Design*, see Ludington 1980, 443.

23. John Dos Passos, *Chosen Country* (Boston: Houghton Mifflin, 1951) (hereafter cited in text as *Chosen*).

24. Dos Passos published his theory about the incident and expressed his outrage at the murder of his friend Tresca in "Carlo Tresca," *Nation*, January 23, 1943, 123–24, an article later reprinted in *Il Martello*, of which Tresca had been editor.

25. Ernest Hemingway, *A Moveable Feast* (New York: Charles Scribner's Sons, 1964). Hemingway never names Gerald and Sara Murphy, patrons and hosts to many American artists in France in the 1920s and 1930s. Nor does he

name Dos Passos, who in the course of his long friendship with them introduced Hemingway to the elegant couple. In the final chapter of the book, Hemingway does mention by name Scott and Zelda Fitzgerald, both of whom had died by the time he published the book. But anyone familiar with the associations among the prominent "Lost Generation" figures can discern the group of friends in Hemingway's description: "The rich have a sort of pilot fish who goes ahead of them, sometimes a little deaf, sometimes a little blind. . . . Then you have the rich and nothing is ever as it was again. The pilot fish leaves of course. . . . He enters and leaves politics or the theater in the same way he enters and leaves countries and people's lives in his early days" (207).

26. Granville Hicks, "The Fruits of Disillusionment," *New Republic,* September 27, 1954, 18; Harold Clurman, "Communists by Dos Passos," *Nation,* October 9, 1954, 310.

27. James T. Farrell, "How Should We Rate Dos Passos?" *New Republic,* April 28, 1958, 17–18; Malcolm Cowley, "Success That Somehow Led to Failure," *New York Times Book Review,* April 13, 1958, 45.

28. John Dos Passos, *Midcentury* (Boston: Houghton Mifflin, 1961) (hereafter cited in text).

29. John Dos Passos, "What Union Members Have Been Writing Senator McClellan," *Reader's Digest,* September 1958, 25–32.

30. John Dos Passos and Paul Shyre, "The Complete Text of U.S.A.," *Theatre Arts* 44 (June 1960): 24–50. The play, performed in the round on a bare stage, had a successful run of over seven months at the Hotel Martinique in New York City. But a contract with cowriter Paul Shyre and promoters Nick Spanos and Howard Gottfried prevented Dos Passos from responding to potentially lucrative offers from Hollywood agents for developing the play into a feature film. Because of the growing number of people involved who wanted a share of the profits, the project stalled, much to Dos Passos's frustration.

31. Harry T. Moore, "Proud Men in an Age of Conformity," *New York Times Book Review,* February 28, 1961, 1, 61. For other positive reviews that emphasize Dos Passos's integrity in maintaining his principles and advocating for the individual, see Jack Conroy, "Our Soul-Sick Century," *Chicago Sun-Times,* March 5, 1961, and Granville Hicks, "Of Radicals and Racketeers," *Saturday Review,* February 25, 1961, 25–26.

32. John Dos Passos, "Mr. Rip Van Winkle, Wake Up Some More," *National Review,* January 18, 1964, 71–74; John Dos Passos, "The New Left: A Spook Out of the Past," *National Review,* October 18, 1966, 1037–39.

33. Granville Hicks, "John Dos Passos Reminisces," *Saturday Review,* November 26, 1966, 33–34; Dan Wakefield, "Return to Paradise," *Atlantic Monthly,* February 1967, 102–7; Robert Sklar, "Dos Passos' Restless Times," *Nation,* January 16, 1967, 87–88.

34. John Dos Passos, *Century's Ebb* (Boston: Gambit, 1975) (hereafter cited in text). The publisher's foreward, xi-xiii, details the efforts of the editors and Elizabeth Dos Passos to compose and arrange the existing manuscript.

Rosen, 171 n. 89, conjectures that *Century's Ebb* would have been "less co-herent" than *Midcentury* even if Dos Passos had finished it. One of the most complete discussions of the editing and final form of the book is in Wagner, 159–76.

35.   These five segments were originally published as "U.S.A. Revis-ited," *Atlantic Monthly,* April 1964, 47–54. Their original title provides a clue to his intentions for these segments in *Century's Ebb.*

36.   The crux of Jay's story is clearly the politics. But in a hurried final segment on Jay's life, Dos Passos attempts to resolve the narrative via a felici-tous marriage, as he had in the first Jay Pignatelli novel. Both the account of the automobile accident that claims the life of Lulie Harrington Pignatelli and the account of Jay's second marriage, to Emily Merlin, a talented and dark-eyed beauty whom he meets through mutual friends, are autobiographical accounts of parallel events in Dos Passos's life. Narratively, however, the some-what contrived resolution of *Century's Ebb* works no better than the one in *Chosen Country* did.

37.   John Dos Passos, "Acceptance by John Dos Passos," *Proceedings of the American Academy of Arts and Letters and the National Institute of Arts and Letters,* 2d ser., no. 8 (1958), 193 (hereafter cited in text as "Acceptance"); reprinted in Pizer 1988, 221.

Selected Bibliography

PRIMARY SOURCES

Novels

One Man's Initiation: 1917. Ithaca, N.Y.: Cornell University Press, 1969.
Three Soldiers. New York: George H. Doran, 1921.
Streets of Night. New York: George H. Doran, 1923.
Manhattan Transfer. New York: Harper and Brothers, 1925.
The 42nd Parallel. New York: Harper and Brothers, 1930. First vol. of *U.S.A.*
1919. New York: Harcourt, Brace, 1932. Second vol. of *U.S.A.*
The Big Money. New York: Harcourt, Brace, 1936. Third vol. of *U.S.A.*
U.S.A.: The 42nd Parallel, 1919, The Big Money. New York: Library of America, 1996.
Adventures of a Young Man. New York: Harcourt, Brace, 1939. First vol. of *District of Columbia.*
Number One. Boston: Houghton Mifflin, 1943. Second vol. of *District of Columbia.*
The Grand Design. Boston: Houghton Mifflin, 1949. Third vol. of *District of Columbia.*
Chosen Country, Boston: Houghton Mifflin, 1951.
District of Columbia. Boston: Houghton Mifflin, 1952.
Most Likely to Succeed. New York: Prentice-Hall, 1954.
The Great Days. New York: Sagamore Press, 1958.
Midcentury. Boston: Houghton Mifflin, 1961.
Century's Ebb. Boston: Gambit, 1975.

Nonfiction

Rosinante to the Road Again. New York: George H. Doran, 1922.
Facing the Chair. Boston: Sacco Vanzetti Defense Committee, 1927.
Orient Express. New York: Harper and Brothers, 1927.
"Translator's Foreword." *Le Panama et mes sept oncles* (Panama or the Adventures of My Seven Uncles), by Blaise Cendrars. New York: Harper and Brothers, 1931, vii–viii.
In All Countries. New York: Harcourt, Brace, 1934.
"Satire as a Way of Seeing." In *Interregnum,* by George Grosz. New York: Black Sun Press, 1937.
Journeys between Wars. New York: Harcourt, Brace, 1938.
The Villages Are the Heart of Spain. Chicago: Esquire-Coronet, 1938.
State of the Nation. Boston: Houghton Mifflin, 1944.
Tour of Duty. Boston: Houghton Mifflin, 1946.

The Prospect before Us. Boston: Houghton Mifflin, 1950.
The Theme Is Freedom. New York: Dodd, Mead, 1956.
Brazil on the Move. Garden City, N.Y.: Doubleday, 1963.
Occasions and Protests. Chicago: Henry Regnery, 1964.
The Best Times. New York: New American Library, 1966.
John Dos Passos: The Major Nonfictional Prose. Edited by Donald Pizer. Detroit: Wayne State University Press, 1988. This volume collects the most reve- latory and influential of Dos Passos's prolific journalistic writings and essays. The selections document clearly the transitions in Dos Passos's political thinking and his own concept of the relationship between his social and political aims and the forms of his novels and plays.
"Art and Baseball." John Dos Passos Papers. University of Virginia Alderman Library.

Short Fiction and Poetry

"The Almeh." *Harvard Monthly* 56 (July 1913): 172–79.
Book of Verses, 1914–1917. John Dos Passos Papers. University of Virginia Alderman Library.
Literary Diary of John Dos Passos, 1914–1916. John Dos Passos Papers. Uni- versity of Virginia Alderman Library.
"Malbrouck: A Sketch." *Harvard Monthly* 59 (March 1915): 192–94.
"An Aesthete's Nightmare." *Harvard Monthly* 60 (May 1915): 77–80.
"An Interrupted Romance." *Harvard Monthly* 60 (June 1915): 119–22.
"First Love." *Harvard Monthly* 61 (October 1915):22–25.
"Prairies." *Harvard Monthly* 61 (November 1915): 55.
"Romantic Education." *Harvard Monthly* 61 (October 1915): 1–4.
"Orientale." *Harvard Monthly* 61 (November 1915): 43–49.
"A Pot of Tulips." *Harvard Monthly* 61 (December 1915):77–83.
"From Simonides." *Harvard Monthly* 61 (January 1916): 110.
"The Shepherd." *Harvard Monthly* 61 (January 1916): 115–21.
"The Cardinal's Grapes." *Harvard Monthly* 61 (February 1916): 152–55.
"Les Lauriers Sont Coupés." *Harvard Monthly* 62 (April 1916): 48–49.
Cummings, E. Estlin, et al. *Eight Harvard Poets.* New York: Laurence J. Gomme, 1917.
A Pushcart at the Curb. New York: George H. Doran, 1922.
Afterglow and Other Undergraduate Writings. Edited by Richard Layman. Detroit: Omnigraphics, Inc., A Manly Book, 1990. Provides facsimile and tran- script copies of some of Dos Passos's earliest writings at Harvard, includ- ing a fragment of a novel that demonstrates the origins of themes and characters that emerge in later fiction.
"Bubbles and the Sea Wind." John Dos Passos Papers. University of Virginia Library.
"The Past." John Dos Passos Papers. University of Virginia Alderman Library.

Histories

The Ground We Stand On. New York: Harcourt, Brace, 1941.
The Head and Heart of Thomas Jefferson. Garden City, N.Y.: Doubleday, 1954.
The Men Who Made the Nation. Garden City, N.Y.: Doubleday, 1957.
Prospects of a Golden Age. Englewood Cliffs, N.J.: Prentice-Hall, 1959.
Mr. Wilson's War. Garden City, N.Y.: Doubleday, 1962.
Thomas Jefferson: The Making of a President. Boston: Houghton Mifflin, 1964.
The Shackles of Power: Three Jeffersonian Decades. Garden City, N.Y.: Doubleday, 1966.
The Portugal Story: Three Centuries of Exploration and Discovery. Garden City, N.Y.: Doubleday, 1969.

Drama

Three Plays: The Garbage Man, Airways, Inc., Fortune Heights. New York: Harcourt, Brace, 1934.

Letters

The Fourteenth Chronicle: Letters and Diaries of John Dos Passos. Edited by Townsend Ludington. New York: Gambit, 1973.
John Dos Passos' Correspondence with Arthur K. McComb or "Learn to sing the Carmagnole." Edited by Melvin Landsberg. Niwot: University Press of Colorado, 1991.

SECONDARY SOURCES

Bibliographies

Potter, Jack, comp. *A Bibliography of John Dos Passos.* Chicago: Normandie House, 1950. Selected primary works and secondary sources through 1949.
Rohrkemper, John, comp. *John Dos Passos: A Reference Guide.* Boston: G. K. Hall, 1980. Annotated secondary bibliography.
Sanders, David, comp. *John Dos Passos: A Comprehensive Bibliography.* New York: Garland, 1987. This bibliography, the most recent, the most complete, and accurate of the three, contains extensive publication information on primary listings and helpful annotations on secondary sources through 1983.

Biographies

Carr, Virginia Spencer. *Dos Passos: A Life.* Garden City, N.Y.: Doubleday, 1984. Offers exhaustive details about Dos Passos's youth, life within his family, and life after the Spanish Civil War. Carr's impressionistic chapter introductions echo the style of the *U.S.A.* "Camera Eye" sections. Extensive notes.

Landsberg, Melvin. *Dos Passos' Path to U.S.A.: A Political Biography, 1912–1936.* Boulder: Colorado Associated University Press, 1972. Emphasizes the political aspects of Dos Passos's intellectual and literary development through the first half of his career.

Ludington, Townsend. *John Dos Passos: A Twentieth Century Odyssey.* New York: Dutton, 1980. A balanced, readable biography with helpful notes. Explains the relationships among the biographical, cultural, artistic, and political bases of Dos Passos's literary development.

Books and Parts of Books

Aaron, Daniel. *Writers on the Left: Episodes in American Literary Communism.* New York: Harcourt, Brace, 1961. Discusses the reasons for Dos Passos's political shift to conservatism in midcareer and the results of that shift on his writing. Finds the change in his political attitudes consistent with his lifelong principles.

Astre, Georges-Albert. *Themes et structures dans l'oeuve de John Dos Passos.* Paris: Lettres Modernes, 1956. The first of a two-volume study of Dos Passos's work in all genres. This volume covers the work through *Manhattan Transfer* and includes a close reading of texts and an overview of literary influences. Not translated into English.

———. *Themes et structures dans l'oeuve de John Dos Passos.* Paris: Lettres Modernes, 1958. The second volume of Astre's work ends with *The 42nd Parallel.*

Becker, George J. *John Dos Passos.* New York: Ungar, 1974. Critical overview of Dos Passos' works; biographical outline; brief summaries of novels; and separate chapters on *Manhattan Transfer* and *U.S.A.*

Bogardus, Ralph, and Fred Hobson, eds. *Literature at the Barricades: The American Writer in the 1930s.* Tuscaloosa: University of Alabama Press, 1982. Contains a revealing essay by Townsend Ludington on the ideological conflict over the American Communist Party between Dos Passos and John Howard Lawson.

Bradbury, Malcolm, and David Palmer, eds. *The American Novel in the Nineteen-Twenties.* Stratford-Upon-Avon Studies 13. London: Arnold, 1971. Contains general essays by Henry Dan Piper, Malcolm Bradbury, and others on social and literary contexts of the decade; it includes an essay by Brian Lee, "History and Dos Passos," tracing the emergence of the theme of depersonalization in the novels through *U.S.A.*

Brantley, John. *The Fiction of John Dos Passos.* The Hague: Mouton, 1968. A study of the novels through *Midcentury.* Highlights the "machine" as symbol of impersonal forces that threaten individuality in U.S. culture.

Clark, Michael. *Dos Passos' Early Fiction, 1912–1938.* London: Associated University Presses, 1987. The most detailed study to date of Dos Passos's apprentice fiction. Explores the influence of American intellectual history on his work through *U.S.A.*

Colley, Iain. *Dos Passos and the Fiction of Despair.* London: Macmillan, 1978. Studies Dos Passos's growing pessimism evidenced in his fiction. Suggests that the quality of the later works does not decline because of his political shifts but because of his "creative exhaustion."

Cowley, Malcolm. *Exile's Return: A Literary Odyssey of the 1920s.* New York: Penguin Books, 1934. Early study by critic of Dos Passos's own generation places the writer in the social and historical context of the era.

————. *After the Genteel Tradition: American Writers since 1910.* New York: W. W. Norton, 1936. Traces Dos Passos's development from "romantic" to "radical" in his early career.

Diggins, John P. *Up from Communism: Conservative Odysseys in American Intellectual History.* New York: Harper and Row, 1975. Places Dos Passos in the context of major radical writers in the United States who shifted to political conservatism and valuably examines reasons for that transition in Dos Passos's politics.

French, Warren, ed. *The Thirties: Fiction, Poetry, Drama.* Deland, Fla.: Everett Edwards, 1967. Besides other critical articles about major works of the decade, contains Eleanor Widmer's "The Lost Girls of *U.S.A.*: Dos Passos' Thirties Movie," one of the earliest essays to focus on women in the novels.

Gelfant, Blanche H. *The American City Novel.* Norman: University of Oklahoma Press, 1954. Explores technique in *Manhattan Transfer* and *U.S.A.* and traces the development of characterization toward figures representative of conflicting factions in American culture.

Hjerter, Kathleen G., ed. *Doubly Gifted: The Author As Visual Artist.* New York: Harry N. Abrams, 1986. Provides examples of the visual art of several noted literary figures, including Dos Passos and Cummings.

Knox, George, and Herbert M. Stahl. *Dos Passos and the Revolting Playwrights.* Upsala: A.-B Lundequistka Bokhandeln, 1964. The most complete treatment of Dos Passos's involvement with the New Playwrights, with synopses and criticism of his plays.

Lawrence, D. H. *Phoenix: The Posthumous Papers of D. H. Lawrence.* Edited by Edward D. McDonald. London: Heinemann, 1936. Lawrence's review of *Manhattan Transfer* is the first exploration of the novel's filmic structure.

Magny, Claude-Edmonde. *The Age of the American Novel: The Film Aesthetic of Fiction between the Two Wars.* Translated by Eleanor Hochman. New York: Frederick Ungar, 1972. Defines the film aesthetic in the American novel and discusses *U.S.A.* as the most important example of it.

Pizer, Donald. *Dos Passos' U.S.A.: A Critical Study.* Charlottesville: University of Virginia Press, 1988. Straightforward analysis of the composition, organization, and style of the trilogy, with a separate chapter explaining the four modes of the novels. The only full-length study devoted entirely to *U.S.A.*

Rosen, Robert. *John Dos Passos: Politics and the Writer.* Lincoln: University of
Nebraska Press, 1981. A concise overview of the political transitions in
Dos Passos's career. Analyzes fiction and nonfiction in terms of their
political contexts and messages. Is critical of both the quality and biases
of works after *U.S.A.*

Sartre, Jean-Paul. "John Dos Passos and 1919." In *Literary and Philosophical Essays.*
Translated by Annette Michelson (London: Rider, 1955), 88–96. Landmark
essay in which Sartre declares Dos Passos "the greatest writer of our time."

Shloss, Carol. *In Visible Light: Photography and the American Writer, 1840–1940.*
New York: Oxford University Press, 1987. Contains a comprehensive and
provocative chapter on Dos Passos's exposure to Soviet film theory and
practice and how Eisenstein and Vertov may have influenced the writer's
adaptation of montage for his modernist narratives.

Strychacz, Thomas. *Modernism, Mass Culture, and Professionalism.* Cambridge:
Cambridge University Press, 1993. Strychacz responds to Shloss in his
chapter "Reading John Dos Passos Reading Mass Culture in *U.S.A.*," in
which he uses Marxist and cultural studies' methodologies to discuss the
problems of narrative form and readership in the trilogy.

Tichi, Cecelia. *Shifting Gears: Technology, Literature, Culture in Modernist America.*
Chapel Hill: University of North Carolina Press, 1987. A wonderfully
readable study of relationships between the growth of modernism and
the culture of the machine age in the early twentieth century. Explores
Manhattan Transfer and *U.S.A.* as "machine" novels.

Wagner, Linda W. *Dos Passos: Artist as American.* Austin: University of Texas
Press, 1979. Critical study of all genres includes Harvard writings, discusses the process of Dos Passos's Americanization culminating in later
novels. Extensive selected bibliography.

Wilson, Elena, ed. *Edmund Wilson: Letters on Literature and Politics, 1912–1972.*
New York: Farrar, Strauss and Giroux, 1977. Cross-referenced to Dos
Passos's letters in *The Fourteenth Chronicle,* this collection completes the
record of the lively, enduring correspondence between two of the central
literary figures of their time.

Wrenn, John H. *John Dos Passos.* New York: Twayne Publishers, 1961. The first
Twayne volume on Dos Passos, written during his lifetime and with his
cooperation.

Articles

Aaron, Daniel. "*U.S.A.*" *American Heritage* (July-August 1996): 64–72. Concise explanation of the workings and significance of the trilogy for a general reader.

Bernardin, Charles W. "John Dos Passos' Harvard Years," *The New England
Quarterly* (March 1954): 3–26. Important early essay characterizing Dos

Passos as a college student, his activities at Harvard, and his academic career there.

Brevda, William. "How Do I Get to Broadway? Reading Dos Passos's *Manhattan Transfer* Sign." *Texas Studies in Literature and Language* 38, no. 1 (Spring 1996): 79–114. A provocative semiotic reading of the visual signs of popular culture in the novel.

Carr, Virginia Spencer. "Dos Passos, Painter and Playwright: New Possibilities in Research." *Resources for American Literary Study* 13 (Autumn 1983): 207–14. Covers areas available to Dos Passos scholars for further research on his dramatic and visual works.

Epstein, Joseph. "*U.S.A.* Today." *New Yorker,* August 5, 1996, 68–74. An overview of Dos Passos's career and reputation for the general reader, and a writer's testimony to his literary influence.

Fleming, Robert E. "The Libel of Dos Passos in *To Have and Have Not.*" *Journal of Modern Literature* 15 (Spring 1989): 597–601. Hemingway's depiction of his character Richard Gordon libels Dos Passos and Katy, a depiction Arnold Gingrich persuaded Hemingway to delete from the published edition. What remains in the novel is nevertheless an attack on social novelists of the 1930s.

Foley, Barbara. "From *U.S.A.* to *Ragtime:* Notes on the Forms of Historical Consciousness in Modern Fiction." *American Literature* 50 (March 1978): 85–105. Foley places modern historical novels into the context of Dos Passos's pioneering uses of history.

Galligani, Janet Cosley. "Nancibel Taylor and the Dos Passos Canon: Reconsidering *Streets of Night.*" *Studies in the Novel* 24 (Winter 1992): 410–22. One of a number of recent feminist considerations of Dos Passos's women characters in his work through *U.S.A.*

Knönagel, Axel. "The Interchapters in John Dos Passos's *Number One.*" *Journal of Modern Literature* 19 (Fall 1995): 317–22. Whitmanesque interchapters are "the heart of the novel's ideological and aesthetic intentions" and describe "representations of the people who—ideally—occupy the first position of power in a democracy."

Lewis, Sinclair. "Manhattan at Last!" *Saturday Review of Literature* 2 (December 1925): 361. Vigorous early review that recognizes the goals and achievements of *Manhattan Transfer.*

Ludington, Townsend. "The Ordering of the Camera Eye in *U.S.A..*" *American Literature* 49 (November 1977): 443–46. Concise and insightful analysis of the significance of the order and placement of the "Camera Eye" segments as they reveal the growth of the observer's individual consciousness and vocation.

————. "Dos Passos: New Possibilities in Biographical Research." *Resources for American Literary Study* 13 (Autumn 1983): 195–200. Areas available to Dos Passos scholars for further research on his life and times.

————. "Spain and the Hemingway-Dos Passos Relationship." *American Literature* 60 (May 1988): 270–73. Interesting analysis of the two writers' differing attitudes toward bullfighting as representative of their respective ways of understanding Spain. Dos Passos documents his perception of the ritual and his satiric view of its brutality in a letter written four years before Hemingway publishes his vision of it as embodying "man's struggle in an alien world."

Reinitz, Neale. " 'Revolt, however, brews': An Unpublished Dos Passos Letter." *English Language Notes* 32 (December 1994): 53–65. Biographically interesting analysis of a letter to Roland Jackson in Madrid on the occasion of the declaration of World War I; reveals how Dos Passos's grief at his father's death conflicted with his reluctance to return to the United States from Spain.

Spindler, Michael. "John Dos Passos and the Visual Arts." *Journal of American Studies* 15 (December 1981): 391–405. A sound general overview of visual influences and devices in the modernist works.

Trumbold, John. "Popular Songs As Revolutionary Culture in John Dos Passos' *U.S.A.* and Other Early Works." *Journal of Modern Literature* 19 (Fall 1995): 289–316. The most complete description available of the sources of the songs Dos Passos uses in the trilogy and how they are used, and cultural analysis of songs' contexts. Songs in the "Newsreels" are listed and dated.

Vanderwerken, David L. "U.S.A.: Dos Passos and the 'Old Words.' " *Twentieth Century Literature* 23 (May 1977): 195–228. Useful examination of how the trilogy focuses on the misuse of language in American culture and the need for the redemption of the "old words."

————. "*Manhattan Transfer*: Dos Passos' Babel Story." *American Literature* 49 (May 1977): 253–67. The Babel myth applied to the novel to demonstrate the causes of Herf's escape from the city's corruption.

Wagner, Linda W. "Dos Passos: Some Directions in the Criticism." *Resources for American Literary Study* 13 (Autumn 1983): 201–6. Areas to which Dos Passos literary criticism is being directed and possible fruitful subjects for future criticism.

Collections

Belkind, Allen, ed. *Dos Passos, the Critics, and the Writer's Intentions.* Carbondale: Southern Illinois University Press, 1971. Collects previously published early critical articles including seminal essays by critics such as Malcolm Cowley, Blanche Gelfant, Granville Hicks, Alfred Kazin, and Jean-Paul Sartre.

Hook, Andrew, ed. *Dos Passos: A Collection of Critical Essays.* Englewood Cliffs, N.J.: Prentice-Hall, 1974. Features Dos Passos's own comments on the "situation in American writing," along with important essays by E. D. Lowry, Claude-Edmonde Magny, and John William Ward.

Maine, Barry, ed. *Dos Passos: The Critical Heritage*. London: Routledge, 1988. The most complete overview of the critical reception of Dos Passos's writing from *Three Soldiers* through *Century's Ebb*.

Sanders, David, comp. *The Merrill Studies in* U.S.A. Columbus, Ohio: Charles E. Merrill, 1972. Previously published essays on the trilogy by critics such as Lionel Trilling, John Wrenn, and George Knox.

Unpublished Dissertations

Evans, Thomas G. "Persistence of Vision: Reception and the Cinema Aesthetics of Novels by Dos Passos, Doctorow, and Mailer." Ph.D. diss., University of North Carolina, 1992. A thorough analysis of the use of cinematic techniques and the origins of the methods.

Strickland, Ruth Liggette, ed. "An Edition of John Dos Passos' 'Seven Times Round the Walls of Jericho.' " Ph.D. diss., University of South Carolina, 1981. The only version of the text of his first attempt at a novel available outside the collection at University of Virginia, the document reveals origins of characters, themes, and methods in his early work.

Miscellaneous Materials

The Odyssey of John Dos Passos. Produced by Stephen Talbot. 57 min. Educational Film Center, 1993. Videocassette. Lively overview of life and works sets the writer vividly in historical context; features moving and still footage of Dos Passos, interviews with modern critics, and visual explication of the modes of *U.S.A.*

Index

The Author

Lisa Nanney earned her Ph.D. in twentieth-century literature from the University of North Carolina at Chapel Hill in 1989 where, as a faculty lecturer, she also taught writing, literature, and film criticism. Subsequently, in visiting positions at Emory University and Georgetown University, she has taught interdisciplinary American studies courses as well as writing, literature, and women's studies courses. In 1990, she was awarded a Fulbright Lectureship in American literature at the University of Valencia in Spain. Currently, she teaches and helps design American studies curricula at the North Carolina School of Science and Mathematics, a residential preparatory school for advanced students that is affiliated with the University of North Carolina system. She has published and lectured in America and Europe about modernism and gender in the works of writers such as Nathanael West, Zelda Sayre Fitzgerald, and F. Scott Fitzgerald, and about relationships between the visual arts and literature in the work of writers and painters such as Dos Passos and Fernand Léger.

The Editor

Joseph M. Flora earned his B.A. (1956), M.A. (1957), and Ph.D. (1962) in English at the University of Michigan. In 1962 he joined the faculty of the University of North Carolina, where he is professor of English. His study *Hemingway's Nick Adams* (1984) won the Mayflower Award. He is also author of *Vardis Fisher* (1962), *William Ernest Henley* (1970), *Frederick Manfred* (1974), and *Ernest Hemingway: A Study of the Short Fiction* (1989). He is editor of *The English Short Story* (1985) and coeditor of *Southern Writers: A Biographical Dictionary* (1970), *Fifty Southern Writers before 1900* (1987), and *Fifty Southern Writers after 1900* (1987). He serves on the editorial boards of *Studies in Short Fiction* and *Southern Literary Journal*.